MATHEMATICS FOR YOUNG CHILDREN

JEAN M. SHAW
University of Mississippi

SALLY S. BLAKE
University of Texas—El Paso

Merrill,
an imprint of Prentice Hall

Upper Saddle River, New Jersey   *Columbus, Ohio*

Library of Congress Cataloging-in-Publication Data

Shaw, Jean M.
  Mathematics for young children / Jean M. Shaw and Sally S. Blake.
      p.   cm.
  Includes bibliographical references and index.
  ISBN 0-02-409764-0
      1. Mathematics—Study and teaching (Elementary)   I. Blake, Sally.
  II. Title.
  QA135.5.S478   1998
  372.7—dc21   97-1900
                                                                         CIP

Cover photo: © Superstock
Editor: Bradley J. Potthoff
Production Editor: Julie Peters
Text Design and Production Coordination: Custom Editorial Productions, Inc.
Cover Designer: Russ Maselli
Cover Design Coordinator: Karrie M. Converse
Production Manager: Patricia A. Tonneman
Illustrations: Custom Editorial Productions, Inc.
Director of Marketing: Kevin Flanagan
Advertising/Marketing Coordinator: Julie Shough

This book was set in Bookman ITC by Custom Editorial Productions, Inc. and was printed and
bound by Quebecor Printing/Book Press. The cover was printed by Phoenix Color Corp.

Photos supplied by Nancy P. Alexander.

Extracted text on pp. 53, 55, 57, 79, 80, 112, 115, 137, 138, 164, 169, 187, 212, and 235 is
taken from the following sources, with permission: *Curriculum and Evaluation Standards for
School Mathematics* by the National Council of Teachers of Mathematics, copyright 1989, Reston,
Virginia, and *Developmentally Appropriate Practice in Early Childhood Programs Serving Children
from Birth Through Age 8* by Sue Bredekamp, Ed., copyright 1987, National Association for Education of Young Children, Washington, DC.

Printed in the United States of America

10 9 8 7 6 5 4 3 2

ISBN 0-02-409764-0

Prentice-Hall International (UK) Limited, *London*
Prentice-Hall of Australia Pty. Limited, *Sydney*
Prentice-Hall of Canada, Inc., *Toronto*
Prentice-Hall Hispanoamericana, S. A., *Mexico*
Prentice-Hall of India Private Limited, *New Delhi*
Prentice-Hall of Japan, Inc., *Tokyo*
Simon & Schuster Asia Pte. Ltd., *Singapore*
Editora Prentice-Hall do Brasil, Ltda., *Rio de Janeiro*

This book is dedicated to
Kay Steinsiek Snipes, Lee Holcombe,
and Mary Jo Puckett Cliatt,
to our students,
and to our children . . .
Candice, Vicki, Bill, and Dave.

Preface

Children are the future—everyone's future. In our increasingly complex, technological world, efforts to enhance children's learning in appropriate ways are needed now more than ever. Children learn best when they are actively involved in exploration of topics of interest to them. When supportive adults help children communicate about and interpret what they are doing, learning is developed even further.

This book is about teaching mathematics to children ages three through eight. It is intended for preservice and inservice teachers, but its contents will also interest curriculum planners and administrators as they work to provide quality programs for children. In addition, parents may find items of interest as they seek to support school programs and extend learning at home.

This book is based on ideas from the National Council of Teachers of Mathematics (NCTM), the National Association for the Education of Young Children (NAEYC), and the National Science Teachers Association (NSTA). It is based on research and ideas from effective practice; the book supports the importance of quality early education and the need for better mathematics for all children.

ORGANIZATION AND FEATURES

The book is organized in two parts. The first part (Chapters 1–5) describes the need for and nature of mathematics education reform: how young children learn and how educators can plan and implement learning activities. It also describes multifaceted approaches to assess learning. The second part (Chapters 6–11) focuses on mathematics topics and ways to facilitate young children's learning.

This book includes several features intended to make it a usable resource. Each chapter begins with an outline to guide reading of the sections. Within each chapter, "What Do You Think?" questions will prompt reflection on important points.

Many chapters feature descriptions of children's learning activities. They are set off graphically from the text, but may be read with the text or separately. These learning activities, intended to enhance young children's understanding, are formatted to include NCTM's areas of focus and describe what to do when working with young children. They include adjustments—ways to adapt the learning activities to meet the needs of individuals and groups. Although each activity has suggested ages, educators can adapt most activities for children of different ages. Finally, the activities provide ongoing assessments—a variety of ways to gather data about children's progress. Readers will also find boxed assessment suggestions in the topical chapters describing a variety of ways to gather data about children's learning.

Each chapter concludes with a section called "Applications: Thinking and Collaborating," or "Applications: Thinking and Problem Solving." This section offers several choices of adult-level learning options and suggests ways to apply and extend the ideas presented in the chapter and share results. These applications may be used in college courses, for staff development, or for self-development and personal challenge.

CHAPTER OVERVIEWS

Chapter 1 offers an overview of mathematics for young children as we enter the twenty-first century. Building from NCTM's *Curriculum and Evaluation Standards for School Mathematics* (1989) and other reform documents, this introductory chapter describes the need for reform and the roles for many people in improving mathematics teaching and learning. The chapter, and the rest of the book, focuses on "math power"—problem solving, communicating mathematically, reasoning, and connecting mathematics to the real world and to other school subjects.

In Chapter 2 we present theories of psychologists and educators who describe children's development and their learning of mathematics. Stressing a constructivist view, the chapter presents theories and research that affect planning and guiding children's work.

Chapter 3 relates standards for teaching mathematics and developmentally appropriate practice as described by the NAEYC. In this chapter we describe a classroom environment that encourages positive growth in mathematics for young children.

All children must have opportunities to learn good mathematics. Chapter 4 presents many ways to work toward this goal, including equity issues and the role of parents and family members in young children's education. More suggestions for enhancing classroom climate and environment are also included.

Assessment is a key issue as educators improve children's learning of mathematics. Chapter 5 presents a variety of ongoing, formative evaluation techniques as well as information on summative assessment and evaluation. Educators at many levels are realizing the need for reform in assessment, so the chapter includes suggestions for implementing changes.

In the book's second half, each mathematics-specific chapter includes ideas from the NCTM standards documents. The chapters also present details of mathematics topics to be learned and suggest materials to enhance children's learning. The chapters offer classroom vignettes as well as delineated learning activities. Children's literature can be used to promote children's understanding of math topics, so each topical chapter includes an annotated list of related children's books.

Chapter 6 focuses on problem solving and reasoning, vital areas for young children's mathematics growth. It offers suggestions for infusing problem solving and reasoning through all mathematics activities. Communication, connections, and technology are part of this and the other math-specific chapters.

Numeration and number sense—the quantitative aspect of mathematics—is the focus of Chapter 7. Suggestions for helping young children learn about whole numbers and fractions are described. Ways to introduce numbers, develop their meanings, work with symbols, and develop number sense are included, as is attention to estimating.

Chapter 8 focuses on operations with whole numbers—addition, subtraction, and introducing informal multiplication and division. The chapter describes ways to present operations in problem situations, develop an understanding of the meanings of operations, model the operations, help children learn basic facts, and work with multidigit operations.

Important in today's mathematics curriculum is work with data and probability. Chapter 9 begins with descriptions of sorting, an important prerequisite for organizing data. The chapter also includes ways to help children gather and organize data, and make and interpret displays of data. The chapter ends with techniques for helping children explore probability and chance.

Geometry, the spatial aspect of math, involves concepts such as position, two- and three-dimensional figures, and symmetry. Using the NCTM standards and the van Hieles' theory about geometry learning, Chapter 10 describes active, hands-on experiences for children—experiences to develop spatial sense.

Chapter 11 presents ideas for enhancing young children's measurement concepts and skills. Since measurement is a mathematics topic that combines numbers and geometry, it is especially useful and engaging. The chapter focuses on developing children's understanding of the measurement process and its various attributes—length, weight, volume, and time, for example.

Appendix A features names and addresses of suppliers of mathematics materials. Appendix B is a form for a mathematics autobiography for readers.

ACKNOWLEDGMENTS

Thanks are due to many persons for the development of this book. We are grateful to the many authors of reform documents for helping us develop our thinking about sound, powerful mathematics for young children. We thank our own students who have tried and implemented most of the ideas included in this book, and we thank the many teachers who have tried the ideas in their classrooms. Our editors, Linda Sullivan, Linda Scharp, and Brad Potthoff, were very helpful and supportive in the publishing process. Our reviewers, Cecelia Benelli, Western Illinois; Jane Billman, University of Illinois, Urbana-Champaign; Grace M. Burton, University of North Carolina, Wilmington; Karen Colleran, Pierce College; Ann Harsh, Hattiesburg Public School District; Betty K. Hathaway, University of Arkansas, Little Rock; Michael Henniger, Western Washington University; Jane Ann McLaughlin, Trenton State College; Garry W. Quast, Slippery Rock University; and Mary L. Snyder, University of Scranton, offered many useful and thought-provoking suggestions as well as encouragement. We are indebted to our department chairs, Dr. Peggy Emerson, Curriculum and Instruction at the University of Mississippi, and Dr. Jim Milson, Teacher Education at the University of Texas at El Paso, for their leadership and support.

Jean M. Shaw
Sally S. Blake

Contents

Chapter 6 Problem Solving and Reasoning 111

Chapter 7 Numeration and Number Sense 135

Chapter 8   Operation Concepts and Skills   161

Chapter 9   Working with Data and Probability   185

A New Vision of Mathematics for Young Children

1

◆◆◆

In October of her first year of teaching, Candice Madison must make a short talk to the parents of her kindergarten class about the mathematics program she is implementing. She wants to present the program as one that is in tune with current ideas about what children should be learning and how they should be taught. What are some things Miss Madison might include in her talk? How might she show as well as tell the parents about her math program?

s part of a three-week unit, "Growth and Change," Ms. Roderiguiz introduced "growing" patterns to her class of six-and seven-year-old children. She led the children in making rhythmic patterns such as these: clap, snap; clap, clap, snap; clap, clap, clap, snap. The children enjoyed performing the patterns and describing them. They then settled to help write a group composition about what they had been doing. Along with a narrative, the children also recorded some of their patterns with symbols such as those shown in Figure 1.1. The children counted numbers of movements in the patterns and found that number patterns also emerged: 1, 1; 1, 2; 1, 3; 1, 4; 1, 5; . . . .

The children then moved into small groups to make growing patterns with pattern blocks. One group used triangular blocks to create a pattern like the one shown in the photograph. When Amy suggested counting the blocks in each pattern, Carlos noted that the number of blocks in each row of the triangles was an odd number. Because the children knew that they would later share their work with the rest of the class, Juana drew some of the patterns and recorded some of the numbers the children discovered. Ms. Roderiguiz observed for a while, then asked the children to find the total number of blocks they used in each design. The group members mentally added the blocks in some of the rows; James got a calculator to add other numbers. They recorded these totals to share with their classmates (Figure 1.2).

This vignette illustrates some aspects of a new vision of mathematics for young children: hands-on exploration, active investigation and problem solving, use of manipulatives and calculators, and blending of mathematics topics such as geometry and numbers. It shows the involvement,

Pattern blocks make it easy for children to create growing patterns.

Figure 1.1   *Example of symbols used to record "clap" and "snap" patterns.*

interest, and confidence of the children as they worked on an activity introduced in a thematic context, and illustrates the use of reasoning and communication as the children work together. The description also depicts the teacher facilitating the children's work in ways compatible with a new vision of mathematics for young children.

Why do we need a new vision of mathematics for young children? What is this vision? Who has promoted the new vision and who can implement and refine its implementation in schools and classrooms? How and when can it be implemented? These questions and their answers form the basis of this chapter.

Figure 1.2   *Growing patterns using triangular pattern blocks.*

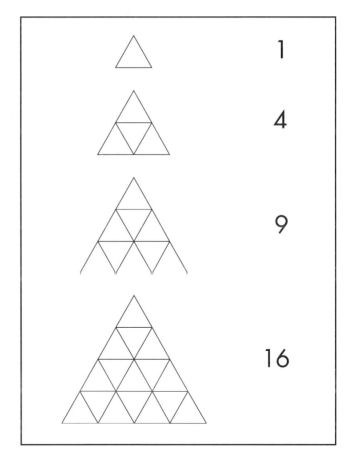

WHY DO WE NEED A NEW VISION OF MATHEMATICS FOR YOUNG CHILDREN?

The context of mathematics education has been influenced by many demands and changes starting in the mid-1980s. The authors of *Reshaping School Mathematics: A Philosophy and Framework for Curriculum* (National Research Council [NRC], 1990) discuss five important changes: (1) Needs for mathematics have changed. More and better mathematics is required for all citizens and for all workers, not just a select few. People in most jobs and walks of life need mathematics. Dealing with the mathematical ideas presented in the media requires sophisticated quantitative literacy. (2) The nature of mathematics has changed; varied, complex problems confront people today and in the future. (3) Technology has changed; thinking and problem-solving skills are needed more than routine computations. (4) Views of learners have also changed. Children are no longer seen as passive "absorbers" of knowledge, but as active learners who construct ideas for themselves, verify answers, and communicate about what they are doing. (5) Changes in international economic competitiveness have encouraged changes in mathematics education at all levels.

The authors of the well known *Curriculum and Evaluation Standards for School Mathematics* (National Council of Teachers of Mathematics [NCTM], 1989) assert that society's goals indicate a need for reform. Pointing out the need for mathematically literate workers in technology based jobs where people formulate and solve problems, they emphasize the necessity for lifelong learning in a changing society. The authors stress mathematical opportunities and equitable treatment of all racial, ethnic, and gender groups. They state that dealing with society's problems—the environment, space exploration, and economic crises—requires a well-informed electorate that is able to interpret data and is mathematically literate.

WHAT IS THE NEW VISION OF MATHEMATICS FOR YOUNG CHILDREN?

"Mathematics curricula at all levels must introduce more of the breadth and power of the mathematical sciences" (NRC, 1989). With these words, the authors of another reform document, *Everybody Counts*, assert that mathematics is a sense-making activity that lets people "perceive patterns, comprehend data, and reason carefully", and that "truth and beauty, utility and appreciation" are parts of mathematical power (p. 43).

The *Curriculum Standards* (NCTM, 1989) define mathematical power as students' abilities to solve problems, use mathematical language to communicate ideas, reason and analyze, understand concepts and perform procedures, and integrate aspects of mathematics. Mathematical power also includes attitudes: valuing of mathematics and believing that mathematics makes sense.

The NCTM's vision of mathematics for young children is based on several assumptions (NCTM,1989): children in grades K–4 must build a strong, broad background of concepts through active involvement; children must *use* the mathematics they are learning; and children must think and reason. We believe that these vital assumptions apply equally well to prekindergarten children. The *Curriculum Standards* authors see the development of understanding and relationships as central to curriculum planning. Though concept development—building math *ideas*—takes time, it establishes a strong foundation for later work with skills and procedures. When people understand concepts, working with skills makes sense and takes less time in the long run than a "skills only" approach. Concept development builds confidence in learners who have a sense of whether answers are right or wrong.

Working with a broad range of content—measurement, geometry, probability, and statistics, as well as numbers and operations—exposes children to important, intriguing math topics. It reflects the true nature of mathematics and the connectedness of math topics. For example, attention to areas such as measurement and geometry also helps children see the applicability of mathematics to other school subjects and to real life. Mathematics is a vital, practical subject. Using topics that arise in the world and in the classroom promotes learning.

Learning and using mathematics must be an active process. Children learn best when they explore, share ideas, use materials and symbols to express ideas, and solve problems. Physical and mental engagement foster learning. As they learn mathematics, children need manipulatives and tools (rulers, calculators, scales). A list of selected suppliers of mathematics materials for young children is included in Appendix A; materials for specific math topics are included in Chapters 6–11 of this book.

Active learning for young children includes the use of technology: calculators, computers, and other tools. Calculators let children explore math ideas and patterns and enhance problem solving, focusing on thinking rather than tedious calculation done by hand. Although calculator usage does not replace mental math and the need to know basic facts, calculators are one of many valid ways of performing calculations. Calculators, properly used, do not depress learning and retention of basic facts (Hembree & Dessart, 1986; Souviney, 1995). Computers motivate children and promote their knowledge of geometry, problem solving, and numbers.

Overall the new vision of mathematics for young children, and for all students, involves many factors. Learners must problem solve and reason, express and clarify their ideas with varied communication forms, and share their ideas with others. Learners must see strong connections between mathematical ideas and powerful connections between mathematics and the real world. They must develop positive attitudes toward math—interest, perseverance, confidence, and the belief that math makes sense. This vision presents a vital challenge to educators.

WHAT DO *YOU* THINK?

What are your initial reactions after reading about the *Curriculum Standards?* Which ideas from these standards have you already experienced? What parts intrigue you? Keep these parts in mind to focus your future reading.

WHO HAS SUPPORTED THE NEW VISION OF MATHEMATICS FOR YOUNG CHILDREN? WHO MUST WORK TO IMPLEMENT THE NEW VISION?

Many teachers have long recognized the need for a new vision of mathematics for young children. Informed parents have supported teachers and helped to provide some of the resources necessary for improvements. Community agencies and professional organizations have pressed for good mathematics as part of a well-balanced program for young children.

Reports such as *A Nation At Risk* (1983) helped to set the stage for concentrated reform efforts. The NCTM prepared their *Curriculum Standards* (1989) to give direction to mathematics education reform. Numerous mathematical science organizations endorsed the document and many professional organizations offered support.

Many people must work together to realize the new vision of mathematics education. The authors of *Everybody Counts* (NRC, 1989) assert that there are roles for everyone in realizing goals of improving mathematics education: national agreement about improvement, state and local resources allocated for change, and acceptance by parents and the public. Jack Price (1995), NCTM president, names three interrelated aspects of mathematics education to take people into the twenty-first century: good math for *all* students, caring teachers, and mathematics taught in ways compatible with students' learning styles.

What are the individual's roles in implementing the new vision of mathematics for young children? The authors of *Everybody Counts* detail the following (NRC, 1989, pp. 93–95):

◆ *Teachers:* Talk with each other about mathematics, examine current practice and debate new proposals, and engage students actively in the process of learning.

◆ *Parents:* Demand that schools meet the NCTM standards, encourage children to continue studying mathematics, support teachers in curricular reform, and expect homework to be more than routine computation.

◆ *Principals:* Provide opportunities for teachers to work together, become educated on issues in mathematics education, and support innovation.

If people are to play a part in reform of mathematics education, they must be informed of current recommendations and ways to implement them. Often educators must help others learn about reform, and value and support it. The NCTM standards documents were written by professionals—teachers, professors, supervisors—not mandated by outsiders. Such groups must again work together to make changes.

Guided by the NCTM standards, teachers can work together to decide, plan, and implement changes in mathematics education. They can invite parents to visit classes and inform them of changes and innovations through newsletters, notes on open-ended homework, and personal contact. They can lead "Family Math" (Stenmark, 1989) meetings where parents, children, and teachers work together solving problems, using calculators, and making geometric models.

Teachers can also form study groups, conduct action research on effects of innovative practice, visit each others' classrooms, and attend NCTM conferences. Teachers might also learn from reading journals such as the NCTM publication *Teaching Children Mathematics* (which was, until 1994, called *Arithmetic Teacher*). This journal offers many stimulating articles as do NCTM *Standards Addenda* books, available for K–6 grade levels and on several mathematics topics. Based on readings, teachers might implement ideas, discuss their readings, and conduct in-service sessions focused on improving mathematics education.

HOW CAN THE NEW VISION OF MATHEMATICS FOR YOUNG CHILDREN BE IMPLEMENTED?

Implementing the new vision of mathematics for young children requires teachers to devote attention to four vitally important areas suggested by NCTM's *Curriculum Standards* (1989). The four areas are problem solving, communicating mathematically, reasoning, and building connections between math topics and among subject areas. The writers of these standards include the four areas not only in their recommendations for grades K–4, but also for grades 5–8 and 9–12, enhancing the broad curriculum recommended for all levels.

 WHAT DO *YOU* THINK?

Before you read further, make notes about how you might involve children in problem solving, communicating, and reasoning activities as well as connecting math to other subjects and to everyday life.

In the following sections, we will provide an overview of each of the four areas deemed important by the NCTM. Each of these areas is also developed in subsequent chapters of this book. Problem solving and reasoning are the focus of Chapter 6. Communication and making connections are inherent in each chapter.

Problem Solving

"Problem solving should be the central focus of the mathematics curriculum. . . . [It is] not a distinct topic but a process that should permeate the entire program and provide the context in which concepts and skill can be learned" (NCTM, 1989, p. 23). These words describe the importance and role of problem solving in the curriculum.

The authors of the NCTM *Curriculum Standards* recommend that young children "use problem-solving approaches to investigate and understand mathematical content" (NCTM, p. 23). Problem solving need not wait until children have mastered arithmetic operations or fully understand concepts; indeed problem solving can be used as a means of introducing and developing ideas and skills. For example, before kindergarten and primary children are introduced to the subtraction sign and basic subtraction facts, they can act out "take away" situations. They can arrange counters or coins to figure out answers to problems such as "Chelsea needs 14 cents to buy a pencil. She has 5 cents. How much more does Chelsea need?" Thus they develop ideas of the subtraction concept through problem solving.

To acquire confidence in using mathematics, children should have opportunities to formulate their own problems, typically from school and real-life situations. They should use a variety of strategies for problem solving, and verify and interpret their results. "Classrooms with a problem-solving orientation are permeated by thought-provoking questions, speculations, investigations, and exploration..." (NCTM, 1989, p. 23). Alert educators use everyday situations to enhance problem-solving skills and to build the idea of mathematics' usefulness.

Many opportunities for problem solving occur each day in the early childhood classroom. Teachers must be sure that children actually become involved in problem solving rather than always providing them with quick, easy answers. It is only through participation that children learn to use their minds in the important problem-solving process. Following are examples of some problem-solving situations for young children.

 LISTEN AND FIND IT

In a unit on autumn, four-year-olds can use careful listening and the process of elimination playing a game to identify pumpkins.

Focus: Problem solving, communicating, reasoning.

What To Do: Using pumpkin faces such as the ones pictured on page 9, give the children a series of clues like these: "I'm tall. I have a smiling face and square eyes.

Which pumpkin am I?" or "I have a triangle for my nose. I'm about as tall as I am wide. My eyes are round. Can you find me?"

Adjustments: After you offer several sets of clues, many children will be ready to pose clues for their classmates.

Ongoing Assessment: Watch the children's reactions, keeping the game brief and lively. Make notes about the children's abilities to base judgments on the clues you offer.

 CONDUCTING BUSINESS

As the children are studying their communities, they can role play "business" situations.

Focus: Problem solving, working with money, communicating, connecting to the real world.

What To Do: Help four- or five-year-old children set up a restaurant and make menus with pictures of foods. They can mark prices using cut-out coins or coin stamps, and can pay for their purchases with play money. For children who are ready to trade coins (five pennies for a nickel), use reference cards to show coin equivalents.

Adjustments: Use the children's suggestions for other types of "businesses." With primary children, pose questions such as, "Rashid paid 35 cents with a quarter and a dime. Was this right? What are other ways to make 35 cents? What coins might we use?" Encourage the children to verify their answers.

Ongoing Assessment: Let the children talk about what they are learning in their "businesses." Encourage them to suggest needed changes and to identify areas to help each other.

Communicating Mathematically

Communication is important in every aspect of life, and mathematics is no exception. The social nature of humans and their abilities to use language and other symbolic forms makes communication possible. Doing mathematics is largely a social activity; math is much more than isolated manipulation of symbols.

Educators often think of communication as involving talking, listening, writing, and reading. Communication in mathematics can extend to other forms: drawing complements writing—pictures often convey ideas that words alone cannot. Young children's emerging writing abilities are extended when adults take dictation of what the children say, or write experience charts as a group of children discusses a situation. Using manipulatives, models, charts, graphs, and diagrams clarifies and stimulates communication in mathematics.

The authors of the NCTM *Curriculum Standards* (1989) state that children need numerous opportunities to "relate physical materials, pictures, and diagrams to mathematical ideas; reflect on and clarify their thinking about mathematical ideas and situations; relate their everyday language to mathematical language and symbols; and realize that representing, discussing, reading, writing, and listening to mathematics are a vital part of learning and using mathematics" (NCTM, 1989, p. 26). Children need situations in which they use a variety of language forms as they learn mathematics. Children can construct questions for others about almost any situation (Menon, 1996). Following are some examples of activities to emphasize communication and reasoning.

 GROUPING PICTURES

With sorting, opportunities for communication abound.

Focus: Communication, reasoning.

What To Do: Have three-year-olds work in small groups; let each cut or tear several clothing pictures from a catalog. Have the children describe their pictures and sort them many ways. They might start by clothing types—shirts, pants, and hats. They might next sort the pictures as items worn above the waist, below the waist, or at the waist. Next they could sort their pictures by color or by pattern. After grouping the pictures many ways, have the children glue the pictures to a large paper using one sorting scheme. Take dictation as they describe their categories.

Adjustments: Older children might also classify their pictures by the prices of the items (those costing $20 or more and those costing less), then make a picture graph.

Ongoing Assessment: Let the children decide on questions they can ask their classmates as they talk about and show their pictures.

 THE COMMUNICATION GAME

Clear communications are vital in this engaging game.

Focus: Communication, reasoning, spatial sense.

What To Do: Have kindergarten or primary children work in pairs, sitting back to back. One draws a simple picture or arranges pieces on a small felt board. Step by step, he tells his partner what he is doing, and the partner tries to duplicate it. As they compare results, have the partners talk about how and why their arrangements varied, and discuss clues that were particularly helpful. Then have the partners switch roles.

Adjustments: Let the children work with blocks, clay, or modeling dough, making three-dimensional arrangements.

Ongoing Assessment: Observe the children as they work, noting their abilities to give and follow directions, then discuss the effectiveness of their communications.

To enhance communication skills, children as young as three or four can make their own math books. For almost any topic—numbers, geometric shapes, or sizes—each child can complete a page with narration and an illustration (Merenda, 1995). A committee can then create a title page and cover, and bind the pages together. The teacher can read the books to the children, then place the books in the class library area; perhaps the children can check out the books to share at home.

Even five-year-olds can regularly write in journals or learning logs. The process provides opportunities for children to express and reflect on ideas, and it gives adults insights into the children's thinking. Journal entries made throughout the year provide evidence of children's growth over time. Children can use invented spelling, and supplement their writing with pictures and diagrams. Buschman (1995) suggests that children write newsletters for their families sharing ideas about the mathematics they are exploring and problems they have created.

The communication game. After one child gives directions to the other for creating a picture, the children might ask, "How will our pictures compare?"

Calculators, like other math tools, enhance communication. Primary children might press in numbers to make their calculators show a pattern—12121212, for example. They can then describe the pattern and translate it different ways: with blocks (one red, one blue, one red, one blue, . . .), with body instruments (clap, snap, clap, snap, . . .), or with letters (ABABABAB. . .).

A single number sentence can represent an almost endless number of situations. Having kindergarten and primary children communicate about these situations is often a profitable activity. The children might use the number sentence 2 + 6 =__ , work with partners, and act out stories to fit the number sentence. Each child can draw or write a story to match the number sentence and display the work on a bulletin board.

Diagrams and maps are common communication forms. Children five years and older might make diagrams of toys on a shelf and use positional words to describe the placement of objects. Visual memory skills are enhanced by having the children look at a toy shelf, then look away and try to draw it. Making classroom maps is also a profitable venture and one in which children must solve many problems: What details will they show? How will they determine the proportions of the room? What materials do they need? How will they judge the accuracy of their map?

Communication plays a vital role in mathematics achievement and in developing positive attitudes toward math. To realize the new vision of mathematics for all young children, educators are moving beyond the idea that children are passive receptors of narrow, preset knowledge. They treat children as active participants who build and share ideas. Using a variety of communication forms is essential in this process.

Reasoning

For young children, reasoning involves several components that are closely related to problem solving and communicating mathematically. According to the NCTM *Curriculum Standards,* reasoning involves children "drawing logical conclusions; ... explain[ing] their thinking; justifying answers and solution processes; using patterns and relationships; and believing that mathematics makes sense" (NCTM, 1989, p. 29).

These behaviors can be fostered in a classroom where teachers and children question, investigate problems, and respect each others' ideas. "Children need to know that being able to explain and justify thinking is important and that how a problem is solved is as important as its answer" (NCTM, 1989, p. 29). Allowing time for children to converse and express their reasoning is vital. Creating an environment where children feel free to "take intellectual risks by raising questions and formulating conjectures" is part of the teacher's job (NCTM, 1991, p. 57). Following are descriptions of reasoning activities for young children.

ARRANGING NUMBERS

Reasoning is important as children explore numbers.

Focus: Reasoning, communicating, number meanings.

What To Do: Work with a group of kindergarten children to explore a number such as 8. Have them arrange blocks of various colors in a line to represent the number. Help children record symbols for their arrangements—4 and 4, 1 and 5 and 2, 2 and 2 and 4, or 6 and 2. Encourage the children's reasoning by asking questions such as, Do we have all the arrangements? What patterns do you notice here? Do all of these make 8? Are 3 and 5, and 5 and 3 related? How?

Blocks or inter-locking cubes let children explore the many ways to compose a number such as 8.

Adjustments: Have the children use the calculator, enter some of their number combinations, and see what happens.

Ongoing Assessment: Observe the children's work and mark on a checklist the abilities to count, represent numbers, use the calculator's symbols, and explain their reasoning.

REASONING CARDS

Use Fitzgerald's (1990) suggestion to enhance primary children's reasoning and problem-solving abilities.

Focus: Reasoning, problem solving, communicating.

What To Do: Prepare small manila-paper squares, cutting 1, 2, and 3 corners off some of them and leaving about one-fourth of the squares intact. Hole-punch one-fourth of the squares with 1 hole, one-fourth with 2 holes, one-fourth with 3 holes, and leave one-fourth without holes to make a set of squares as pictured.

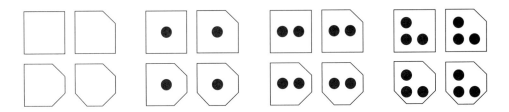

Ask the children to examine the attribute pieces and describe them, then ask them to arrange their pieces to "organize them" however they wish, and check each others' arrangements. Have the children work with partners. One child closes her eyes while a partner removes a piece. The first child then tries to identify the piece that was removed. Knowledge of the arrangement scheme helps the child reason about the missing piece.

Adjustments: Invite the children to invent other games and activities for their attribute pieces.

Ongoing Assessment: Listen to the children's explanations to gain ideas of their reasoning processes and communication skills.

Primary children can practice drawing logical conclusions in a questioning game. A child can arrange shapes on a flannel or magnet board, then secretly select one shape. The others can try to guess the secret shape by asking questions that can be answered as yes and no. The children will find that they must focus on attributes such as shape, position, and color to determine the "secret shape." Perhaps they can eliminate several shapes with one question, selecting an attribute common to two or more shapes.

Reasoning activities such as the ones suggested strengthen children's reasoning abilities as well as their communication and problem-solving skills. Reasoning activities also show children that often in mathematics there are many good, valid ways to think about situations; frequently there are many good answers to problems. Reasoning should be addressed in almost every math activity so that the children's understanding and confidence are built and the children see that mathematics makes sense.

Making Mathematics Connections

People use mathematics in a variety of situations. Areas within mathematics are closely related. It is also important to connect mathematics and other areas of the curriculum. The NCTM standards stress these relationships as well as "linking conceptual and procedural knowledge, relating various representations of concepts or procedures to each other, and recognizing relationships among the different topics in mathematics" (NCTM, 1989, p. 32). Connections are important because they make mathematics realistic and whole, not a narrow school subject comprised of unrelated parts.

The NCTM standards authors advocate children having opportunities to explore ideas thoroughly. In classrooms where connections are fostered, a variety of mathematical ideas are incorporated into several lessons rather than each lesson focusing on a single, narrow idea. Teachers help children build bridges from concrete situations to abstract ideas. Children are encouraged to exchange ideas and relate concepts and procedures.

In a position paper published in *Teaching Children Mathematics* (NCTM, 1995), the NCTM asserts that "curriculum should center on children's natural curiosity and inclination to construct and reconstruct meaning and on relationships among and within disciplines to provide instruction that enhances skillful problem solving and decision making." It recommends "natural and logical connections ... organized around questions, themes, or projects" and responsive to children's needs and related to their lives so that children develop and maintain positive attitudes towards school and learning (NCTM, 1995, p. 386).

Areas of mathematics can be related in natural ways that make sense to children. As they make and interpret graphs, children count, classify, and compare sets. They often use geometric representations of data. As children work with fractions, common representations of the fractions are geometric figures. To make such connections clear, educators must be aware of opportunities for children to explore and discuss them. Children should connect mathematics to everyday life as well.

Mathematics is easy to connect to other areas of the curriculum, as illustrated in "Planting Seeds."

PLANTING SEEDS

Several areas of mathematics connect in this science activity.

Focus: Communicating, measuring, graphing, connecting to everyday life and to science.

What To Do: As nursery school children grow plants as a science investigation, help them record the progress of their plants on a calendar. Count the number of seeds planted, then see how many seeds sprout. Keep records so the children can see, for example, that it took 4 days to see plant growth above the soil, then constant growth for 3 days, and finally a growth spurt. The children can picture and graph the growth of their plants using paper strips cut or torn to the heights of their plants.

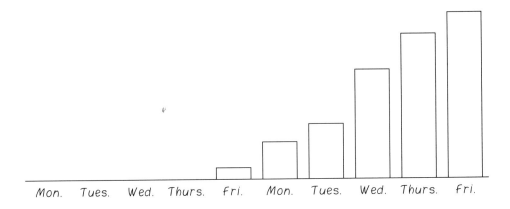

Mon.   Tues.   Wed.   Thurs.   Fri.   Mon.   Tues.   Wed.   Thurs.   Fri.

Adjustments: Have older children draw pictures or make a time line to document the growth of their plants.

Ongoing Assessment: Take dictation as the children describe what happened. Use photographs for the children's portfolios.

Books stimulate making connections. For example, *Nature's Wonderful World in Rhyme* (Sheehan, 1993) can be used with young children of any age. Discussion of the vivid and detailed pictures and verses exposes children to shapes, sizes, positions, and time concepts. The book also connects well to language arts and science.

Many books are available to help educators choose literature with mathematics connections and to suggest activities to complement stories in children's books. For example, *The Wonderful World of Mathematics* (Theissen & Matthias, 1992) includes critical annotations of about 500 books for preschool through grade 6. *Read Any Good Math Books Lately?* (Whiten & Wilde, 1992) features reviews and teaching suggestions of books for mathematics lessons for grades K–6. Ramirez and Lee's (1993) *Multiethnic Children's Literature* suggests fine children's books that emphasize a variety of lifestyles. Burns's (1992) *Math and Literature* describes sample lessons for 10 books and additional ideas for about 20 others. The journal *Teaching Children Mathematics* includes "Links to Literature" columns starting in the fall of 1994; articles by various authors describe literature-based learning.

Building connections within mathematics and relating mathematics to other curricular areas and to the real world is vital. When educators help children make such connections, they are likely to be more confident in their work and more interested in the subject. Mathematics can become a vital, natural part of in- and out-of-school activities for young children.

WHAT DO *YOU* THINK?

At the beginning of this section, you thought about problem solving, communicating, reasoning, and making connections with young children. How did your ideas compare to those that were presented? Share some of your ideas and reactions with others.

WHEN WILL THE NEW VISION OF MATHEMATICS EDUCATION FOR YOUNG CHILDREN BE IMPLEMENTED?

The "when" is now! Many teachers have long used principles and activities like those described here. Realizing that math must be connected to the children's lives and to other school subjects, teachers have used problem solving, reasoning, and communication as important parts of their math programs, stressing active learning and participation by all children. Other teachers are beginning to become aware of mathematics education reform efforts (Souviney, 1995). They are working alone and with others to learn about content and techniques they should use to help *all* children participate and learn.

Even though the standards have impacted curriculum in virtually every state, teachers must still be aware of recommendations for improving the teaching and learning of mathematics. Administrators can support teachers by providing the time, education, and materials needed to actualize reform. Parents and other community members must be apprised of needed changes.

Changing and improving mathematics for young children is not a quick, easy process. It cannot be accomplished by a single individual or in a year. Instead it requires sustained effort, commitment, and focus and the work of many individuals. Children are our future. Improving their educational opportunities will enhance children's lives, but will also improve the world for all people. Change—starting or continuing *now*—is essential.

PARALLEL REFORM EFFORTS IN SCIENCE EDUCATION

Efforts at reform and change are not isolated to the mathematics education community. Paralleling efforts by mathematics educators, science educators have produced documents such as *Science for All Americans: Project 2061 Report on Literacy Goals in Science, Mathematics, and Technology* (American Association for the Advancement of Science [AAAS], 1989), *Benchmarks for Science Literacy* (National Science Teachers Association [NSTA], 1993), and *National Science Education Standards* (National Science Teachers Association [NSTA], 1996).

These reports point out the need for all children—especially minority children who have been underrepresented in science education—to receive a quality education in science, mathematics, and technology. The reports recommend attention to many of the same areas of mathematics as do the NCTM standards, highlighting the importance of patterns, problem solving, numbers, probability, graphs, and geometric concepts in science. Reasoning, a powerful process that often demands creative thought, is used in both mathematics and science.

SUMMARY

A need for more and better mathematics for all citizens has prompted attention to mathematics education at all levels. Concern for economic competitiveness as well as the changing nature of mathematics set the stage for reform efforts by members of the NCTM and others. Documents such as *Curriculum Standards* (NCTM, 1989) present a new vision of mathematics, its teaching, and its learning. They are complemented by documents from professional organizations such as the NSTA. We will present related recommendations for teaching young children as proposed by the National Association for the Education of Young Children in subsequent chapters, addressing curriculum and classroom practice based on the developmental needs of children.

Work with young children is especially important in improving mathematics education. At the early childhood level children's confidence and foundations of understanding can be built. By connecting mathematics to children's everyday experiences and to other school subjects, and by building connections among math topics, educators can present a complete, engaging, useful view of mathematics. They can enhance the children's opportunities for problem solving, reasoning, and communicating about mathematics.

The efforts of many people are needed to implement changes in curriculum, classroom practice, and evaluation of learning. Efforts have already begun and must continue if we are to successfully implement a new vision of powerful mathematics for young children. Readers of this book have started their efforts to improve the teaching of math by learning more about recommendations for improving mathematics education for young children. By considering and implementing the suggestions in this book, readers can do even more to make mathematics interesting and meaningful to young children. In the process, most readers will find that by challenging themselves, they find additional fulfillment and pride in teaching.

◆ *APPLICATIONS: THINKING AND COLLABORATING*

This chapter presented aspects of a new vision of mathematics for young children. Now it's your turn to extend the chapter's content by completing one or more of the following.

1. Start a mathematics autobiography using the form provided in Appendix B or devising one of your own. Mark your opinion of your competence on the lines, then describe your experiences with and feelings about mathematics. Exchange math autobiographies with a friend; discuss your past experiences and points of view.

2. Reflect on reasons for reform of school mathematics in light of your own background. Do you need different mathematics than you were taught in school? What technology was available when you studied mathematics, and now? Were all students encouraged to study mathematics and take higher-level math classes? Did you learn mathematics as an active participant or as a passive "sponge"? After reflecting about your own background, discuss some reasons for reform efforts with colleagues.

3. Can you discuss "math power"? What do phrases like problem solving, communicating mathematically, and reasoning mean for young children and for you as a teacher? Reread the chapter and compare answers with colleagues to refine your answers.

4. The authors of *Everybody Counts* (NRC, 1989) outline roles for many persons in mathematics education reform. Study teachers' roles and, with a partner, list at least 10 appropriate actions. Add five things you could do to help parents or administrators act more effectively in the roles described in *Everybody Counts*.

5. Start a file of problem-solving and reasoning activities for young children. Collect or create at least 10 selections. To start you might adapt activities from this chapter or Chapter 6. Add to your file as you work with children.

6. Connecting math topics is an important part of the new vision for mathematics. For example, children can use a reasoning skill— sorting—as they work with geometry; they combine numbers and problem solving as they make and interpret graphs. Generate at least five more examples of connecting math topics. Discuss how the connections would help children.

7. Mathematics should be connected to everyday life and to other school subjects. List at least 10 ways you could help children make such connections. Share ideas with colleagues or implement them with children.

◆ REFERENCES

American Association for the Advancement of Science. (1993). *Benchmarks for science literacy.* New York: Oxford University Press.

_____. (1989). *Science for all Americans: a project 2061 report on literacy goals in science, mathematics, and technology.* Washington, DC: Author.

Burns, M. (1992). *Math and literature.* Sausalito, CA : Math Solutions.

Buschman, L. (1995). Communicating in the language of mathematics. *Teaching Children Mathematics,* 1, 324–329.

Fitzgerald, D. (1990). *Manipulatives for developing prenumber logic and problem-solving skills.* Paper presented at the National Council of Teachers of Mathematics Conference, Salt Lake City, UT.

Hembree, R., & Dessart, D. (1986). Effects of hand-held calculators in pre-college mathematics education. *Journal of Research in Mathematics Education,* 17, 83–99.

Menon, R. (1996). Mathematical communication through student-constructed questions. *Teaching Children Mathematics,* 2, 530–532.

Merenda, R. (1995). A book, a bed, a bag: interactive homework for 10! *Teaching Children Mathematics,* 1, 262-266.

A Nation at Risk. (1983). Report from the National Commission on Excellence in Education. Washington, DC: Author.

National Council of Teachers of Mathematics. (1989). *Curriculum and evaluation standards for school mathematics.* Reston, VA: Author.

National Council of Teachers of Mathematics. (1991). *Professional standards for teachers of mathematics.* Reston VA: Author.

National Council of Teachers of Mathematics. (1995). Position paper on interdisciplinary learning, pre-K–4. *Teaching Children Mathematics,* 1, 386–387.

National Research Council. (1989). *Everybody counts.* Washington, DC: Author.

National Research Council. (1990). *Reshaping school mathematics: a philosophy and framework for curriculum.* Washington, DC: Author.

National Science Teachers Association. (1996). *National science education standards.* Washington, DC: National Academy Press.

Price, J. (1995). *NCTM standards: the non-rigid triangle.* Speech presented at the National Council of Teachers of Mathematics Conference, Birmingham, AL.

Ramirez, G. & Lee, J. (1993). *Multiethnic children's literature.* New York: Delmar.

Souviney, R. J. (1995). *Learning to teach mathematics* (2nd ed.). New York: Merrill.

Stenmark, J. K. (1989). *Family math.* Berkeley, CA: EQUALS.

Theissen, D. & Matthias, M. (Eds.). (1992). *The wonderful world of mathematics.* Reston, VA: National Council of Teachers of Mathematics.

Whiten, D. J., & Wilde, S. (1992). *Read any good math books lately?* Portsmouth, NH: Heinemann.

◆ **SELECTED CHILDREN'S BOOK**

Sheehan, W. (1993). *Nature's wonderful world in rhyme.* Santa Barbara, CA: Advocacy Press. Featuring about 30 poems that "arouse a sense of wonder and desire to cherish and protect the remote and nearby natural world," this book includes realistic pictures. It may inspire discussions of sizes, shapes, and positions.

Developmental Expectations in Math

2

✓ **Developmentalism and Constructivism**

✓ **Influences on Developmental Theories**
     Jean Piaget
     Zoltan P. Dienes
     Maria Montessori

✓ **General Implications of Constructivist Theories**

✓ **Planning for Developmental Levels**
     Mathematics development

✓ **Summary**

◆◆◆

Candice, a three-year-old, is working in the math center at her day care center. Her teacher wants her to learn to count. The teacher says the number words from one to ten, pausing after each word for Candice to repeat it. When Candice says the word ten, the teacher claps and praises her effort. After several minutes of this Candice immediately says "ten" after the teacher cues her with the word "one"; she waits for praise.

This story illustrates how maturity levels may affect learning. Candice is not mature enough to understand seriation or numbers. How does maturation relate to concept development? How can teachers of young children use theories of development to plan an appropriate mathematics curriculum? This chapter explores developmental influences and how they might affect mathematics learning.

T he *American Heritage Dictionary* defines learning as "acquired wisdom, knowledge, or skill" (p. 744). The process of learning has engaged scholars for centuries, yet it is unknown precisely how humans really do learn. Numerous theories have emerged describing both learners and the manner in which people acquire knowledge. Some theorists see students as vessels waiting to be filled with mathematical knowledge. Others contend that active involvement is necessary to acquire mathematical understanding. Others feel that mathematics is a subject that only "gifted" students may ever understand. Many students, even by early elementary school years, fear mathematics and feel that they cannot succeed at this subject.

A growing body of research has emerged affirming that children learn more effectively through a developmental or constructivist approach to mathematics education that includes the necessary thought processes fundamental to mathematics understanding. In this chapter we will discuss the basis for developmental and constructivist theories and ways to plan for these levels in relation to mathematics. First, however, it is important to understand developmentalism and constructivism. What does a developmental approach mean?

What exactly does constructivism mean? How can these theories influence mathematical learning and instruction?

DEVELOPMENTALISM AND CONSTRUCTIVISM

Developmentalism and constructivism have emerged from theories based in cognitive psychology that provide the rationale for supporting active involvement in the learning process. Developmental psychologists propose the existence of stages of development concerning growth and cognition in humans and that all humans experience certain perceptions and exhibit similar behaviors at predictable times as they mature. Some studies indicate that these stages occur in sequential order (Bjorklund, 1989; Bruner, 1960; Dienes, 1960; Elkind, 1981; Erikson, 1968; Piaget, 1952). In children these stages occur in all domains of development: physical, emotional, social, and cognitive (Bredekamp, 1993). These four domains are interactive, and each area influences the other three concerning growth, development, and learning.

A constructivist teaching practice can be defined as any deliberate, thoughtful educational activity that is designed to facilitate students' active understanding (Henderson, 1996). Developmentalists and constructivists theorize that true understanding of mathematics involves the internalization of concepts and relationships by the individual involved. Individuals may interpret information regarding mathematics in varying ways.

Lourdes and Francisco are both in Mrs. Arnez's third grade class. Lourdes comes from a family that always reads to her, takes her many places, and spends a lot of time preparing her for school. Francisco comes from a single-parent family whose mother must work unusual hours to support her family. Francisco's mother cannot afford the time away from work to travel. During a mathematics lesson on map skills, the teacher asks the children to find a place far from their home. Lourdes selects a country on the other side of the globe, Francisco selects a neighboring part of the city. Which is correct? As far as the experience of each child is concerned, each is quite correct. Each child relates the concept to past personal knowledge.

As you explore developmentalism and constructivism, it is important to approach teaching from the viewpoint that each student is unique, with an individual personality, learning style, and family background, and to realize that these unique characteristics influence and create the behaviors indicative of each stage of learning. When their mental structures are ready to receive new information, children are motivated and eager to act on their environment to assimilate this information into their conceptual frameworks (Althouse, 1995). The teacher's understanding of each student's individual impact on learning plays an important role in analyzing and building mathematical learning. Mathematical learning involves far more than observable behaviors. What is happening with the student's thinking is as important as what is seen in the classroom.

Developmental and constructivist theorists emphasize active student involvement in the learning process. They assert that the degree of meaning increases when individuals interact personally with various aspects of their environment. Positive personal interactions, with adults and peers, enhance the development of mathematics meaning for children. Therefore mathematics experiences should include the use of manipulatives and real objects that children can handle and move, conversation with peers and adults, and activities that include seeking solutions to concrete real-world problems.

Developmentalists and constructivists emphasize learning large conceptual structures or overall ideas rather than the mastery of large collections of isolated bits of information. Noddings (1990) asserts that teaching isolated skills is not an appropriate approach for teaching children. Conceptual knowledge of mathematics builds on relationships connecting to other mathematical ideas and concepts and other curriculum areas. A conceptual approach allows children to acquire clear and stable ideas by constructing meanings in the context of physical situations; it allows mathematical abstractions to emerge from empirical experience (National Council of Teachers of Mathematics [NCTM], 1989).

How does conceptual teaching differ from traditional, skill-based teaching? The following examples illustrate traditional skill- and conceptual-based teaching. Carlos has been working in a classroom where mathematics instruction is taught through skill emphasis alone. Math is taught as a separate subject at a scheduled time each day. A math textbook with accompanying workbook, practice sheets, and board work are the focus of this instruction. Carlos's daily work this week has consisted of a series of worksheets on which he adds 2 to other numerals. He has spent five hours this week on these worksheets. Problems he has been working on include 2 + 4 = _____, 2 + 5 =_____, and so on. After trial and error, Carlos has memorized the symbols that combine to produce several sums. However, when he gets nervous Carlos forgets the facts he has learned and does not know how to figure out the answers.

Carlos's lessons probably bring back math memories from elementary school experiences. Traditional teaching follows an absorption theory of learning. The student is a passive receptor of knowledge, taught best by repetition of procedures involving pencils, worksheets, sitting still, and being quiet. By contrast, developmental teaching emphasizes a web of connected ideas rather than isolated bits of mechanically learned rules. Any one group of students may all hear the same lecture, but each learner is interpreting and analyzing the material in a personal manner.

Gilbert is in a developmentally appropriate classroom. There are learning centers, open spaces for group work, and places where children may work alone if they choose. Children in this classroom use and learn mathematics through exploration, discovery, and by solving meaningful problems. The teacher plans activities that will engage the children through active involvement. One day Ms. Munzo gives the children a piece of paper that is about 5 inches long. She has Gilbert find something in the room that is as long as, longer than, and shorter than his piece of paper. As Gilbert solves this problem he talks to other children to see what they have found and compare results. Gilbert and the other children in this class are learning about measurement, problem solving, and communication. Dusty, a more mature child, wants to use standard measurement to see how long her piece of paper is and compare with the other children. Dusty uses a measuring tape to determine the length of her paper and the other things she has found. She writes her measurements in her mathematics journal. Dusty and Dwight work together to calculate the differences in their measurements. The children in Ms. Munzo's class are working at different developmental levels. She walks around the class and talks to each child to analyze where each child is in relation to understanding measurement.

Another element of the developmentalist and constructivist approaches is an emphasis on the process dimension of learning. *How* children learn is as important as *what* children learn. The manner in which children approach and solve a problem is as important as the end answer. Spontaneous play, projects, and situations of daily living develop mathematics skills. Developmentalists and constructivists encourage teachers to engage children in mathematical conversations in classroom settings to develop mathematics thinking on an individual basis. Teachers work one-on-one or with small groups of children to discuss, illustrate, and encourage mathematics concept development. The children should connect existing understanding with new concepts through participation and direct involvement in this process. Constructivists view teachers as mathematical guides. The teachers provide the setting, organize the challenges, and guide the conversation and thought processes around the children's own view of mathematics.

 WHAT DO *YOU* THINK?

"Students decide early in their schooling that the mathematics they learn in school has nothing to do with their real world outside school. They do mathematics in school to please the teacher or their parents, or they do it to get done with it so people will stop bothering them, or for some other reason—but almost never do they do such problems because they want to know the answer. And almost never do they have any reason to believe that the problem, or its solution, has anything whatsoever to do with their real world" (Willoughby, 1990, p. 11). How do you use mathematics in your daily life? Why do students need to learn mathematics?

Developmentalists and constructivists advocate children's input into math content and planning curriculum exploration. Children brainstorm with the teacher to determine mathematics interests. Teachers then web ideas with the children to outline plans for learning. Teachers should encourage children to discover the connection between mathematical learning and the real world. They must listen to children explain their understanding of and interest in mathematics topics. Children help the teacher chart out future mathematical learning based on their interests and developmental levels.

Stacy Harper, a multiage class teacher at Cravens Elementary, uses the webbing technique with her children. She starts with a mathematics area like addition. The children name what the word *addition* makes them think of. One child might say "problems," another might say "more things," another might say "money," or any variety of answers. Stacy writes their ideas in circles and draws lines to her original word. Next she asks the children what they would like to learn about their individual ideas. "What would you like to learn about addition and money?" The children help Stacy plan the direction of their mathematics exploration.

Often connections between existing knowledge and new material do not happen automatically. The teacher must help the children build the bridge between personal experience and mathematical concepts. As each day unfolds there are many opportunities for the teacher to point out how

Mathematics is a natural part of real life, and of everyday life too.

mathematics is used in the classroom or to help children think about how they use mathematics in their homes. This integration of ideas requires working, reflective thinking by both the learner and teacher.

INFLUENCES ON DEVELOPMENTAL THEORIES

In the following sections we will discuss the theories of Piaget, Dienes, and Montessori as these theories apply to mathematics education for young children. Each of these individuals has made direct contributions to the developmental or constructivist theories of learning mathematical concepts. Their influences on developmentalism and constructivism are acknowledged worldwide.

Jean Piaget

Jean Piaget was a Swiss psychologist who was professionally active from the 1930s until the late 1980s. Piaget studied stages of intellectual development and their relationships to the development of cognitive or intellectual structures. He viewed intelligence as an evolving phenomenon that occurs in stages that are constant and relatively easy to identify. Piaget believed that intelligence involves continuous organization and reorganization of one's perceptions of and reactions to the environment. Development occurs as newer and more complex mental structures evolve. In order for this development to occur, children must interact with their environment and other people. Piaget states, "The essential functions of intelligence consist in understanding and in inventing, in other words in building up structures by structuring reality" (Piaget, 1969, p. 27).

Piaget's Sequence of Development

Piaget's four stages of development are useful to educators because they emphasize the development of children's thinking. He believed that children's thought processes, language, and actions differ in quality and quantity from adults. The educator should be aware of these differences in order to plan and implement appropriate activities for young children.

Sensory-Motor Stage of Development. According to Piaget, children are in the *sensory-motor stage* of development during the first two years of life. During this period children form the basis for subsequent symbolic thought through physical actions. Children in this stage spend their time looking at things, manipulating things, and placing things in their mouths. Once an interesting event occurs, children attempt to repeat it, learning new behaviors in the process. For example, babies may try to reproduce noises they have made by hitting a toy on the side of the crib. Budding concepts of time, space, and causality emerge.

In the sensory-motor stage, children may exhibit the beginning of mental representations to think about their available schemes, to predict what effect each action might have, and then apply the scheme they perceive as appropriate. During this period adults should talk to children about what they are discovering. Say things such as, "You have crawled a long way," or "The toy fits nicely in that space. It is the same size." Use basic math words that explain size and space relationships. As young children explore their environment, adults should comment on cause-effect situations. "You hit the pan lids together, that caused a noise," or "You threw your bottle, so I picked it up."

Children also discover that certain actions have effects on the environment and this provides the basis for *causality*, a thought process necessary for mathematical thinking. Mature mathematics thought includes an "if I do this, then this should happen" concept for equations. During this sensory-motor stage children gradually become aware that there is a difference between self and others; this leads the child to a more objective thought process.

An important concept that develops during the sensory-motor stage is that of *object permanence.* Through interactions, maturation, and experimentation the infant discovers that objects and people do not simply disappear when they are out of sight. All subsequent logical thought necessary for math exploration hinges on this discovery. During this stage the child discovers that while objects or people may appear in different contexts, their identities do not change.

Preoperational Stage of Development. Piaget called his second stage of development the *preoperational stage.* During this stage, language accelerates. At this stage most children talk continually and their vocabularies grow dramatically, providing an excellent opportunity for adults to introduce and encourage the use of math words. While children are discussing their environment, adults can emphasize math words or concepts as children show an interest. When young children talk they generally use ideas that make sense to them within their intellectual frameworks. This allows adults to gain insight into the children's understanding and thinking. Adults listen and extend these thoughts as children express themselves.

Usually children in the preoperational stage can classify based on one attribute. However, children may not identify like characteristics among people or objects. For example, a child may understand that red and blue shapes can be sorted by color, but not by shape or angles. Attribute recognition helps young children develop mathematical reasoning and problem-solving skills and develop trial-and-error strategies. Adults can verbalize their own thought processes for sorting and classifying in daily activities, thus helping young children focus on attributes and how objects in one set share characteristics of other sets.

Transductive reasoning is evident during the preoperational stage. A broken sequence may cause the child to disassociate from the logical pattern: cause-effect may be unclear. For example, Twana always watches cartoons on Saturday morning. One Saturday morning she oversleeps and does not see her usual programs. Later in the day her mother suggests a trip to the zoo to enjoy the pretty weather and the freedom of no school on Saturday. Twana tells her mother it can't be Saturday since she saw no cartoons that morning. Twana has established an association of cartoons with Saturday. Because she was in the preoperational stage when this pattern was broken, she disassociated from her usual thinking pattern. The cause (Twana oversleeping) did not connect to the effect (missing cartoons), therefore Twana could not believe it was Saturday. Transduction is normal for the preoperational stage of development. Discrepancies in young children's environments motivate them to find answers. In this way children structure their own knowledge (Althouse, 1995).

By the approximate age of six, children are growing out of the preoperational stage of development. According to Piaget, during this time children should begin to classify materials by more than one attribute. They might be able to sort geometric shapes by both color and shape. During this stage quantitative thinking begins. This means that children are capable of expressing quantity or numbers and amount. They can apply number ideas to sets of objects. Children should be able to understand relationships founded on numerical order. This involves the transition from counting actual objects to the use of numbers as symbolic referents.

Concrete Operational Stage of Development. Around the age of six or seven children enter what Piaget calls the *concrete operational* stage of development. At this point logical or adultlike reasoning develops in situations involving real or concrete objects and events. The most important single proposition an educator can derive from Piaget's work is *children* *learn best from concrete experiences.* In order for mental structures to change children must act on their environment (Althouse, 1995). Children need to handle, move, and use real materials to illustrate mathematics concepts.

During this period, objectivity increases in children. The child may now begin to separate his or her thinking from an egocentric perception of the world. Concrete operational thinking involves a higher degree of logic than previous levels. Children may now begin "if-then reasoning" or "eliminating cases."

One thing an adult can do to focus on this type of logical thinking is to make a chart like Figure 2.1. The children can write or dictate possible connections. Chart entries could stand for possible pairings and the strategy is to eliminate those that do not fit the conditions of the problem.

Transitivity is what Piaget called the thought process that involves using children passing from one point to another along a conceptual continuum. Children at this stage may be able to solve a problem such as the following:

> If a block is heavier than a toy car and a toy car is heavier than a crayon, which is heavier, a crayon or a block?

Transitivity is critical for continued development of number concepts. It also underlies the process necessary for arrangement of objects in a series along a continuum, such as heavier to lighter in weight. Piaget calls this *seriation.* Children can arrange sets of objects to literally show their work and then draw their sets to illustrate their work.

Development of *class inclusion* ideas is evident during the concrete operational stage. The child can now think about parts and whole independently in whole-part relationships. When shown a set of 15 red crayons and 7 green crayons and asked, "Are there more red crayons or total crayons?", the child can realize there are more crayons than the total number of red crayons. A less mature child would base an answer on the more prominent visual stimulation of red crayons and say there are more red crayons than the total number of 22 crayons. Class inclusion is the basis for understanding rational numbers, which is the first set of numbers children experience that are not based on a counting algorithm of some type. Rational numbers describe the

Figure 2.1   *Children dictate or write possible results or extensions of problem solving.*

if..............	then..........

property that between any two numbers in a system, there are other numbers. For example, between 1 and 2 there are numbers such as 1 1/2 or 1 3/4; between 0 and 1 there are numbers such as 1/4 and 2/3.

Children in this stage are ready for more sophisticated classifying and patterning activities such as making sets and subsets or multiple classification. For example, a concrete operational child may be able to sort squares and triangles into sets by shape, then make subsets by size (large squares, small squares, large triangles, small triangles). Sophisticated classification skills require a more mature level of logical thinking.

In the concrete operational stage, *reversibility* becomes evident. The children realize that for many actions there exist other actions that cancel the others out. This is a necessary thought process for addition, subtraction, and negative numbers. Breaking down a block structure reverses building a block structure; subtraction reverses addition. Reversibility is a prerequisite for acquisition of *conservation.* Piaget uses the term *conservation* to mean that certain properties of an object remain unchanged despite rearrangement or displacement of the object. The following activity concerns conservation of continuous quantity.

 CONSERVATION ACTIVITY: CONTINUOUS QUANTITY

This activity is considered a classic Piagetian activity for young children. Piaget used tasks such as this to help in his determination of developmental levels.

Focus: Conservation of continuous quantity.

What To Do: Place equal amounts of water in two identical containers. Ask the child if the glasses contain the same amount of water? If the child says "no," adjust the amount until the child agrees that the amounts are the same. Now pour the contents of the containers into a taller container with a lesser diameter.

Piaget's conservation of continuous quantity.

Ask the child about the relation of the water in the third container: "Is there more, less, or as much as in the first container?" Ask why or why not.

Interpreting Responses: A child who does not understand conservation often believes that the amount of water in the third container is more than in the comparison container. Such a child might answer, "There's more in the tall one—see it's so high." This answer reveals that the child focuses on one factor, the height of the water. She ignores the fact that the third container is thinner than the others. She also is unable to consider the fact that no water was added or taken away. She may also think the third container now holds less because the water level is low; again she focuses on only one feature of the situation—the depth of the water.

On the other hand a child that conserves will typically offer one of the following explanations.

"They're the same. You didn't add or take away." (Piaget calls this an *identity* explanation; it means that the child understands that the amounts of water stay identical even though the water is "rearranged".)

"They're the same. Look, this one is tall, but it is skinny. This one is wide, but it's not very deep." (This explanation is known as *compensation* and shows that the child is able to consider two factors for each container, depth as well as width. The child does not focus on just one characteristic and ignore the others.)

"They're the same. You could pour it back and it would be the same." (This explanation, *reversibility,* shows that a child can mentally reverse the pouring action and "see" or visualize the results.)

The concept of conservation of amount or continuous quantity develops, according to Piaget, toward the end of the preoperational stage. Typically children conserve amount and number first. They usually develop conservation concepts of area, weight, and volume during the concrete operational stage.

Associativity also develops during the concrete operational stage. Associativity allows a child to discover that different routes can lead to the same point. The child can now understand problems like $(2 + 3) + 4 = 2 + (3 + 4)$. The child realizes the possibility for combining parts in different ways or that objects of varying sizes and colors can have equal values or equal weights.

Formal Operational Stage of Development. Piaget's fourth and final stage of development is called formal operations. In the formal operational stage, the child's thought systems integrate to form more sophisticated mental structures so the child can now generate hypotheses and logical conclusions or deductions on a symbolic level. The child can now visualize the necessary manipulation of mathematical symbols internally. This is considered adult-level thinking.

Use of Piaget's Theories
A number of researchers have modified Piaget's conception of development to incorporate new empirical findings (Inagaki, 1992). Later research

indicates that sociocultural influences also affect the growth and development of children (Althouse, 1995). This suggests that developmental stages may not progress as Piaget stated, but are hindered or advanced by certain domain-specific conditions (Inagaki, 1992). Social conditions or cultural influences may slow or accelerate the stages of development.

Piaget's theories of constructivist development are still widely accepted and have greatly influenced educators. His emphasis on play as a vehicle for learning is considered an important element in intellectual development. Piaget remains the pioneer of constructivist theory.

Zoltan P. Dienes

Dienes's theories focus on mathematics. Dienes recommends that mathematics does and should have intrinsic value to the learner; the student should learn and enjoy mathematics because of the personal satisfaction derived from such work. Dienes says that mathematics learning should be integrated with the learner's personality, leading to genuine personal fulfillment (Dienes & Golding, 1971). Dienes's theory of mathematics learning has four basic principles. His first component, the dynamic principle, forms the framework for his other three principles. As you read about Dienes you will notice many similarities to the work of Piaget.

The Dynamic Principle

Dienes's *dynamic principle* states that learning proceeds from experience to the actual act of categorizing (Dienes, 1968). Thought begins with play or experimentation, and as children work a natural order of classification or sorting emerges. A young child might play with counting blocks, stacking, lining them up, or matching. At first the child randomly plays with and explores the arrangement of blocks. As the child experiments, a natural organizational thinking process emerges. Soon the child is classifying the blocks and sorting according to a personal criteria that has evolved through free exploration. This indicates that involvement is necessary for conceptual understanding and that true understanding of a new concept is an evolutionary process. Intellectual development builds on previous knowledge and experiences connected by past and new knowledge.

Dienes envisions concept understanding as evolving through three learner-involved stages. First the learner experiences the play or preliminary stage. The concept is introduced through *exploration* of materials in a free environment. Exploration appears to be a relatively unstructured activity, but the children's actions are not without organization because the teacher provides the materials and plans activities for children to have opportunities to manipulate materials. The teacher has one or two outcomes in mind and places the types of materials out that should guide the child toward understanding.

After a discovery period the teacher introduces the second stage of the dynamic principle: *structured activities* using the materials. The teacher plans these activities to guide children toward development of specific concepts. For example, the teacher might ask the children to arrange pattern blocks according to selected attributes or to follow a preassigned pattern card. The teacher might see if children can create patterns and explain their work. She may then show the children how to make a tessellated pattern covering a surface with no "holes," then encourage children to try their own.

After the children have mastered these activities, the third stage evolves: *mathematical concept development.* During this stage the teacher plans activities that imprint and foster retention of the mathematical concept. It is important that the teacher provide application of the content to the child's real world. An example of appropriate third-stage activities follows. Patterning, an important mathematical concept, takes many forms in a child's exploration of the time patterns that occur naturally in the classroom. The daily class schedule might be a time pattern children can understand. The teacher can make a "child response chart," recalling daily activities like large group time, center time, clean up, and other activities over a five-day period. On the fifth day the adult can help the children analyze the chart to look for patterns. The teacher also encourages children to look for music patterns in repeating songs. The important idea is to point out patterns in a variety of activities and contexts. This is the stage where mathematical conceptualization should occur.

Dienes calls this three-stage process a *learning cycle* (Dienes & Golding, 1971). According to Dienes the cycle must be completed before any mathematical concept becomes meaningful. He believes that all concept development should follow this sequence of learning. Dienes's next three principles all fall within the sequence of this first principle.

Perceptual Variability Principle

Dienes's second principle, the *perceptual variability principle,* states that conceptual learning occurs through exposure to a concept in a variety of physical contexts or embodiments. Educators should use a variety of materials illustrating the same conceptual structure to promote abstraction of concepts. For number understanding, the teacher might provide materials such as paper clips, pencils, crayons, or counting bears for use with any activity teaching number concepts. This allows the child to see the concept in different ways and under different conditions. As the following vignette illustrates, the child soon realizes that the concept remains constant regardless of the materials used.

Mrs. Freeman introduces linear measurement to her five- and six-year old children. Mrs. Freeman provides a variety of activities to develop this concept. She has her children use yarn to measure the lengths of the tables and other objects in the room. She provides paper clips for the children to use as units of measure; next they use interlocking cubes to form equal lengths. She has the children use adding machine tape to measure these same lengths and other lengths as well as their heights and other body parts. Mrs. Freeman helps the children make charts that compare their measuring units (10 paper clips = 7 interlocking cubes). The children write in or dictate for their math journals the different things they measured and the tools or units they used. After Mrs. Freeman provides many experiences with linear measurement, her children are ready for the introduction of standard measurement devices—rulers.

Mathematical Variability Principle

Dienes called his third principle the *mathematical variability principle*. He states that the generalizations of mathematics concepts develop when variables irrelevant to the concepts are systematically varied while keeping relevant variables constant. An example follows.

Mr. Snipes teaches his primary students about triangles. He provides a wide variety of materials that have the characteristics of triangles. He allows the children to explore triangle-shaped attribute blocks, pattern blocks, building blocks, triangles made of pipe cleaners, and other triangle shapes and pictures. He varies the length of the segments, angle sizes, and proportions, but keeps the crucial attribute—three sides—constant. The children soon realize that the size of a triangle may vary but the three sides are always present, therefore that is an important characteristic of a triangle.

Mr. Snipes wants his children to be able to identify triangles. He provides different types of materials so his class can eliminate variables that are not vital to triangle identification. Younger children seem to find generalizations on a narrow front, that is, within certain well-defined fields, easier to grasp (Dienes, 1968). The variance of materials is not a random occurrence. The teacher gathers specific materials and plans activities that guide children to discover generalizations.

Dienes recommends using the two variability principles, perceptual and mathematical, in an integrated manner. The perceptual variability principle states that "to abstract a mathematical structure effectively, one must meet it in a number of different situations to perceive its purely structural properties. The mathematical variability principle states that as every mathematical concept involves essential variables, all these mathematical variables need to be varied if the full generality of the mathematical concept is to be achieved" (Dienes, 1968, p. 223). Effective mathematical thinking must take into account the abstraction and the generalization process illustrated by these two principles. They lend nicely to interchangeable work and planning.

Constructivity Principle

Dienes's *constructivity principle* states that construction should always precede analysis. This means that an idea may be constructed before the child can analyze the components that influence the concept. With children there is usually a preponderance of constructive thinking over analytical thinking (Dienes, 1968). Unstructured play is assumed fundamental to Dienes's theory. Play leads to the construction of more and more complex categories or mental classifications as the cycles progress; play enables the child to discover the regularities and commonalties relating to concept construction. These regularities or patterns of structure can then be subjected to analysis. Young children may not consciously analyze this rule structure. Often it is imprinted and made acceptable and operational by repeated use and practice in recognizing situations where a rule structure is applicable (Dienes, 1968). For example, young children playing with a set of interlocking blocks may start building towers using blue blocks only. The children's own play experience provides the base for conceptual development that emerges in an intuitive manner. Development of analysis, or the ability to see a relationship between concepts, occurs at some future time. Dienes states that it is not possible for children to analyze what is not yet there in concrete form. Like Piaget, Dienes believes that concept development requires active involvement based on concrete experiences.

Dienes classifies two stages of thinking: *constructive thinking,* similar to Piaget's concrete operational thinking, and *analytical thinking,* similar to Piaget's formal operational thinking. For young children in the constructive stage of thinking, teachers should provide a variety of experiences that allow involvement and encourage children to construct mathematical concepts. The following is a classic problem used by Dienes.

IDENTIFYING ATTRIBUTES: THE SQUARE PROBLEM

This activity was one Dienes used to determine if a child could generalize.

Focus: Generalization.

What To Do: Provide the children with one large square, small squares, and paper strips. Ask the following questions:

- Is it possible to make a square with what you have?
- Is it possible to make one if you are allowed to have some small squares as well?
- Is this always possible whatever the number of strips that you took in the beginning?
- If it is sometimes possible to make the square and sometimes impossible, can you say what makes it possible or impossible?

Interpreting Responses: Dienes observed the children to determine if they have analytical insight into the structure and if the child could verbalize the relationship between the number of strip lengths and the number of squares. He concluded that narrowly defined immediate generalizations are found quite easy by children when it is an extension from a finite class to an infinite class of which the finite class forms a part (Dienes, 1968). Young children may or may not realize that they have the potential to create many squares with the materials provided. Some will choose only the obvious squares, while more mature children will realize the possibilities of many combinations.

Dienes expresses some concerns about the traditional mathematics education in the United States. He believes that most schools focus on narrow mathematics program objectives. When instruction includes only traditional computation skills, it limits the scope and expansion of mathematical thinking. Programs that include a wide variety of mathematics content are more appropriate for construction of mathematical thinking (Dienes & Golding, 1971).

Further, Dienes questions the use of large-group mathematics instruction. Traditionally this method exposes all children to one element of mathematics at the same time and does not address individual differences or levels among learners. Large-group mathematics instruction limits active, individual exploration of materials and does nothing to encourage analysis of materials.

Dienes also points out that traditional grading systems could actually inhibit learning. Dienes believes that mathematical learning grows from intrinsic motivation or each individual's respect for self-learning. Traditional grading encourages children to memorize facts in order to receive high grades and does not teach children to value learning. Competition often arises among children and devalues the importance of lifelong development or encourages short-term learning. Competitive grading systems based on narrow measures do not encourage learning for the pure joy of self-satisfaction; learning often is temporary, not connecting to any other concepts.

Maria Montessori

Maria Montessori, founder of the Montessori method of education was the first woman doctor of medicine in Italy. Maria Montessori became interested in learning problems through her contact with children who, at the time, were labeled mentally retarded or disturbed. As her work progressed she began to question the effectiveness of traditional instruction used with all children.

Montessori's Components

Montessori stresses the first six years of life as the most critical for developing thinking skills. Montessori emphasizes the importance of a *prepared environment.* She states that an organized and coordinated set of materials and equipment should promote significant learning in a child

(Montessori, 1965). A Montessori room has a highly ordered room arrangement. All things have a place and all things are in place. The children are responsible for learning and maintaining this order.

Montessori's *motor education* emphasizes freedom of movement. Motor education activities are goal oriented and functional for the child in managing and responding to the real-world environment. Activities include such things as lacing, typing, cutting, pouring water, and other small muscle involvement fundamental for development of practical life skills. Integrated into motor education are responsibility training activities.

The second component of Montessori's method is *sensory education*, which uses motor activities to explore beginning mathematical concepts. She designed elaborate teaching materials that built sensory discrimination skills. Concepts of form, size, weight, temperature, and texture evolve from these activities. Children study sequenced activities and materials simultaneously. These materials and activities foster the children's techniques of observation and decision-making abilities. Montessori's objectives for the sensory component are important mathematical skills:

◆ The ability to recognize and match identities.

◆ The ability to discriminate differences among items that are similar in shape, color, texture, weight, and other properties.

◆ The ability to discriminate and classify sensory attributes.

One example of Montessori's sensory materials is the cylinder block. This block of wood has bored sockets of graded sizes. There are wooden cylinders that correspond to and fit into the sockets. The cylinders are identical in form and color. They vary in two attributes, width and length. The cylinder block lends itself to size comparison and seriation activities (Figure 2.2).

Montessori's *language education* occurs in conjunction with sensory education and focuses on a lot of vocabulary development. This sequence of development starts with naming, then recognizing, and last pronouncing related words. The teacher initiates naming during a demonstration period. For example, a teacher shows a rectangle to the children and says, "This is a rectangle." Next the children respond to identifying statements as the teacher says things like, "Give me the red rectangle," or "Show me the largest rectangle." The last stage, pronunciation, requires the child to respond to questions such as, "What is this?" or "Tell me its name."

Figure 2.2 *Maria Montessori's cylinder blocks.*

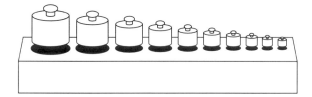

Formal Instruction

Academic learning or "essential culture," according to Montessori, begins at age four. Children engage in activities that teach writing, reading, and arithmetic. Formal mathematics instruction starts during this stage. Number introduction begins with red and blue rods, a set of materials Montessori designed. These rods, based on the decimal system, are carefully scaled so that the largest rod is twice the length of the next rod, the third rod is three times the length of the first rod, and so on. These rods are graded in succession from 1 through 10. Number names and their corresponding symbols are taught in the customary sequence.

Greater levels of complexity follow exercises with the number rods. These include experiences that teach the meaning of zero, odd and even numbers, and the decimal system, which was taught with a device known as the golden bead material in which a single bead represents a unit. A vertical row of beads represents the quantity 10. A square composed of 10 vertical rows of 10 beads each represents a unit and a cube comprised of ten 100-squares indicates 1000. Activities that require the child to count large numbers of beads dramatize the need for a more economical strategy than counting out single beads. Thus substitutions, exchanging one 10-bar for 10 units, can be made when necessary. The golden bead materials are also used for games that teach basic mathematics operations.

GENERAL IMPLICATIONS OF CONSTRUCTIVIST THEORIES

A reform of existing educational practice, teacher-student interactions, mathematical content, and teaching methods is called for if the ideas of Piaget, Dienes, and Montessori are to be implemented. One major developmentalist and constructivist concern deals with teaching methods or the actual processes of instruction. How a teacher relays information could be as important as the information itself.

Teaching that focuses on developmentally appropriate methods should enhance constructivist principles. Althouse (1995) suggests that teaching developmentally should (1) allow choice from among many teaching themes as long as children have some prior knowledge of the topic; (2) allow teachers to direct and facilitate children's acquisition of knowledge by encouraging children to pursue topics in depth; and (3) allow children to define and solve problems through interactions with their peers. The classroom focus is on the student not the teacher. This approach to teaching is called learner *centered instruction.*

Developmental and constructivist teaching requires a flexible room arrangement to allow children to move freely and have the space to investigate problem-solving situations. These types of rooms do not use straight rows of desks, but usually have tables or desks grouped in a manner that allows small-group work. Children move between small groups for investigations or learning centers that address individual levels of thinking.

It is also important to analyze teachers' attitudes toward mathematics. Teachers are often among the first causes in what has become a vicious circle of discouragement about and failure in mathematics (Cipra, 1992). Many teachers feel inadequate concerning their own mathematics ability. Often teachers fear mathematics instruction or are uncomfortable in a facilitating role of instruction because of personal insecurities. Special training sessions to encourage a more positive learning environment will help educators accept this role.

Although the developmentalist-constructivist position originated in the 1960s and 1970s, it is as important today as when it was originally conceived (Post, 1992). More recently several national educational organizations have developed topic-related position documents that advocate developmental teaching. The National Council of Teachers of Mathematics (NCTM, 1989) supports these theories and calls for reform following developmental and constructivist teaching methods. The National Association for the Education of Young Children (NAEYC) has published position statements and guidance documents to support and implement developmental teaching in the primary schools. Many other groups recommend that mathematics be taught in such a way that children not only will be able to use and understand mathematics, but also will *want* to use mathematics.

PLANNING FOR DEVELOPMENTAL LEVELS

Planning is a vital part of any successful teaching experience. Whatever the type of activity, teacher directed or student directed, the key to success lies in organization. Planning facilitates the teaching process and allows teachers to reflect on their work. Planning for developmental mathematics instruction takes careful thought and needs to be flexible.

It is important to remember that the individual child's characteristics should be considered first. Setting the goals without considering the children first is ineffective and inappropriate (Taylor, 1995). Planning is like creating a new recipe for successful mathematics. Many ingredients are blended to achieve the best possible product. Cooks may vary individual ingredients until they find that perfect combination. Planning requires constant experimenting and blending to find the appropriate mixture of content and method for each child.

Most states have mandated expectations for mathematics instruction. Teachers can write or call their state department of education, located in each state capitol, and request mandated curriculum requirements. These should be used as a teaching guide and introduced as individual children mature. It is important to remember that all children will not be ready for

Children can discover many things about balance and shape as they work with blocks.

the same skill or concept at the same time, but curriculum guides are useful for directing goal planning. Some school districts have set curriculum expectations. Wherever teachers live, it is important to consider state and district guidelines when designing lessons.

In addition it is vital for teachers to keep up with professional societies' recommendations for teaching methods and content. This book includes recommendations from the NCTM and the NAEYC. Both organizations provide sound advice for developmental teaching of mathematics. Mathematics is traditionally considered cognitive development, yet all four domains—emotional, social, physical, and cognitive— interact and influence each other.

Mathematics Development

Traditionally, counting is one of the earliest mathematics experiences for young children. They may name a series of number names or express large numbers such as two zillion. Children do not recognize symbols yet, but have heard the names, and repetition follows (Taylor, 1995). Many researchers question the value of drilling young children in number sequence. Developmentalists recommend concept development before number recognition. Piaget wrote, "When adults try to impose mathematical concepts on a child prematurely, his learning is merely verbal; true understanding of them comes only with his mental growth." Piaget proposed mathematics concept development as follows:

- ◆ Classification—the process of making sets in which objects within the sets are alike according to some property.
- ◆ Seriation—arranging materials in order, such as from shortest to longest.
- ◆ Spatial relationships—understanding of pictures of three-dimensional solids as well as orientation of figures.

◆ Temporal relationships—understanding of time relationships.

◆ Conservation—properties remain the same although materials are rearranged.

Dr. Stanley Ball from the University of Texas at El Paso has been collecting data regarding developmental levels. In his mathematics class he presents a wide variety of problems and asks his students to arrange them in order according to complexity, from easiest to hardest. Dr. Ball has found that almost all students agree on the easiest and the hardest problems. However, the progression of levels in between are rarely consistent among students. This supports the constructivist view of mathematics learning. Each student views the complexity of mathematical tasks from their own individual knowledge base. Developmental levels are different for each individual, and the educator should be aware of this when working with children.

SUMMARY

Developmentalist and constructivist theories have influenced mathematics instruction in this country. These theories propose that learning is a highly individual process and that many things influence the development of mathematics understanding. Children grow through developmental stages that influence their perceptions of mathematics. Chronological ages of children in these stages of development vary, depending on factors such as physiological maturation, meaningful social and educational interactions, and the nature and degree of relevant intellectual and psychological experiences. Play is considered an important element for development of thought. Hands-on concrete materials are recommended for mature construction of concepts. The thinking and learning processes are active rather than passive. Relationships connect mathematics concepts to other mathematics areas and the individual learner.

Piaget, Dienes, and Montessori have all contributed to the developmentalists' mathematics research. There are common themes among their work. All support movement and active involvement. Traditional teaching methods do not address the key points of these developmental learning theories. Planning should allow for individual differences among learners. A learning center room arrangement lends itself to developmental teaching.

◆ REFERENCES

Althouse, R. (1995). *Investigating mathematics with young children*. New York: Teachers College Press.

Bjorklund, D. F. (1989). *Children's thinking: developmental functions and individual differences*. Pacific Grove, CA: Brooks/Cole.

Bredekamp, S. (1993). *Developmentally appropriate practice in early childhood programs serving children from birth through age 8.* Washington, DC: National Association for the Education of Young Children.

Borko, C. & Borko, H. (1992). Becoming a mathematics teacher. *Handbook of research on mathematics teaching and learning.* New York: MacMillan Publishing Company, 1992.

Bruner, J. S. (1960). *The process of education.* Cambridge, MA: Harvard University Press.

Cipra, B. (preparer), & Flanders, J. (compiler). (1992). *On the mathematical preparation of elementary school teachers.* Report from the University of Chicago supported by the National Science Foundation and Exxon Education Foundation.

Dienes, Z. P. (1968). *Building up mathematics.* London: Hutchinson Educational Ltd.

Dienes, Z. P., & Golding, E.W. (1971). *Approach to modern mathematics.* New York: Herder and Herder.

Elkind, D. (1981). *Children and adolescents: interpretive essays on Jean Piaget.* New York: Oxford University Press.

Erikson, E. H. (1968). *Identity, youth, and crisis.* New York: W. W. Norton.

Henderson, J. (1996). *Reflective teaching.* Columbus, OH: Merrill.

Inagaki, K. (1992). Piagetian and post-Piagetian conceptions of development and their implications for science education in early childhood. *Early Childhood Research Quarterly.* 7, 115-133.

Montessori, M. (1965). *The Montessori elementary method.* Cambridge, MA: Robert Bentley.

National Council of Teachers of Mathematics. (1989). *Curriculum and evaluation standards for school mathematics.* Reston, VA: Author.

_____. (1991). *Professional standards for teaching mathematics.* Reston, VA: Author.

Noddings, N. (1990). Constructivism in mathematics education. In B. Davis, C. Maher, & N. Noddings (Eds.), *Constructivist views on the teaching and learning of mathematics.* [Monograph]. *Journal for Research in Mathematics Education,* 4, 7–18.

Piaget, J. (1952). *The origins of intelligence in children.* (M. Cook, Trans.). New York: W. W. Norton.

Piaget, J. (1969). *The theory of stages in cognitive structure.* New York: McGraw Hill.

Piaget, J. (1970). *Science education and the psychology of the child.* New York: Grossman.

Post, T. R. (1992). *Teaching mathematics in grades K-8.* Needham Heights, MA: Allyn and Bacon.

Taylor, B. J. (1995). *A child goes forth.* Columbus, OH: Merrill.

Willoughby, S. (1990). *Mathematics education for a changing world.* Alexandria, VA: Association for Supervision and Curriculum Development.

Mathematics Standards and Developmentally Appropriate Practice

3

◆◆◆

Ms. Snipes teaches in a preschool where her students practice writing numerals, matching numerals, and counting out loud. All the other teachers have the children do the same thing. Sometimes her children complete and take home 20 or more worksheets a week. Ms. Snipes is not sure she is teaching the children what they really need to know about mathematics. She asks her coworkers for help but no one knows what to tell Ms. Snipes. They learned mathematics in this manner and have always taught this way. Ms. Snipes's director has no answers for her either. Where can Ms. Snipes find the answers to questions like this? Where do teachers look for guidance about teaching mathematics to young children?

Mathematics education in the United States is a vast enterprise involving millions of teachers and tens of millions of students. Yet by nearly every measure, mathematics education in the United States today is a failure (Garfunkel & Young, 1992). Although the National Science Foundation (NSF) reports more time is being spent on mathematics in the elementary schools, little progress has been made toward raising mathematics scores nationally (National Science Foundation [NSF], 1996). Many studies document our nation's failure to provide students with a mathematical background adequate to meet our society's needs, not only for careers in science and engineering, but for jobs in offices and on factory floors (Cipra & Flanders, 1992). This mathematics crisis has forced educators to closely examine every aspect of mathematics education.

Mr. Garland has been teaching first grade mathematics for 25 years. He was a student himself when the Russians conquered outer space and remembers how his "arithmetic" class changed as "new math" became the rage. When he entered high school, "new math" disappeared and Mr. Garland had to spend many hours catching up in order to pass his required courses. In college his education classes focused on basic operations and skills. In addition, his college professors demanded he learn the metric system because the United States was changing to this system.

Mr. Garland, like other teachers who survived the "new math" programs of the 1950s and 1960s, the "back-to-basics" movement of the 1970s, and the "critical thinking" movement of the 1980s, may view recent reform efforts with doubt and apathy. Some traditional veterans of education see no need to reform anything at all, but consider current reform efforts as mere fads or change for the sake of change. However, many educators agree that this new mathematics reform is substantive and will change the what and how of instruction. Current reformers view mathematics as thinking and reasoning; they view teaching as involving and guiding students in the process of making sense of mathematical ideas (Battista, 1994).

Many elements influence mathematical curriculum reform. The National Council of Teachers of Mathematics (NCTM) (1989) advises teachers to remember that learning mathematics has a purpose. Young children use mathematics to understand and interpret their world and solve everyday problems. Mathematics application in the daily environment allows children to appreciate mathematics and see a real reason why they need to learn the subject. Mathematics lessons should fit into individual children's level of understanding.

DEVELOPMENTALLY APPROPRIATE PRACTICE

Carol Gestwicki (1995) defines developmentally appropriate practice as "applying child development knowledge in making thoughtful and appropriate

WHAT DO *YOU* THINK?

"The public's first intimation that there might be something seriously wrong with mathematics education came with the publication of results from the first International Study in Mathematics Education in 1964. The United States was outranked by many countries. If you talk to educators, parents, or even children in these other countries, you are struck with the fact that they are, in general, not satisfied with their mathematics education. However, in the United States, where children are demonstrably learning less mathematics, and learning it less well than other industrialized countries, teachers, parents, and children are convinced that they are doing well in mathematics" (Willoughby, 1990 p.4). How do you account for this difference in perceptions? How do you feel about your mathematics education? Jot some answers down and compare them with a colleague's.

decisions about early childhood program practices." Developmentally appropriate practice does not prescribe a curriculum but rather an approach to teaching. The National Association for the Education of Young Children (NAEYC) describes characteristics of programs considered developmentally appropriate. A series of documents have been published through the NAEYC to guide educators of young children.

Background

Early childhood education programs began in the United States during colonial times. There has been a wide variation among program approaches throughout the history of the United States. While the proportion of children enrolled in primary schools has remained constant since World War II, the proportion of children enrolled in preprimary school (preschool and kindergarten) has increased (Spodek & Saracho, 1994a).

Because of the increasing population of young children in child-care facilities the NAEYC began an investigation into the quality of these programs. The NAEYC leaders expressed concern that many individuals without early childhood backgrounds were designing programs for young children (Spodek & Saracho, 1994a). As a result, the NAEYC developed a document of early childhood standards to provide guidance to child-care providers.

National Association for the Education of Young Children

A developmentally appropriate curriculum builds on each child's previous knowledge to design an array of opportunities for learning. An approach to developmentally appropriate practice is explained in two documents from the NAEYC. In *Developmentally Appropriate Practice in Early Childhood Programs Serving Children from Birth Through Age 8*, the NAEYC defines developmentally appropriate practice in terms of parent relationships, staffing patterns, and curriculum (Brewer, 1995). This document defines age and individual appropriateness and includes many meaningful suggestions for early childhood curriculums.

Age appropriateness. Human development research indicates that there are universal, predictable sequences of growth and change that occur in children during the first nine years of life. These predictable changes occur in all domains—physical, emotional, social, and cognitive. Knowledge of typical development of children within the age span served by the program provides a framework from which teachers prepare the learning environment and plan appropriate experiences.

Individual appropriateness. Each child is a unique person with an individual pattern of timing of growth, as well as individual personality, learning style, and family background. Both the curriculum and the adult's interaction with children should be responsive to individual differences. Learning is the result of interaction between the child's thoughts and experiences with materials, ideas, and people. These experiences should match the child's developing abilities while also challenging the child's interest and understanding (cited in Brewer, 1995, p.2).

The curriculum framework is extended in a second NAEYC document, *Reaching Potentials: Appropriate Curriculum and Assessment for Young Children* (Bredekamp & Rosegrant, 1992). The NAEYC documents are based on important principles relating to how children learn. Educators need to be aware of these principles and how they apply to mathematics education. Adults have many decisions to make as they translate knowledge of child development into practical implications for mathematics education (Gestwicki, 1995). Influenced by changing views concerning how children learn, there is a movement away from a traditional teacher-directed curriculum toward a more developmentally appropriate child-centered approach (Althouse, 1994).

 WHAT DO *YOU* THINK?

A second grade teacher tries to get away from her mathematics workbook and drill sheets. She wants to try a broader curriculum and use a lot of manipulatives. Her student's parents are upset when they do not get weekly worksheets. Most of the parents in her classroom attended school when emphasis was on skill acquisition. How can she explain to the parents why she is working like this? How will you explain to parents why developmentally appropriate mathematics is important to young children?

Principles and Implications

Some educators contend that curriculum develops in response to pressures to provide coverage of content and to enhance performance on standardized tests (Texas Education Agency, 1994). But most informed professionals believe that curriculum should instead evolve from knowledge of individual children's stages of development and principles of appropriate practice.

The NAEYC presents eight principles that apply to mathematics instruction. Much of the literature on child development reinforces basic concepts from constructivist theories and recommended national standards. The principles are stated in broad terms for curriculum development, but the discussion of implications of each clarifies how the principles may apply to mathematics programs.

1. *The curriculum is consistent with current recommendations from professional societies and research on how children learn. The curriculum has intellectual integrity.*

Curriculum for young children should follow guidelines from professional societies such as the NAEYC and NCTM. Educators, aware of national societies recommendations, apply this knowledge to their planning and work. Although the NCTM standards do not include three- or four-year-olds in the recommendations for grades K–4, they include topics such as estimation, measurement, number, problem solving, spatial

Seriation materials enhance children's concepts of position and size. Hand-eye coordination is also strengthened as children work independently with such materials.

sense, patterns, and communication. These topics are developmentally appropriate for children as young as age three (Althouse, 1994).

2. *Curriculum addresses a broad range of content that is relevant, engaging, and meaningful to students. This content develops through a wide variety of learning experiences, materials and equipment, and instructional strategies.*

To become mathematically literate, children must know more than arithmetic. They must acquire knowledge of such important topics as measurement, geometry, statistics, probability, and algebra (NCTM, 1989). Educators of young children must prepare them for the world in which they will live, one where mathematics is an everyday occurrence not a score on a worksheet. They need opportunities to use number concepts and skills to explore, discover, and solve meaningful problems (Gestwicki, 1995). The following vignette illustrates how a child solves a problem that is meaningful to her.

Marisela is five years old. Her birthday is next week and she plans to have her friends to a party. Marisela wants her whole class to attend, but her mother has limited the number of guests to six because of the limited space in their apartment. Marisela looks at the space in the living room and agrees that there is not much room. However, Marisela moves some of the furniture into her room and shows her mother how more children could fit into the apartment. Marisela experiments with space by pretending to be doing things that could happen at her party. Her mother agrees four more guests can come. Marisela has solved a problem that is meaningful to her. She had a real reason to work on spatial arrangement and number relationships. Opportunities to use mathematics in contexts that are personally meaningful to children help them develop strong mathematical concepts (Gestwicki, 1995).

3. *Curriculum allows for focus on topics while integrating across curriculum areas through thematic/project-type planning.*

Very young children are capable of assimilating thoughts and seeing connections (Althouse, 1994). Young children make sense of mathematics when connections to other curriculum areas and daily activities are emphasized. Integrating mathematics with daily events and other curriculum subjects fosters a strong sense of community and provides many opportunities for critical thinking and choice as well as cooperative work with others. Integrated curriculums provide time to develop self-knowledge and competency (Charbonneau & Reider, 1995).

Mr. Newman integrates mathematics and language arts as he prepares a story for his first grade children. His story relates to the theme "The World Around Us." He has copied today's story on large charts and displayed them on the wall. The table in front of the story charts has paper and pencil, as well as manipulative materials.

After reading the story to his class, Mr. Newman helps the children identify the nouns from the story he has read. Mr. Newman provides this list of nouns and he encourages a small group of children to tally the number of nouns from the story on a tally sheet. He helps the children interpret the results from this sheet and prepare a graph of their results. Some children use interlocking cubes to represent the numbers of nouns, others choose to color in centimeter-square paper. Other areas of the room have activities emphasizing other curriculum skills that relate to the book he has read.

The real world provides challenges that are complex and require integration of subject-area information, knowledge, and prior experience (Texas Education Agency, 1994). Thematic or project planning with subject areas integrated creates a meaningful context for instruction. Children see how concepts relate to each other and why it is important to connect their learning to the world. Skills become tools that children use to enhance understanding, not a base for learning.

4. *Curriculum actively engages children in the learning process.*

Appropriate plans for young children's instruction emphasize learning as an interactive process. The environment allows children to learn through exploration and interaction with adults, other children, and materials. The room arrangement lends itself to movement and communication. Children are encouraged to share ideas and interact with one another (Althouse, 1994).

5. *Curriculum emphasizes reasoning, problem solving, and decision making.*

Problem solving is a process that should permeate the entire mathematics curriculum and provide the context in which concepts and skills are learned (NCTM, 1989). The thought processes involved in reasoning influence the ability to solve problems. How children perceive their mathematical learning and why they have made a mathematical decision is as important as the answer. Children do not arrive at school with empty minds. Children are constantly engaged in the business of making sense of their world, a process that involves much reasoning and problem solving (Clinchy, 1995). Mathematics reasoning and thought processes are with children from birth. Children explore problems naturally; they want to make sense of their world and themselves. The emphasis in developmentally appropriate primary classrooms is on developing the thinking that underlies a child's ability to deal with mathematical symbols (Kamii & Kamii, 1990).

Decision making directly relates to problem solving and reasoning. Future generations face more complex and vital decisions than any that have come before. World population growth, accompanied by overcrowding and hunger, environmental destruction, new diseases, and political and ethical considerations are but a few of the problems these children must solve. The children of tomorrow must be prepared to make informed logical decisions in order to sustain life on Earth. Mathematics plays an important role in finding solutions to these and other societal problems. Adults in developmentally appropriate programs help children define problems, seek answers, and organize information (Althouse, 1994).

6. *Curriculum builds the children's sense of competence and an enjoyment of learning.*

Another important goal of the primary mathematics curriculum is to help children develop confidence in their ability to think things through (Gestwicki, 1995) and to instill in students a sense of confidence in their ability to think and communicate mathematically (NCTM, 1989).

Educators must provide activities that allow success and reinforce independence for children. Open-ended activities allow children to develop confidence in their abilities to analyze. Ideas such as "one answer only" or "teacher as the only right person" inhibit children's expanded thinking.

One related goal of an appropriate mathematics program is to help children develop the belief that they have the power to do mathematics and that they have control over their successes and failures. Belief in their ability to control problem-solving success encourages children to continue and extend their problem-solving skills. This autonomy develops as children gain confidence in their ability to reason and justify their thinking (NCTM, 1989).

Learning should be pleasant and enjoyable for children. Early childhood educators have long advocated play as a means of teaching young children. A play environment is conducive to eliciting the child's highest skill level (Linder, 1993). Many teachers feel that fun is directly opposed to learning: "Children have to learn that life is not all fun and games." Making mathematics fun can enhance concept development and lay a basis for wanting to continue the lifelong pursuit of learning. The mathematical ideas that children acquire in the early years build a foundation for all future study of mathematics (NCTM, 1989).

7. *Curriculum acknowledges the importance of social interactions to learning.*

"Social interaction" refers to needed skills for communicating and working with other people as well as to behaviors that lead to peer acceptance or popularity. These skills are vital for working with others in the real world and influence the perception of self-esteem among children and adults. Social interactions in the early years will affect children's later academic performance, feelings about themselves, attitudes toward others, and future social patterns (Spodek & Saracho, 1994b).

WHAT DO *YOU* THINK?

Children act, believe, and feel in ways that are consistent with the mores of their communities. Young children who speak a language other than English or a nonstandard dialect are reluctant to give up this connection to members of their own group. Attending school often makes these children feel inadequate and left out. The same curriculum and one lesson level for everyone should not be used for all children. Children socialized in different worlds will not understand the material in the same way (Bowman, 1989).

How does the above relate to constructivist theories? How can a teacher use this information to plan for mathematics instruction? Make a list of approaches to teaching mathematics that can meet the needs of all children.

Social interactions are inseparable from communication skills; they directly affect learning. Young children learn language through open communication, so it would seem reasonable that open communication also enhances mathematical learning. Children need to talk and communicate in a friendly, relaxed manner during class time. Such interaction with classmates and educators helps children construct mathematical concepts and enhances social competence. The socialization aspect encourages clearer mathematical thinking by encouraging children to share ideas and interact with one another (Althouse, 1994).

8. *Curriculum builds on children's prior knowledge and fosters acquisition of new skills and concepts.*

Mathematics is not something that waits until a child enters a formal classroom at a prescribed age (Taylor, 1995). Mathematics instruction should start with what a child already knows and build from there. The work of Constance Kamii (1973) explains that children structure their mathematical knowledge from their own actions and the logical sense of these actions. Children's understanding of mathematics evolves from an individual frame of reference, unique to the individual's environment and experiences, and builds from each child's perception of the learning experience. Kamii's work reinforces the constructivist view of learning and suggests that educators change from the traditional whole-group, one-lesson approach to more individualized methods.

To emphasize applications and to relate the use of mathematics to everyday life, teachers might use story problems dealing with their local community to maintain the children's interest. For example, Mr. Casillas teaches in a school on the border of the United States and Mexico. He has his children make tortillas at the mathematics center. The children use their measuring skills to mix the flour or corn meal. Then they estimate the circumference of the tortillas and think of ways to determine the actual measurement. Children look for other things in the classroom that might have the same circumference and compile a list on the board. Then they investigate their comparisons through actual measurement of circumference while more mature children work with diameter. Younger children might focus on the characteristics of a circle and finding similar shapes in the environment. Another teacher helps children to plan a week's snacks, estimate the cost, shop for the food, and prepare the snacks.

NCTM PROFESSIONAL STANDARDS

A second set of standards published by NCTM deals with a variety of topics relevant to the act of teaching mathematics in the classroom. The Professional Standards for Teaching Mathematics (NCTM, 1991) discusses the role of the teacher, the nature of the classroom environment, the process of teacher evaluation, and teachers' professional development. The intention of the teaching standards is not to create another endless checklist of concepts, skills, and behaviors that teachers must have, rather the standards outline a set of principles that will be of value for judgment regarding mathematics instruction. The emphasis is on creating a learner-centered approach to teaching. The following example illustrates one approach to a learner-centered primary classroom.

Ms. Harper's classroom is arranged in learning centers. She has a research center where she provides theme-related books on many reading levels. Her mathematics center contains a variety of mathematical tools that encourage exploration. Other centers include science materials, art supplies, and computers. One day Ms. Harper places a large bowl of multicolored cereal in the mathematics center. The cereal includes red, yellow, and orange pieces. The children fill a cup with cereal, estimate how many pieces of each color are in the cup, and record their estimates in their math journals. After they separate and count each color of cereal, they record the data and make a graph to illustrate their discoveries. The children subtract to find the difference between their estimations and the actual number of each color of cereal. Some children use a scale to weigh the cup full of cereal and an empty cup. Others decide to use the cereal as a unit of measurement to determine the capacity of the measuring cup. The teacher monitors the work in the centers. She talks to the children about their investigations and clarifies concepts. As Ms. Harper talks to her class she makes short notes about the level of understanding her students display while they work. She keeps notes in their files so she can write narratives about their work at report card time. Ms. Harper's classroom encourages mathematics investigation as children are free to explore mathematics and are allowed to initiate mathematical learning.

Principles for Teaching

The NCTM standards (1989) recommend a significant departure from traditional practices of mathematics teaching. It suggests change in not only what is taught but how it is taught. The NCTM's 1991 document recommends needed changes to implement the curriculum standards in an appropriate manner. The first section presents teaching methods and how they influence mathematics educators. The following paragraphs summarize the four main areas from this document.

Tasks

The first teaching standard relates to mathematical instruction "tasks," that is, the projects, questions, problems, constructions, applications, and exercises in which students engage. Tasks provide the stimulus for students to think about concepts and procedures, their connections with other mathematical ideas, and their application to real-world contexts. Tasks also convey messages about what mathematics is and what doing mathematics entails. Tasks should create opportunities for students to develop mathematical understandings, competence, interests, and dispositions. The tasks standard (NCTM, 1991, p. 25) includes the following:

> The teacher of mathematics should pose tasks that are based on

- ◆ sound and significant mathematics;
- ◆ knowledge of students' understandings, interests, and experiences;
- ◆ knowledge of the range of ways that diverse students learn mathematics.

Following is an example of a teacher allowing students to explore sound and significant mathematics in a variety of ways.

Mr. Sheffield introduces perimeter to his third grade class. He passes out plastic one-inch squares to his class. He also gives them a prepared sheet that looks like Figure 3.1. He demonstrates on an overhead projector how to find perimeter by tracing along the edges of the figures, and the children work in small groups or with partners to arrange their

Figure 3.1 *Mr. Sheffield helps his students learn about perimeter by using Diene's perceptual variability principle.*

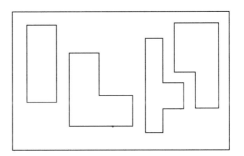

squares on worksheets like the one pictured. Mr. Sheffield gives the students another set of problems to solve with their plastic squares. He walks around the classroom and talks to the children about what they are doing.

Mr. Sheffield next challenges the students to find the perimeter of their mathematics books, their desks, and four other things of their choice in the classroom. Soon a child excitedly tells the teacher that she has found a shortcut. "If you double the length and width and add them together, you get the right number for the perimeter." Another child discovers that you can represent this idea symbolically. Other children are including the handlelike part on their desk. One child explores his shoe while others investigate other things in the classroom. Mr. Sheffield helps the students share what they have found and write their discoveries in a formula form. He accepts a range of numbers on the classroom tasks he gives the children.

 WHAT DO *YOU* THINK?

Means and Knapp (1991) recommend that educators make connections with students' out-of-school experience to increase learning by using realistic problems to solve in class, but also encouraging students to bring their own real-life problems for classmates to solve. Think about the community in which you live. How could you relate your community to your mathematics instruction? What types of realistic problems could you include when teaching mathematics to young children?

Sound mathematics tasks are ones that do not separate mathematical thinking from mathematical skills and concepts. That is, the thought processes behind problem solving connect to concepts and include skills. Learning is not an isolated event, but rather a blend of all three areas, the mathematics content, the students, and the way the students learn mathematics. The idea that children should act on their environment through hands-on approaches to learning, that they should manipulate concrete materials in ways that are parallel to mental operations, and that they should learn to solve mathematical problems is good education (Spodek & Saracho, 1994).

Students should be involved with task planning. What do the students already know? What do they need to work on? What are the students' interests, dispositions, and experiences? Sensitivity to the diversity of students' backgrounds and experiences is crucial in selecting mathematical tasks (NCTM, 1991).

WHAT DO *YOU* THINK?

Often teachers believe that a "quiet" classroom is a learning classroom. How do you feel about this? What do you remember about mathematics classes? Were you allowed to talk or not? Did you really pay attention to everything your mathematics teacher said or did your mind wander to other topics while he or she talked?

Did your classroom provide activities that helped visual learners, auditory learners, or kinesthetic learners? Jot down a few ways that you can teach children who learn best through movement or by a combination of learning styles. How do you best learn mathematics? Total quiet? Bright or dim lighting? By drawing representations as you think? What kind of mathematics learner are you?

Discourse

Students' actual opportunities for classroom application of tasks depends on the type of discourse that the teacher allows. Discourse refers to ways of representing, thinking, talking, agreeing, and disagreeing. Discourse includes values about knowledge and authority. How are ideas discussed? What do the ideas include? What makes something true in mathematics? How do students know mathematical ideas make sense? The NCTM (1991, p. 35) recommends the following:

The teacher of mathematics should orchestrate discourse by

♦ posing questions and tasks that elicit, engage, and challenge each students' thinking;

♦ listening carefully to students' ideas;

♦ asking students to clarify and justify their ideas orally and in writing.

The teachers' role is to initiate and guide the discourse in the classroom, so they must be observant and sensitive to student participation. The culture of the classroom should include an environment in which everyone's thinking is respected and in which reasoning and arguing about mathematical meanings is encouraged (NCTM, 1991).

Ms. Ainsa works with a group of children ages three and four. She arranges the tables in her room so that a small number of children sit at each table. At snack time she allows the children to help set up the tables. She talks to them during the entire process, listening carefully to everything they say. She asks Ava to please help decide how many cups, napkins, and other snack things they need at her table. Ava and Jorge talk about how many chairs are at the table and who they think will sit there.

Ms. Ainsa suggests they place one napkin at each chair. When Jorge decides to also place one cup with each napkin, Ava looks at the children and tries to determine if each child will have a cup and napkin. Ms. Ainsa helps Ava count the children and then the snack supplies. Jorge says there are two extra cups and napkins and picks them up. Ms. Ainsa asks Ava and Jorge to count all the children that will sit at their table and say the names of each child. Ava realizes that they forgot to include themselves when counting children. Ms. Ainsa helps the children recount the number of children at the table and finish setting the table. Ms. Ainsa changes the number of chairs at each table throughout the year and allows different children to be snack helpers.

This vignette illustrates a teacher who uses the idea that children modify and construct ideas by interacting with their physical world, materials, and other children (NCTM, 1989). Ms. Ainsa provides many opportunities for her children to interact in their classroom through daily activities. She encourages her children to talk, discussing real mathematics problems they encounter.

The teacher should orchestrate discourse by posing questions and tasks that elicit, engage, and challenge thinking, listen carefully to students, ask students to justify answers, and guide the mathematical analysis of all instruction. Mathematics journals also allow children and educators to reflect on their thought processes and analyze the development of concepts. The following example comes from a multilevel classroom at Cravens Elementary School. Children in this classroom work in learning centers and write journals that reflect daily work. The following excerpt illustrates the child's thinking process.

> I gest that my tape would be 14 inches long. But it was 12 inches long. I had the longest tape in my group.
> I gest I was 41 inches.
> I am 51 inches long. I am 132 centimeters long. Next time I will know how to do this better. I will look at what I am measuring first and then try to gess. I could use myself as a way to help gess.

This journal excerpt illustrates a reflective thought process as the child writes about her work. The children at Cravens Elementary School engage in active communication; written and oral language abound as children work. A conceptual approach enables children to develop and acquire clear and stable concepts by constructing meaning in the contexts of physical situations (NCTM, 1989). A conceptually oriented curriculum can result in better balanced, more dynamic programs that are more appropriate for the intellectual needs and abilities of children.

Students also play an important role in discourse. Children are doers—their thinking patterns do not allow them to sit and listen or absorb ideas (Taylor, 1995). They must listen, respond to, and question the teacher.

Students initiate problems and questions, make conjectures and explore examples to investigate conjectures, and defend their thinking. They should learn to verify, revise, and discard claims on the basis of mathematical evidence.

Classroom Environment

The mathematics classroom creates an intellectual environment that allows engagement in mathematical thinking. The environment of the classroom creates the foundation for learning, illustrating what really counts in learning. The learning environment standard (NCTM, 1991, p.57) includes the following:

> The teacher of mathematics should create a learning environment that fosters the development of each student's mathematical power by
>
> ◆ providing and structuring the time necessary to explore sound mathematics and grapple with significant ideas and problems;
> ◆ using the physical space and materials in ways that facilitate students' learning of mathematics;
> ◆ respecting and valuing students' ideas, ways of thinking, and mathematical dispositions;
>
> and by consistently expecting and encouraging students to
>
> ◆ work independently or collaboratively to make sense of mathematics;
> ◆ take intellectual risks by raising questions and formulating conjectures;
> ◆ display a sense of mathematical competence by validating and supporting ideas with mathematical argument.

When you think of learning environments you may think of only the physical environment—things like seat arrangement, lighting, or learning centers. You may notice that the above standard includes more than room arrangement, it refers to an emotional climate as well. Let's explore some elements of the classroom environment and ways to enhance the mathematical learning climate.

One key dimension of a learning environment encourages serious mathematical thinking that takes time as well as intellectual courage. An environment that supports problem solving allows students to think, make mistakes, try new approaches, and discuss their work with each other and adults. Students are comfortable with not getting the right answer the first time and not afraid of saying the wrong thing. Students are allowed to be wrong and are encouraged to try another solution. Students are not humiliated for missing problems.

Respect for all students—their ideas and backgrounds—is another important element relating to a productive learning environment. All children

*Opportunities for working to-
gether enhance peer support
and increase children's comfort
level in the classroom.*

enter programs with different mathematical backgrounds and experiences. Early childhood programs must use a range of teaching techniques, demonstrate relationships between mathematical experiences and mathematical language, and focus on methods that promote all areas of mathematical understanding (Spodek & Saracho, 1994a). Students are not grouped according to scores on standardized tests, nor are they labeled as "the slow group" who are placed in a corner while "gifted" students investigate problems and work on projects. Demonstrating respect for students' ideas does not imply that teachers or students accept all ideas as reasonable or valid (NCTM, 1991). Teachers must dignify incorrect responses, help children find where their thinking failed, and pursue better answers.

Teacher Evaluation

The teacher is the key to high-quality mathematics education for children (NCTM, 1991). Most school districts have teacher evaluation systems which influence career ladder decisions or judgments about teacher competence. Rarely do these evaluations allow teacher reflection or encourage the teacher to address plans for future improvement. A typical example of a teacher evaluation follows.

Mr. Torres teaches second grade. Today is his formal observation from his principal. Mr. Torres has spent many days arranging his room to comply with district requirements. He has coached his children on correct answers and ways to behave during the observation; his evaluation is a one-shot chance and he wants everything to really look good. This one hour of observation will determine his job contract for the next year. The principal arrives during mathematics instruction. As Mr. Torres works, the principal writes rapidly. Most of the children do as they have practiced; however, a few do not remember and give wrong answers. Mr. Torres glares at the children. After the observation Mr. Torres has a meeting with the principal. The principal evaluates Mr. Torres on what the school district thinks is important. Mr. Torres gets very angry as the principal talks. He thinks that no one has a right to criticize his work. After all, he is the one putting up with those children and he'd like to see the principal deal with that group. Mr. Torres receives a copy of the evaluation. He throws it in a drawer and teaches as he thinks he should. This is the only time that year he will be observed.

The above story is one that happens all too often in our schools. Teachers resent evaluation and often feel threatened. Principals comply with district requirements, but are often too busy to really give constructive feedback and support their teachers. It is ironic that people in a profession that demands so much evaluation of their students would balk at their own evaluations. Let's think about why evaluations might be important for teachers.

The NCTM standards (1991) suggest that evaluations generate information about teachers and provide analyses that lead to rich and appropriate professional development experiences. Information should not be threatening to the teacher. It is a way of thinking about what he/she is doing and ways to improve. Teaching is, after all, a complex act. The NCTM suggests an evaluation process based on information from a variety of sources and a variety of teaching situations. A fair and valid evaluation should include a variety of contexts with enough data to see an overall picture of the teacher's work. The evaluation standards include the following:

The evaluation of the teaching of mathematics should be a cyclical process involving

- the periodic collection and analysis of information about an individual's teaching of mathematics;
- professional development based on the analysis of teaching;
- the improvement of teaching as a consequence of the professional development.

The evaluation of the teaching of mathematics should provide ongoing opportunities for teachers to

- analyze their own teaching;
- deliberate with colleagues about their teaching;
- confer with supervisors about their teaching.

Evaluation should provide teachers the chance to identify their strengths and allow them to think about professional development. The process recommended by NCTM begins by collecting data representative of the teacher's current practice. This might include a videotape of the teacher in action, a written observation, samples of work done in the classroom, awards, or many different types of documentation of mathematics instruction: a teaching portfolio. What is valued in the teaching of mathematics—problem solving, communication, reasoning—should determine criteria for evaluation.

The NCTM advocates teacher participation throughout the evaluation process. Teachers should be given opportunities and encouragement to engage in reflecting on and evaluating their own teaching (NCTM, 1991). Similar to assessing students' mathematical thought processes, supervisors need to understand teachers' thought processes in order to guide planning and growth. It is crucial for teachers to see the evaluation process as one that contributes to their professional growth, not as a threat to their ego.

Supervisors should foster positive relationships with their teachers. Their role is more of a guide than a judge. The notion of "coaching" is relevant here, since regular feedback should be furnished on progress in mastering a greater repertoire of instructional strategies (NCTM, 1991). The relationship should be collegial and mentoring with the goal of improving the mathematics instruction; a continual process of adjustment, dynamic progress, and collaboration should be encouraged. The evaluation process should be a positive one that encourages growth and allows work with colleagues.

Professional Development

The NCTM (1991) states that the first few years of teaching present a unique period in professional development. Beginning teaching assignments and support structures play a significant role in shaping teachers' views of their profession and commitment to it, just as the first years of school are important to the children's attitudes toward education. Planning for instruction, learning to work with parents, managing student behavior, responding to the environment, and many "housekeeping" tasks fill the first few years.

As teachers become more experienced, the type of professional growth changes to fit the teacher. More collegial interactions increase and teachers assume different roles (NCTM, 1991). Training and growth involve more research-based information as new studies and theories are presented to teachers. Often experienced teachers become mentors for new teachers and they work together to avoid burnout or teacher stress.

Those who teach mathematics bring with them experiences as learners in mathematics classes from elementary school through their college careers. These experiences influence the ways they think about the teaching process, their choice of teaching as a career, and the subsequent ways they are involved in professional development (NCTM, 1991). Teachers' mathematical background may or may not be strong. Professional development, constructivist in nature, will depend on the individual's background and perception of learning; this makes professional development an on-going process. Mathematics teachers must become lifelong learners in order to meet the needs of an ever-changing society. Teachers must learn to accept responsibility for their own professional development as they become more experienced. Self-reflection helps teachers make wise decisions about their own teaching. Some teachers keep weekly journals of their thoughts, reactions, and teaching activities. This allows them to really think about their work and decide where personal improvement is needed and how they might improve their performance. Ideally the weave of the professional fabric will evolve and change, reflecting the numerous stages to be explored in the career-long development of mathematics teachers (NCTM, 1991).

MATHEMATICAL ASSUMPTIONS FOR TEACHING

Some basic assumptions emerge from the literature on mathematics and young children. Common threads that emerge from national standards, researchers, and theorists should guide the educator's thinking on teaching mathematics. Following are short discussions of these summary principles.

Teachers should continue to grow as professionals. Teachers need to continue learning about teaching. They may do so by joining professional organizations and reading new books and professional journals, attending professional meetings at the local, state, and national levels, networking with other teachers and sharing ideas and information. They may be able to participate in workshops, and upper-level classes and seminars offered at colleges and universities often address new issues in mathematics education.

Teachers should build connections between mathematics topics and other subject areas. Instruction should connect and make sense to children. One way to achieve this is to teach through interdisciplinary projects or broad thematic units. Literature-based units lend themselves to integrated curriculum planning. Some children's mathematics texts help teachers integrate literature with other curriculum areas. The school's textbook review committee should be aware of this important teaching method as they choose appropriate textbooks for primary children.

Teachers should utilize a variety of teaching methods. Variety addresses not only needs of children, but the nature of mathematics. Learning centers set up with multilevel activities address children with different developmental stages and learning styles. Small-group work that focuses on cooperative learning not only allows socialization, but builds confidence in each child's ability to perform mathematical tasks successfully. Peer tutoring—children helping children—could be utilized to increase mathematical understanding. Teachers could team teach to increase effectiveness and model social interaction.

Teachers should plan and organize rooms to encourage active child involvement. Multisensory activities need to vary and be planned for children's active involvement and exploration. Classroom arrangement should encourage talking, writing, modeling, and acting out mathematics ideas. Concrete materials should be used in a variety of ways to help children represent mathematical ideas. Activities should be learner centered, not teacher centered. Open-ended activities in which children solve real-life problems must be used.

Teachers should model positive attitudes toward math for all children. Teachers need to explore their own attitudes about mathematics; conveying personal enthusiasm builds confidence in children and their ability to do mathematics. Teachers should encourage and accept multiple answers and approaches to problem-solving situations. Activities should be planned to promote children's success, build confidence, and create a positive disposition toward math. A pleasant, stress-free environment encourages children to learn and be secure with mathematics.

Teachers should address children's learning on an individual basis. Each child comes to school with different backgrounds and beliefs. Children from different cultures and backgrounds should be accepted and appreciated. Activities from other cultures should be integrated with mathematics every day. Teachers must model acceptance of differences and encourage each child to be proud of his or her accomplishments. To increase teachers' awareness of the manner in which they interact with children during the course of the day, videotaping might be used to provide data for self-evaluation of the daily interactions.

Teachers should develop partnerships with parents and other family members. The home provides the first learning experiences for a child and will serve as reinforcement for what is taught at school. Parents or other family members can encourage mathematics development after school hours and provide valuable background information for the teacher. Helping parents understand how to help children learn mathematics is an important role for the teacher. Techniques such as welcoming parents into the classroom and encouraging their participation in the school program, visiting in the home to establish mutual respect, and communication with the family helps develop home-school relationships.

SUMMARY

Standards for mathematics education guide teachers toward better teaching performance, set goals for education, and establish principles. The NCTM is a major influence in the national establishment of professional standards.

The NAEYC has established standards for appropriate practice when working with young children. These standards complement the NCTM standards regarding developmental and constructivist approaches of working with young children.

The NCTM has established standards for teaching, as well as curriculum content. These recommendations are greatly influencing the future course of mathematics instruction.

◆ *REFERENCES*

Althouse, R. (1994). *Investigating mathematics with young children.* New York: Teachers College Press.

Battista, M. T. (1994). Teacher beliefs and the reform movement in mathematics education. *Phi Delta Kappa, 75*(6), 462–470.

Bowman, B. T. (1989). Educating language-minority children: challenges and opportunities. *Phi Delta Kappa, 71*(2), 118–120.

Bredekamp, S. (Ed.). (1993). *Developmentally appropriate practice in early childhood programs serving children from birth through age 8.* Washington, DC: National Association for the Education of Young Children.

Bredekamp, S., & Rosegrant, T. (1992). *Reaching potentials: appropriate curriculum and assessment for young children* (Vol. 1). Washington, DC: National Association for the Education of Young Children.

Brewer, J. A. (1995). *Introduction to early childhood education.* Needham Heights, MA: Simon and Schuster.

Charbonneau, M., & Reider, B. (1995). *The integrated elementary classroom.* Needham Heights, MA: Allyn and Bacon.

Cipra, B., & Flanders, J. (1992). *On the mathematical preparation of elementary school teachers.* Report from the University of Chicago supported by the National Science Foundation and the Exxon Foundation.

Clinchy, B. M. (1995). Goals 2000: the student as object. *Phi Delta Kappa, 76*(5), 383–386.

Garfunkel, S. A., & Young, G. S. (1992). *In the beginning: mathematical preparation for elementary school teachers.* Lexington, MA: COMAP, Inc.

Gestwicki, C. (1995). *Developmentally appropriate practice: curriculum and development in early education.* Albany, New York: Delmar Publishers, Inc.

Kamii, C. (1973). A sketch of a Piaget-derived preschool curriculum developed by the Ypsilanti early education program. In B. Spodek (Ed.), *Early childhood education* (pp. 209–229). Upper Saddle River, NJ: Prentice Hall.

Kamii, C., & Kamii, M. (1990). *Negative effects of achievement testing in mathematics.* Washington, DC: National Association for the Education of Young Children.

Linder, T. W. (1993). *Transdisciplinary play-based assessment.* Baltimore, MD: Paul H. Brooks.

Means, B., & Knapp, M. S. (1991). Cognitive approaches to teaching advanced skills to educationally disadvantaged students. *Phi Delta Kappa, 73*(4), 282–289.

National Council of Teachers of Mathematics. (1989). *Curriculum and evaluation standards for school mathematics.* Reston, VA: Author.

_____. (1991). *Professional Standards for Teaching Mathematics.* Reston, VA: Author.

National Science Foundation. (1996). *The learning curve: what we are discovering about U.S. science and mathematics education.* Suter, LE (Ed.). NSF 96-53. Washington, DC: Author.

Spodek, B. & Saracho, O. (1994a). *Dealing with individual differences in the early childhood classroom.* White Plains, NY: Longman.

Spodek, B., & Saracho, O. N. (1994b). *Right from the start.* Needham Heights, MA: Allyn and Bacon.

Taylor, B. (1995). *A child goes forth.* Upper Saddle River, NJ: Prentice Hall.

Texas Education Agency. (1994). *First impressions.* Austin, TX: Author.

Willoughby, S. S. (1990). *Mathematics education for a changing world.* Alexandria, VA: Association for Supervision and Curriculum Development.

Helping All Children Learn Mathematics

4

✓ **Equity Issues in Mathematics**
      Gender Issues
      Cultural Influences
      Socioeconomic Environment

✓ **Building Parents' and Families' Understanding of Their Roles in Equity Issues**
      Involving Parents in Mathematical Programs
      Activities for Involving Parents

✓ **The Classroom Environment**
      Teaching Methods
      Thematic Units

✓ **Summary**

✓ **Applications: Thinking and Collaborating**

◆◆

Eight-year-old Misty loved mathematics; she wanted to be a mathematician when she grew up. When Misty raised her hand in class to answer math questions, her teacher often ignored her and called on the boys, even when they had not raised their hands. Misty could not understand why she was not called on more. When Misty answered correctly, her teacher would say "unhuh" and go on to another problem. When her friend Yurbin answered correctly the teacher said things like, "Great answer, how did you do that?" Misty soon quit raising her hand at all and began to think that she was just not very bright in mathematics. Misty decided to focus on other curriculum areas where she felt successful and left mathematics to the

65

boys, who always seemed to warrant such positive atten-
tion. How could a more encouraging teacher help Misty
better develop her mathematical ability?

Mathematics plays an ever-increasing role in the daily life of all people (Ornstein, 1995). Drivers estimate space before passing cars, adults manage personal budgets, people make decisions based on probability of rewards or consequences, shoppers use percentages to determine good buys. People apply many different mathematical strategies daily. Often people who find themselves in situations that require mathematics don't recognize that good decisions depend on mathematical thought; they don't make the best decisions because they are unwilling or unable to think mathematically (Willoughby, 1990).

Career advancements and educational opportunities often depend on mathematics achievement. As technology increases, the use of mathematics becomes more important for all people and a part of the social process which people need to understand. The interactions of mathematics and technology and the various fields with human social systems and the values that society applies can influence how children learn and apply mathematics (Johnson, 1989). Mathematics is no longer a subject reserved for afternoons in classrooms, it is a vital part of life and survival for the modern population.

Mathematics for young children involves many elements. It is a way of solving real problems and understanding numbers, which includes operations on numbers, functions and relations, probability, and measurement (Brewer, 1995). The world is becoming more mathematical and children need more mathematics to survive daily living, yet there are groups of students who seem destined to fail in this vital curriculum area.

To grasp the magnitude of the current mathematics crisis in education, it is essential to recognize that at least one-third of America's children are at risk of failing in school, even before they enter kindergarten (Sadovnik, Cookson, & Semel, 1994). The term "at risk" has become well used throughout the country to identify children who fall into the category of facing potential school problems. Sadovnik et al. (1994, pp. 366) describe the condition of these children in stark terms: "Since 1987, one-fourth of all preschool children in the United States live in poverty. In 1990, approximately 350,000 children were born to mothers who were addicted to cocaine during pregnancy. Some 15 million children are being reared by single mothers whose family income averages about $11,400 a year. At least 2 million school-age children have no adult supervision after school, and every night between 50,000 and 200,000 children have no home." Teachers must find ways to address the educational needs of all children, and most certainly children who may face a rough entry into and journey through school.

The current educational crisis in mathematics, and all curriculum areas, is complex and solutions are difficult to find. Many sociologists are exploring the relationship between school and society. Studies indicate that social origins affect educational attainment and also occupational attainment after completion of education (Blau & Duncan, 1967; Duncan & Hodge, 1963; Eckland, 1965; Sewell, Haller, & Porter, 1969). Mathematics, and all curriculum areas, suffer when any population of students fail in school. If society directly affects school, then it is important for all teachers to explore how this relationship influences children and their school performance.

Studies comparing the United States with other countries indicate that American students score below the mean among 14 industrial nations, and 15% below Japanese students' scores in both mathematics and science (*Digest of Education Statistics*, 1988). In addition, other countries outperform American students on the International Association for the Evaluation of Educational Achievement (IEA) study in mathematics and science. Considering the fact that we live in a highly technological and scientific society, mathematics achievement has serious implications for the future of our country (Ornstein, 1995). Answers to mathematics learning questions can no longer be ignored; mathematics is too important a subject to consider it unteachable for any child.

EQUITY ISSUES IN MATHEMATICS

From the beginning of America's history the American people have had a deep belief in equity of opportunity. The Declaration of Independence and the Constitution of the United States are considered the voices of people who demand to be treated with respect, dignity, and equality. The founding fathers declared that all people would be guaranteed equal opportunity in the United States, and as America grew its laws were adjusted to ensure equity based on gender, race, handicapping conditions, and age.

Public schools evolved in order to increase the equality chances of all Americans. Horace Mann advocated a system of free education for all students as early as 1837. He was idealistic in his belief in education as a reformer of society, stating in 1842 that, "Education, then, beyond all other devices of human origin, is the great equalizer of the conditions of man— the balance wheel of the social machinery" (Reed & Bergeman, 1995). Mann and other early educators believed equity of educational chance would solve all societal problems. However, as society evolved, different types of problems emerged, and education has had to change in order to address the new population of students.

Equity can be considered that of equal outcomes, not just equal opportunity. The National Council of Teachers of Mathematics (NCTM) standards state that, "Mathematics has become a critical filter for employment and full participation in our society. We cannot afford to have the majority of our population mathematically illiterate. Equity has become an economic necessity" (National Council of Teachers of Mathematics [NCTM], 1989). Yet there appears to be groups of people who are not attaining equal educational outcomes as far as mathematics is concerned. The National Association of Educational Progress (NAEP) data show disparities in mathematics proficiency between groups defined by race/ethnicity and gender. Females and minorities score consistently lower than white males on mathematics tests.

Gender Issues

Women represent 45% of the total work force, but only 13% of these women are scientists and engineers (Taylor, 1995). The largest percentage of females working are in jobs that require little or no mathematics. Females take fewer advanced mathematics, computer, and science courses—courses important for college admission and success in many technological and scientific fields (Grossman & Grossman, 1994). Traditionally gender has been directly related to educational attainment. While women may be rated as better students than men, they often fail to obtain the same level of education (Sadovnik et al., 1994). Educational attainment almost always influences job mobility and promotions.

Boys and girls seem to enter elementary school with about the same mathematical knowledge. The fact that gender differences do not appear to be as strong in elementary school does not mean the gender issue is not important for teachers of young children. What happens in the elementary school provides the basis for what happens later in mathematics (Post, 1992). New knowledge builds on existing knowledge and educators of young children directly influence the well formed beliefs children have about themselves and mathematics, which in turn influences subsequent learning.

Females are outscored by males by an average of 45 points on the mathematics portion of the scholastic aptitude test (SAT) (Educational Testing Service, 1992). Although scores of both females and males increased on this test over the last few years, and increases in linear correspondence with the number of mathematics courses taken, the greatest gap occurs between select cohorts of male and female students who have more than four years of mathematics coursework. Despite outstanding academic records, fewer females are admitted to the most prestigious colleges and universities as a result of SAT math scores (Sadovnik et al., 1994).

Although many educators still tend to speak about, and act on, misleading gender stereotypes, no generalization about male-female behavioral differences applies to all males and females (Grossman & Grossman, 1994). While generalizations about gender differences can be misleading, it is important to recognize that some gender differences cut across class,

WHAT DO *YOU* THINK?

Some studies indicate that teachers allow males more opportunities to answer mathematics questions, encourage them to be more involved with math activities, and praise their answers more when correct. Do you think this is true? Go to a classroom and observe a few teachers working with mathematics and keep a tally of how many questions are asked males and females. Do the teachers seem to show favoritism to the males? Do you remember this happening when you were in elementary school?

ethnic, and geographic boundaries. These gender differences develop gradually. For many years some educators believed that the age when differences between male and female behavior first appeared provided a clue as to whether the difference was innate or environmental; the earlier a particular behavior appeared in the life cycle, the more likely it was influenced by biological behavior (Grossman & Grossman, 1994). If this is true, then the gap in mathematical testing would be more influenced by environment than biology and therefore teachers play an important role in mathematical development.

Research brings awareness that the way we treat boys and girls and what we expect of them shapes their behavior so that the two groups become either more alike or more different (Spodek & Saracho, 1994). Educators should examine how they are teaching mathematics. Boys and girls should have equal encouragement to work in math centers and on mathematics activities. Praise should be given to all children when they show an interest in mathematics. There is ample evidence that adults, including educators, model gender-specific behaviors and communicate gender-specific expectations to children that children tend to copy (Grossman & Grossman, 1994).

Children can change their attitudes, self-concept, and choice of academic subjects to conform to their parents' or teachers' gender expectations. A girl's evaluation of her mathematical abilities and her decision whether or not to take advanced mathematics courses is more influenced by her parents' and teachers' opinions of her abilities and expectations of how she will fare in these courses than by her actual mathematics grades (Grossman & Grossman, 1994). Teachers of young children must model high mathematics expectations for *all* children. Teachers tend to assume that males will do better in mathematics than females, and this may be the most logical explanation for the gender difference in mathematics (Sadovnik et al., 1994).

The fact that educators of young children influence their behavior, attitudes, and opinions have important implications, one of which is to

Even preschoolers show great interest in working with the computer.

closely and objectively analyze teaching methods and interactions with children. To this end a third-grade teacher worked out the following plan.

Mr. Milson teaches mathematics to third-grade children. He is well aware of what research says about gender differences between males and females. He wants to teach in an equitable manner because he realizes how important females and all children will be to a mathematically related future. Mr. Milson videotapes his teaching for one week and then carefully analyzes his interactions with the children during mathematics work. He has another teacher watch and evaluate his work with the children. They both notice that Mr. Milson usually allows males a longer time to answer the questions and spends more time with the boys when they do ask questions. Boys receive more and better feedback. Mr. Milson makes a conscious effort to give the girls equal time and feedback. He videotapes himself after a few weeks and is pleased to notice an improvement in his treatment of both boys and girls.

Cummings (1994) conducted research regarding attitudes toward mathematics. Students in the eleventh grade were interviewed concerning the reasons for higher scores in mathematics for males. The largest category of responses revealed that was "just the way it is." Responses included things like math is natural for boys, boys like hands-on activities, and girls get confused in math. Both sexes saw one sex as innately more intelligent. Other areas of response indicated that boys work on cars, houses, and lighting and therefore use math more than girls. Several boys pointed out that historically men were the hunters, land tillers, or providers and therefore math skills were needed more by males. Other students in the study felt that teachers impacted success in mathematics. One thing is evident: almost all students accepted the statement that males score higher in mathematics than girls without question.

WHAT DO *YOU* THINK?

Wilbur (1991) encouraged teachers to think about reasons to develop a gender-fair curriculum with the following six major benefits.

◆ It acknowledges and affirms variation, similarities, and differences among and within groups of people.
◆ It is inclusive, allowing both males and females to find and identify positively with messages about themselves.
◆ It is accurate, presenting information that is data based, verifiable, and able to stand critical analysis.
◆ It is affirmative, acknowledging, and valuing the worth of individuals and groups.
◆ It is representative, balancing multiple perspectives.
◆ It is integrated, weaving together the experiences, needs, and interests of both males and females.

These recommendations reflect the original goals of education in America, one of which was to provide equal opportunity for all children to learn. What are some ways you can try to ensure that these ideas are used in your classroom?

Cultural Influences

The United States is considered a pluralistic society, one where diversity is common. It has been called the "melting pot" society because so many different cultures have existed here since the country's beginning. Different ethnic groups hold different expectations for education. Researchers indicate that culture influences how children think (Sadovnik et al., 1994). Culture is reflected in a person's lifestyle, including food, language, social patterns, dress, and other indications of ethnicity. Different cultures value different things and expect different behavior from their group. Minorities whose cultural frames of reference are opposite to the cultural frame of reference of American mainstream culture have greater difficulty crossing cultural boundaries at school to learn (Ogbu, 1993). For example, Mexican-American children whose families maintain traditional Mexican standards may have trouble accepting American behavior norms in school. Children from other cultures may be confused regarding expectations in school, or may in some cases feel that expected behaviors are directly opposed to their own cultural expectations.

Students from varied ethnic backgrounds may not behave in the same manner, and in addition there is diversity among students brought up in families with similar ethnic backgrounds. Subgroups within ethnic groups also differ. Even students from the same socioeconomic class may not be equally motivated to maintain their cultural heritage. There are minority groups whose language expressions, mathematical, or number systems might be different enough from White Americans to be considered barriers to learning math and science, but whose individual members learn successfully. It seems that culture alone is not an indicator of mathematics success or failure.

Traditionally minority groups have not done well in mathematics according to educational measurement. The NAEP data reveals large discrepancies between the mathematics achievement of White students and that of their Black or Hispanic age mates. At ages 9 and 13 years, the differences in average proficiency between White and Black students has been decreasing, although data across the years show that there was a substantial narrowing until 1986 and no further progress since that time. The gaps between White and Hispanic students have remained somewhat constant at age 9. The gaps have narrowed at ages 13 and 17, but progress once again seems to have stopped. School learning and the performance of minority children is influenced by complex social, economic, historical, and cultural forces (Ornstein & Behar, 1995).

When young children enter school they may encounter a culture and language that differs from the one in their homes. Differences can exist between the more familiar home setting and the more formal school setting. For many children the switch from home to school is difficult, representing a major break in culture patterns (Spodek & Saracho, 1994). Many educators such as Josefina Tinajero (1996), bilingual expert at the University of Texas at El Paso, believe that children with different home languages should be taught mathematical concepts in their home language. After a child has mastered basic mathematics concepts, English should be used, with the native language reserved for introduction of new concepts.

Other educators believe that mathematics should be taught in English from the beginning of school. This is called *immersion*. The children are not allowed to speak their native language and are instructed in English. Still others recommend pulling non-English speaking students out of regular classes for intense English instruction during the day, and then returning for normal mathematics instruction.

There is evidence from comparative research that suggests that differences in school learning and performance among minorities are not due merely to cultural and language differences (Ornstein & Behar, 1995). Schools contribute to educational problems through tracking, biased testing, curriculum, and misclassification due to low comprehension of the school's predominant language (Ogbu, 1995). Minorities do not fail in school because of mere cultural and language differences but because of the relationship between school and the students.

What goes on inside schools—the kind of curriculum taught—plays a major role in the education of minorities. Many researchers recommend core curriculums be implemented in all schools. Core curriculum refers to a series of courses that all students must take to successfully graduate from school. All students take the same courses which usually cover a broad spectrum of the curriculum. Other countries such as Germany, Japan, South Korea, and Taiwan have core curriculums and their students score well on international tests. Studies indicate that these countries have higher participation in upper-level mathematics classes and an increased emphasis on mathematics-related job entry skills. Curricula based on accepted standards of content and outcomes that are taught consistently in all schools could increase mathematics mastery in our country. The NCTM standards could serve as the guiding document for the mathematics curricula.

Another suggestion relating to curriculum addresses integrating mathematics with multicultural activities. Educators should learn about their students' cultural backgrounds and use that knowledge to organize classrooms and mathematics activities. One example of integrating mathematics with multicultural activities follows.

Mr. Holcombe has several children in his class whose parents came from Vietnam. Mr. Holcombe researches traditional celebrations from Vietnam and presents them, and other cultural activities, daily in his class. During the last of September the people of Vietnam celebrate Tet Trung-Thu, to honor the moon at its brightest time. At Tet Trung-Thu children of Vietnam create lanterns shaped like boats, cranes, dragons, hares—every imaginable creature or object. At night candles are placed inside the lanterns and the children march through the streets to the rhythms of drums and cymbals. Mr. Holcombe uses this activity to reinforce perimeter measurement of the paper the children use to create their boats. He has the children arrange their finished product according to size to reinforce seriation concepts. Mr. Holcombe allows the children to use a water table to race their boats using different sources of air. The children estimate which boat will win when blown by air through a straw, air directly from a child's mouth, and air from a fan. The children record how long each boat takes to reach the finish line. Mr. Holcombe often integrates mathematics with multicultural activities in order to help all children learn.

Almost any activity can be adapted to include teaching mathematics. Educators should be familiar with mathematics concepts and relate them to other activities in the classroom. You may want to check the NCTM standards for ideas on how to integrate mathematics activities. Educators must find ways to address differences among minority learners. However, research indicates that race tends to be less of a factor with similar social and economic background (Ogbu, 1995).

Socioeconomic Environment

From its inception, public education was conceived as a social vehicle for minimizing the importance of class and wealth as a determiner of who should get ahead (Sadovnik et al., 1994). Most people acknowledge that society is stratified—there are rich people, poor people, and people in between. Children are more likely to live in poverty than any other age group, and the numbers are increasing (Reed & Bergman, 1995). One study released by the Census Bureau in March 1990 indicates that American young people are at far greater risk for social, economic, and health problems than are children in the world's other developed countries. American children were the most vulnerable in the number and percentage of youngsters living in poverty.

Sara lives in government housing with her mother and five brothers and sisters. Sara's mother dropped out of school when she was 15 and married a neighbor. Sara's mother gave birth to Sara and her brothers and sisters in five consecutive years. Sara's father left home right after the last child was born and the family has never heard from him again. Sara's mother has no work skills and no degree. Therefore she must take whatever work she can find. Sara's mother earns less than $10,000 a year, and with six children this money does not go very far. Sara's mother loves her children but does not have the skills needed for a high-paying job. She cannot afford to buy books or take time from her job to spend a lot of time with her children or return to school to improve her chances for a better job. Child care is expensive for parents with one child; Sara's family could never afford such a program. Sara is in charge of her brothers and sisters. It is not surprising that Sara does poorly in mathematics, she sees no use for mathematics in her life.

Too many children live like Sara. Millions of children and their parents are unable to enter the middle class because they are locked into inner-city environments. This growing number of poor children could mean a grim future for mathematics and all education. Children who live in poverty may not be able to afford to spend money on well balanced meals and most certainly not on expensive educational programs. Some individuals will become socially mobile through education, yet an overwhelming number of individuals will remain in the social class into which they were born because social stratification seems to cause human differences (Sadovik et al., 1994).

Research indicates that students in different economic classes have different kinds of educational experiences. Education is expensive, and the higher the level of attainment, the higher the cost. This often forces children from lower socioeconomic classes to lose out on educational opportunities and almost condemns them to a life of low-level education in all areas. Middle and upper socioeconomic class families can afford tutors when their children need help in mathematics. Families of middle and upper socioeconomic children expect their children to finish college, while families with fewer assets feel defeated before they start. Often children and young people from such families must drop out of school to help support the family.

Studies indicate that the number of books in a family's home relates to the academic achievement of its children. The parents' level of education also influences the success of their children. Whether parents read to their children can impact the degree of educational success. Class is directly related to achievement and to educational attainment; there is a direct correlation between parental income and children's performance on achievement tests, as well as ability groups and curriculum track placement (Sadovnik et al., 1994). When parents do not have money or time, the children have little chance to achieve success in mathematics or any curriculum area.

Teachers must address the problem of the increasing number of children whose families cannot afford the same types of experiences that can be afforded by children from families with more money. Being poor does not equate to an inability to do mathematics. However, it does relate to the types of experiences a child might have. The constructivist teacher must acknowledge the inequality of these children entering the mathematics classroom. It is indeed challenging for the teacher to think of approaches that could give children the same mathematical opportunities.

One way to address this issue is to teach to individual levels of learning rather than using large-group instruction. Learning centers with a variety of activities encourage each individual child to learn at his/her own pace. Authentic types of assessment, like portfolios, journals, and performance events, can reveal how individual children are thinking and assist the teacher when planning instruction.

BUILDING PARENTS' AND FAMILIES' UNDERSTANDING OF THEIR ROLES IN EQUITY ISSUES

Today's families take many forms. Parents may share the responsibility for their children with others. The child's primary caregivers may be

Informal measurement experiences can take place in a setting such as the classroom's housekeeping center.

both parents, single mothers, stepparents, grandparents, uncles, aunts, sisters, brothers, foster parents, or guardians. Educators must recognize and respect the culture, social background, religious beliefs, and childbearing practices of each family in order to build a working educational relationship. Educators must not be judgmental about families and their lifestyles. Most parents care strongly about their children. There are many reasons why parents do not get involved with schools, but lack of concern about their children is usually not one of them (Brewer, 1995).

Parents or the home care providers are the first teachers children have. The importance of the parents' role has been well documented. Henderson's early research (1988) indicates that children achieve more when parents are involved in school. The major findings on parent involvement are summarized below.

◆ The family, not the school, provides the primary educational environment. Educators must find ways to involve and work with parents if successful mathematics programs are to be implemented. Often parents feel inadequate in mathematics and are insecure working with their children in mathematics. The educator must not only build the children's confidence in mathematics ability but also the parents'.

◆ Parent involvement improves children's achievements. Educators must plan and implement ways to involve parents in the mathematics curriculum. Most parents are sincerely interested in the education of their children and will work to promote education.

◆ Parent involvement is more effective when it is comprehensive, well planned, and long lasting. Educators should work together across grade levels to organize parent involvement in mathematics programs. Vertical grouping of teachers can help identify mathematics goals and develop plans for instruction.

◆ Involving parents when children are young has beneficial effects that persist throughout the children's academic careers. Early childhood programs have long advocated parent involvement. Many federally funded programs mandate parent involvement as an integral element of program success.

◆ Involving parents with children's education at home may not be enough to improve schools. It takes both homes and schools working together to improve mathematics understanding for children.

◆ Low-income and minority families benefit most when parents are involved with schools. Educators need to implement parent involvement programs to ensure equal education for all children.

Parent involvement enhances education in all subject areas. Encouraging parent involvement aids teachers in building children's self-esteem:

it reduces discipline problems and increases children's regard for themselves as learners (Brewer, 1995). Parent involvement should enhance the NCTM goal of building students' confidence in their mathematical abilities.

Involving Parents in Mathematical Programs

Studies indicate that strong parent involvement impacts not only the school but the entire family. Leik and Chalkey (1990) studied the effects of the family involvement component that Head Start uses with their parents. This model involves parent training and home-based instruction. They found parents involved in the training gained significantly in positive attitudes about the importance of education, were more likely to see their children as competent, and felt more secure in their abilities to work with children in the home. It seems apparent that parent involvement needs to be included in a successful mathematics program. Let's look at some ways that mathematics educators can involve parents in strengthening programs.

Bloom (1995) analyzed studies relating to parent involvement strategies. The most effective treatment of parents was a cohort where groups of parents met with a parent educator about two hours twice a month for six months. During parent meetings they discussed ways in which they could support their children's learning in school. An initial presentation was made by the parent educator on one of the home environment processes and parents discussed what they did as well as what they planned to do.

Ysleta Elementary School has a parent coordinator who organizes training sessions for parents. The parents have their own center in the school where they meet and work on different school projects. The parents tutor children in mathematics and other curriculum areas. The parents contribute their time and have become partners in the school, not just parents of children.

Mathematics educators can prepare parent presentations that address home opportunities to teach mathematics. They can organize group meetings and training. An example of such a mathematics-focused parent meeting follows.

Ms. Schrivner is a parent coordinator and meets every two weeks with a group of parents whose children attend the primary school where she works. She has been working with the teachers to design home mathematics activities for her presentation. The teachers and Ms. Schrivner plan carefully, avoiding jargon that parents might not be familiar with and clearly presenting concepts. Ms. Schrivner greets the parents by first name as they arrive. She keeps the relationship one of a friend, not an authoritarian. The parents feel comfortable working with Ms. Schrivner and view her as a confidant, more like a partner in their children's education. The school where Ms. Schrivner works provides a parent room that is furnished in an attractive manner. The parents gather in this room during the day and sometimes on weekends to discuss common problems and work on school projects.

Ms. Schrivner has decided to focus on problem solving and communication for a special session. Ms. Schrivner explains the importance of problem solving and that it is a way of thinking. She has prepared a series of activities that parents can use in their homes. Ms. Schrivner prepares the room so that parents can role play the activities to enhance problem solving. After the parents have participated in the problem-solving activities, they discuss what they have done and how they can use these ideas in their own homes. Ms. Schrivner listens to the parents and encourages them to create new activities for use in their homes. She helps them think throughout their work and praises their efforts.

Every two weeks Ms. Schrivner meets with the parents to introduce new mathematics ideas and to let the parents share what worked for them. This is a typical parent training model. It is important to realize that parents are equals and have valuable insights into the mathematical learning of their children. Educators should promote activities that foster personal growth of parents, such as meetings, workshops, community education programs, and career development as well as topic-related presentations. Teachers are usually less emotionally involved and often act more objective than the parents, but parents are important figures in the educational relationship between families and schools.

Activities for Involving Parents

There are many engaging activities that can be used to involve parents in mathematics learning. Some parents will be comfortable with active roles during class time and others will want to take a passive role. Educators should praise all parent attempts to learn and be involved with their children's work.

Newsletters prepared at school and sent home with the students provide information about the program to parents. It is important to use the families' home language when sending out newsletters. Spanish-speaking parents, or any other language minority, should be respected enough to use the language spoken in the home. Newsletters can share news about mathematics projects being done at school and suggestions for follow-up activities to be done in the home.

Learning cards or packets can be designed for home checkout. Educators should work together to prepare cards or packets in all NCTM-recommended content areas that contain suggestions for hands-on activities. Children or parents can check out these packets and take them home for use. The cards provide directions for engaging activities that parents and children can work on together. Written notices and personal communications by educators can encourage parents to assume increasing responsibility for teaching their children mathematics by using home activity packets.

Inviting parents to share their special talents with the classroom allows parents and other family members to take a lead role and share their skills during visits. In any community there may be parents who can share local stories, play music, or demonstrate individual accomplishments with the classroom. Educators can try to relate the mathematics connection between curriculum areas and the parent's presentation. For example, when a parent presents a musical talent, point out the patterns in the music and the fractional equivalents in the music notes. (Children can listen to the length of notes and possibly compare time relationships.)

Maintaining an open invitation for parents to come to the classroom helps to build personal contacts and positive interactions between parents and staff. Educators should make parents feel welcome in the classroom and allow parents to have input into the way the classroom runs and the methods of teaching. They can encourage parents to join or form support groups, attend mathematics workshops, and present mathematics activities in the classroom.

THE CLASSROOM ENVIRONMENT

Teaching Methods

Some teaching techniques have remarkable effects on learning, while others confer only trivial advantages or even hinder the learning process. In mathematics teaching, problem solving should be the focus of teaching (Walberg, 1995). This type of teaching requires comprehension of mathematical concepts and knowledge of how to apply concepts to a variety of examples. Teachers must model mathematical thinking for young children.

Mathematics instruction focuses on developing students' abilities to explore, conjecture, reason logically, and use a variety of mathematical strategies to solve nonroutine problems. Such a focus requires teachers who are flexible, able to apply mathematics, and willing to try a variety of teaching techniques. Students should be involved in an application content right from the beginning, with an emphasis on authentic problem solving (Brophy, 1995).

The NAEYC's *Developmentally Appropriate Practice* (Bredekamp, 1993, p. 71) identifies the goals of an appropriate mathematics program for young children and explains what is appropriate for mathematics work.

> The goal of the math program is to enable children to use math through exploration, discovery, and solving meaningful problems. Math activities are integrated with other relevant projects, such as science and social studies. Math skills are acquired through spontaneous play, projects, and situations

WHAT DO *YOU* THINK?

The NAEYC documents, like the NCTM publications and constructivists' theories, recommend many similar teaching methods when working with young children. Many of NAEYC's developmentally appropriate practice principles lend themselves to mathematics instruction. Think about what the constructivists say about mathematical learning. How do their ideas on teaching methods relate and compare to current professional standards recommendations?

of daily living. Teachers use the teacher's edition of the math textbook as a guide to structure learning situations and to stimulate ideas about interesting math projects. Many math manipulatives are provided and used. Interesting board and card, paper-and-pencil, and other kinds of games are used daily. Noncompetitive, impromptu oral "math stumper" and number games are played for practice (Bredekamp, 1993).

Teaching for understanding and enhancing the process of learning involves holistic skills instruction. Mathematics skills are taught as strategies adapted to situations, with emphasis on modeling the cognitive components (Brophy, 1995). Activities, assignments, and evaluation methods incorporate a greater range of tasks than the traditional textbooks and tests that focus on recall of information.

Integrated curriculum lends itself to effective holistic instruction. The integrated approach fosters a strong sense of community and provides opportunities for critical thinking and choice. This approach allows children to experience cooperative work with others and gives them time to enhance personal strengths, self-knowledge, and competencies in all areas of development (Charbonneau & Reider, 1995). Schools emphasize rote learning too much and do not put enough emphasis on real understanding and thinking. According to Posner (1995), curriculum recommendations focus on allowing students to construct their own knowledge in purposeful activities requiring decision making, problem solving, and judgments.

An integrated approach requires teachers to utilize developmental principles as the underlying basis for all teacher decision making, multiage groupings to underscore "real world" learning and working conditions, cooperative learning models to encourage interdependency and socially appropriate behavior, a relevant, coherent curriculum, and a direct application of the theory of multiple intelligences (Charbonneau & Reider, 1995). Integrated units address individual learning levels and adhere to the constructivists' theories of learning. Children learn from experiences, those encountered at random and those to which we introduce them deliberately; but these experiences are all-embracing and involve many aspects of knowledge at once (Post, 1992). As an example of integrated learning, let's visit a multiage primary class.

Ms. Svan's class is studying traditional tales. They have read four different versions of "The Three Little Pigs." Several books with this story in them are displayed in the research center. The children are comparing each version and dictating or writing about their discoveries. There is a story comparison chart where children compile the number of elements that are the same in each version of the pigs story. When they have completed this Ms. Svan helps the children make a graph to communicate the results of the research.

In the science center Ms. Svan provides sticks, straw, and bricks. The children experiment with the strength of each material. They use a variety of tools to determine which can withstand the most pressure or weight before breaking. Scales are in the center and children compare the weights of the materials. They place a brick on one side of a balance scale and then add sticks to the other side to determine weight equivalents. In addition the children use the water table to experiment with wind by using different types of air producers like fans, blowing through straws, and fanning by hand. Ms. Svan helps the children record their results.

In the writing center Ms. Svan encourages the children to write their own version of the three pigs. They draft and rewrite the stories and make books. Then the children illustrate their stories and act out their new versions of the story. The children create paper-plate masks in the art center. While the children work Ms. Svan and her assistant discuss the children's work to help the children identify elements of art, theatre, and other curriculum areas.

Mathematics was presented as a strong component in Ms. Svan's classroom, yet it was blended with other curriculum areas. The use of thematic units will enhance this integration of mathematics throughout the curriculum. Connections between curriculum areas allows children to see the practical use for mathematics.

Thematic Units

Thematic units are not new. At the turn of the century, John Dewey advocated the organization of curriculum around projects that would interest or involve children. However, the most common approach to curriculum organization in schools in the United States is subject-matter organization where learning is segmented (Brewer, 1995). Thematic units involve a theme choice and curriculum concepts that are taught through topics within the theme context.

Thematic teaching supports the NCTM belief that connections must be made between mathematics within topics and mathematics with other subject areas. The *Curriculum Standards* justify the need for connections as follows.

> A classroom in which making connections is emphasized exhibits several notable characteristics. Ideas flow naturally from one lesson to another, rather than each lesson being restricted to a narrow objective. Lessons frequently extend over several days so that connections can be explored, discussed, and generalized (NCTM, 1989, p. 32).

If lessons are to flow and promote discussion, then isolated skill teaching is inappropriate. Teachers must teach in a manner that allows for free exploration of ideas across all curriculum areas. One example of a concept that integrates across curriculum areas is patterning. It is generally accepted that patterns play an important role in mathematics learning. Patterning is traditionally taught as a mathematics lesson in isolation, with children looking for and replicating patterns. Examining the thought process behind patterning shows how this same thought process applies to other curriculum areas. When reading, children look for letter patterns, like rhyming words, to help them read. Science uses patterns to identify constancy in life cycles, and certainly allows people to make inferences when a pattern of behavior has been determined. In social studies people look for patterns when analyzing societal behavior and before generalizing about a civilization's characteristics. Patterns are used in music and dance, as well as in artistic composition. Therefore the thought process behind patterning applies to all disciplines and could be called a core curriculum concept.

When teaching thematic units, educators must decide on powerful, engaging themes. Katz and Chard (1989) identify the following five criteria for choosing a theme: relevance, the opportunity for application of skills, the availability of resources, teacher interest, and the time of year.

Brewer (1995) defines relevance as the applicability of a topic of study to a child's life. One reason for teaching relevant topics to the school population is so people will understand the wide range of situations they are likely to face (Posner, 1995). For example, children enrolled at Aoy Elementary live right on the border between Mexico and the United States. According to data from *Characteristics of Schools* (Research and Development, 1994, p. 6), Aoy Elementary School's enrollment is 99% minority, 98% economically disadvantaged, and considered 93% "at risk" of failing. Themes that would be appropriate for this school might include topics dealing with the Hispanic culture, since a large percentage of the children are from a Mexican-American background. Much of what students traditionally learn in schools, they never use explicitly and they quickly forget. Relevance also directly relates to the opportunity for application of skills. When planning a theme, think about what opportunity children will have to apply needed skills. Each theme, in addition to connecting core curriculum ideas, must include skill instruction in natural ways. Opportunities for reading and writing skills need to be included in the theme. Mathematics and science skills need to be taught within the framework of the thematic topic. A valuable question might be: Will the skills be presented in a manner that allows children to answer their own questions and solve their own real-life problems?

Time of year is important because seasonal themes are easier to teach when the environment is exhibiting natural examples of concepts. Teachers will know their children better as the year progresses and this fact will make planning easier. The first themes of the year should not be unfamiliar to students, but should be topics that the teacher knows have been part of their personal experiences and that will interest them (Brewer, 1995).

Of course organization of themes will depend on the area in which you teach and the kinds of topics available for exploration. The key point is to investigate the topics in-depth rather than superficially. Activities that support a theme must be concept and skill-rich in order to provide the types of opportunities children need to succeed.

Integrating mathematics into a school's curriculum and daily events helps children feel comfortable about a subject area that will have applications throughout their entire lives (Krogh, 1995). Mathematics should become a natural part of everyday learning and should be integrated with other areas to allow children to become confident in their abilities. When children become secure in their abilities to work mathematically, they will develop positive attitudes about their work, thus increasing the time spent working with mathematics and enrolling in upper-level mathematics courses.

Effective teachers model enthusiasm, exhibit a zest for inquiry, and empower children to gain confidence to build mathematics understanding (Ward, 1995). Teachers' attitudes influence the attitude being formed by children as they work through problem-solving situations. If students feel in control of learning and feel the teacher believes in their abilities to deal with any mathematical situation they will, in turn, become confident mathematicians.

SUMMARY

The different treatment of males and females is well documented and no doubt influences mathematics learning. A partial result of this treatment is that boys become more independent and feel they are more in control of their own learning. Boys attribute successes to ability, while girls often believe their successes are due to the teacher and their failure is due to a lack of ability (Post, 1992). Educators of young children must provide the opportunity, stimulation, and expectations females need as well as males.

Although many minority children traditionally do not score high on mathematics tests, it is not necessarily due to culture. Membership in a minority group is not sufficient basis for theorizing cultural differences on learning. A more realistic criteria for this failure is the school and teacher. What is taught and how it is taught influences minority learning.

Children from lower socioeconomic families often cannot afford to pursue higher-level education. They cannot afford the materials and experiences that children from middle and upper socioeconomic homes can. Their parents often have lower education expectations and need the children's help at home.

Educators must acknowledge the impact of and important role parents have in mathematics and all education. Teachers and parents can share in the care and education of young children. Parenting is a developmental process where individuals learn and grow according to their past experiences and present lifestyle. Educators must explore the many ways to involve parents in school programs.

The classroom environment affects the teaching of mathematics. Rooms should be arranged in learning centers to enhance mathematics learning. Children need space to explore materials and be close enough to discuss their work. It is important to provide concrete materials for children to manipulate as they work through problems. Many materials are available for teaching mathematics and many can be made.

Teaching methods that reflect the NAEYC and NCTM recommendations call for integrated curriculum. With such a curriculum, the teacher spends most of planning time arranging the environment to allow students to explore and investigate concepts and skills. Teachers serve as a guide or mentor rather than a dictator.

Thematic teaching helps put connections between curriculum areas and concepts and skills. Themes should be relevant to the children's lives, interest teachers and students, be practical for the community, and be appropriate for the time of year.

◆ APPLICATIONS: THINKING AND PROBLEM SOLVING

Apply and extend things you have read about in this chapter by selecting one or more of the following activities. Choose an activity that you could work alone, or better yet choose something that will allow a colleague's input.

1. Mathematics carnivals or mathematics nights can be held at the school. This is a good way to involve parents in the mathematics program. Assist the parents in making up math challenges and setting up math activity booths.

2. Make a list of community resources and resource people that can work with your mathematics program.

3. Organize a potluck dinner to celebrate a local holiday. Invite the children's families to share the social evening together. Discuss

math in an informal environment and see what views parents hold about mathematics.

4. Visit a higher-level mathematics class in your area. Note the number of males and females enrolled in the class. Observe the teacher interactions to determine if, indeed, males are given more positive reinforcement to participate.

5. Call a random selection of accountants and other mathematics-related professionals in your community and gather information on gender and race/ethnicity of employees. Compare your results. What percentages are representative of your community?

◆ REFERENCES

Blau, P. M., & Duncan, O. (1967). *The American occupational structure*. New York: Wiley.

Bloom, B. (1995). The search for methods of instruction. In A. Ornstein and L. Behar (Eds.), *Contemporary issues in curriculum*. Needham Heights, MA: Allyn and Bacon.

Bredekamp, S. (1993). *Developmentally appropriate practice in early childhood programs serving children from birth through age 8*. Washington, DC: National Association for the Education of Young Children.

Brewer, J. A. (1995). *Introduction to early childhood education*. Needham Heights, MA: Simon and Schuster.

Brophy, J. (1995). Probing the subtleties of subject-matter teaching. In A. Ornstein and L. Behar (Eds.), *Contemporary issues in curriculum*. Needham Heights, MA: Allyn and Bacon.

Charbonneau, M., & Reider, B. (1995). *The integrated elementary classroom*. Needham Heights, MA: Allyn and Bacon.

Cummmings, R. (1994). 11th graders view gender differences in reading and math. *Journal of Reading, 38*(3), 196–200.

Digest of Education Statistics. (1988). Tables 289–290, pp. 342–343. Washington, DC: U.S. Government Printing Office.

Duncan, O. D., & Hodge, R. (1963). Education and occupational mobility. *American Journal of Sociology, 68*, 629–644.

Eckland, B. K. (1965). Academic ability, higher education, and occupational mobility. *American Sociological Review, 30*, 735–746.

Educational Testing Service. (1992). *Annual report*. Princeton, NJ: Author.

Grossman, H., & Grossman, S. (1994). *Gender issues in education*. Needham Heights, MA: Allyn and Bacon.

Henderson, A. (1988). Parents are a school's best friend. *Phi Delta Kappa, 70*, 148–153.

Johnson, J. (1989). *Report of the project 2061 phase I technology panel*. Washington, DC: American Association for the Advancement of Science.

Katz, L., & Chard, S. (1989). *Engaging children's minds: the project approach.* Norwood, NJ: Ablex.

Krogh, S. (1995). *The integrated early childhood curriculum.* New York: McGraw-Hill.

Leik, R., & Chalkey, M. A. (1990). Parent involvement: what is it that works? *Children Today,* May–June, 34–37.

National Council of Teachers of Mathematics. (1989). *Curriculum and evaluation standards for school mathematics.* Reston, VA: Author.

Ogbu, J. (1995). Understanding cultural diversity and learning. In A. Ornstein and L. Behar (Eds.), *Contemporary issues in curriculum.* Needham Heights, MA: Allyn and Bacon.

Ornstein, A. (1995). Academic time considerations for curriculum leaders. In A. Ornstein and L. Behar (Eds.), *Contemporary issues in curriculum.* Needham Heights, MA: Allan and Bacon.

Posner, G. (1995). *Analyzing the Curriculum.* New York: McGraw-Hill.

Post, T. (1992). Teaching mathematics in grades K–8. Needham Heights, MA: Allyn and Bacon.

Reed, A., & Bergman, V. (1995). *In the classroom: an introduction to education.* New York: Dushkin Publishing.

Research and Evaluation. (1994). *Characteristics of the Schools, 1993–94.* El Paso, TX: EPISD.

Sadovnik, A., Cookson, P., & Semel, S. (1994). *Exploring education.* Needham Heights, MA: Allyn and Bacon.

Spodek, B., & Saracho, O. (1994). *Right from the start: teaching children ages three to eight.* Needham, MA: Allyn and Bacon.

Sewell, W., Haller, A., & Porter, A. (1969). The educational and early occupational attainment process. *American Psychological Review, 34,* 82–92.

Taylor, B. (1995). *A child goes forth.* Upper Saddle River, NJ: Merrill/Prentice Hall.

Tinajero, J. (1996). Personal interview relating to appropriate teaching methods for second language learners. University of Texas at El Paso.

Ward, C. (1995). Meaningful mathematics with young children. *Dimensions of Early Childhood, 23*(2), 7–11.

Walberg, H. J. (1995). Productive curriculum time. *Peabody Journal of Education, 69*(3), 86–100.

Wilbur, G. (1991). *Gender-fair curriculum.* Wellseley, MA: Wellesley College Center for Research on Women.

Willoughby, S. S. (1990). *Mathematics for a changing world.* Alexandria, VA: Association for Supervision and Curriculum Development.

Assessment and Evaluation

5

✓ **Purposes and Uses of Assessment and Evaluation**

✓ **Techniques for Formative Assessment and Evaluation of Children's Work**

    Observation

    Questioning and Discussion

    Anecdotal Records

    Interviews

    Written Work and Drawings

    Performances and Problem Solving

    Children's Self-assessment and Evaluation

✓ **Techniques for Summative Assessment and Evaluation of Children's Work**

    Projects and Products

    Portfolios

    Tests

✓ **Changing Assessment and Evaluation Techniques**

✓ **Summary**

✓ **Applications: Thinking and Problem Solving**

❖❖

Hong Gao, a teacher at Elton Primary School, feels apprehensive at being assigned to the Assessment Committee during her first year of teaching. As the committee discusses ways to show parents that their children are learning important mathematics in appropriate ways and making real progress in understanding the material, some of the older teachers ask

Hong: "What are some things you learned about assessment in your teacher education program? What are some references and resources we can use?" How might Hong reply?

Assessment and evaluation are vital, ongoing parts of teaching and learning. Assessment and evaluation help educators answer important questions such as, "How are the children doing?" "Is Kevin making the kind of progress I should expect of him?" "How can I tell if Latisha's confidence is improving? How can I have her self-evaluate her work?" "What can I tell parents about their children's accomplishments?"

Assessment and evaluation also help educators reflect on their own performance and the curriculum. Questions such as the following may be posed: "How well-balanced is our math program?" "How can I ask more thought-provoking questions?" "Do my approaches make sense? How can I find out? How can I improve?" "How can I plan lessons to encourage growth in all the children?"

Assessment and evaluation are terms or concepts that are closely related, but different. *Assessment* is the process of gathering useful data or information about a person's or group's knowledge, performance, or achievement (Webb, 1992). "Assessment is [also] a tool that can be used by a teacher to help students attain the goals of the curriculum ... a means to achieve educational goals" (Webb, 1993, p. 1). "Authentic or real assessment" are terms that are emerging in the educational literature. They concern gathering pertinent data from many sources and on varied aspects of development or progress. They involve application of useful skills in realistic situations rather than being based on artificially contrived tests.

Evaluation—note the inclusion of the root "value" in the term—is the process of attaching value, worth, or relative merit to assessment information. It is the process of interpreting information or making judgments, based on criteria, about the information. Educators may evaluate children's work, their own teaching practices, or educational programs.

Routman (1991, p. 301) characterizes evaluation as a problematic process in which educators try to judge student work and progress holistically: "The process is a slow, evolving one that requires lots of risk taking and continuous self-evaluation." Meaningful evaluation, according to Routman, is a challenge. It can become a natural, meaningful process if teachers understand developmental learning processes and curriculum, examine their own beliefs and goals, gain knowledge of collecting and interpreting data, and show commitment to understanding and implementing meaningful approaches to evaluation.

PURPOSES AND USES OF
ASSESSMENT AND EVALUATION

When and how can educators use assessment and evaluation? Good teachers assess constantly and informally, searching children's faces for signs of understanding. They check children's work, looking for evidence that children can follow directions, draw conclusions, and perform mathematical operations. They listen to children's responses in class, group, and one-to-one discussions and discern who can phrase good answers, who is more hesitant, and who gives elaborated responses. They observe and question children to determine their ways of thinking about problems and tasks (Sammons, Kobett, Heiss, & Fennell, 1992).

WHAT DO *YOU* THINK?

Before you read further, jot down several reasons you think teachers use assessment and evaluation. Keep your ideas in mind as you read the following sections.

Why should we assess and evaluate? These processes are integral parts of effective teachers' planning, implementing, and adjusting instruction. Through assessment and evaluation, teachers gain a sense of children's knowledge and interests so they can plan learning activities to build on these strengths and interests. Thus assessment and evaluation serve as guides for instruction and as diagnostic aids. The processes serve to "inform practice," showing educators how to proceed with instruction suited to children's needs.

Verbal or nonverbal input from children—confused looks or confident use of manipulatives, for example—often tells educators how to proceed in lessons. Past experience may guide teachers in determining whether children can proceed quickly through a topic or whether extensive exploration will be needed.

Assessment and evaluation also provide insights affecting decisions about classroom climate (Kroll, Masingila, & Mau, 1992). For example, a teacher's goal might be to personalize each child's use of mathematics. To assess and evaluate this goal she might talk to children in small groups to learn about their interests. She might consult with parents to gain a broader view of the children's interests or have children fill out forms such as the example. Based on this data she could plan open-ended activities for children to pursue their individual interests (Figure 5.1).

Authors of the *Curriculum and Evaluation Standards for School Mathematics* (National Council of Teachers of Mathematics [NCTM], 1989)

Figure 5.1 *A student interview sheet.*

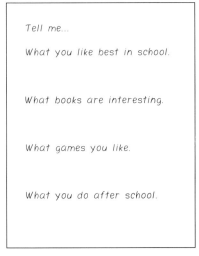

describe evaluation as a process of improving teaching. Stating that evaluation is a cyclical process in which educators collect and analyze representative data concerning their teaching methods, curriculum, time allo-
cations, and goals, they describe evaluation opportunities for teachers to
conduct thoughtful self-review, consult with peers and supervisors, read,
and attend professional meetings to gain and share ideas for improving
mathematics education.

The authors of the *Assessment Standards for School Mathematics*
(NCTM, 1995) describe assessment as a dynamic process that yields information about students' mathematics learning. They offer six standards to
help educators develop effective assessment systems. First, assessment
should *reflect the mathematics that all students should be able to do.* This
body of knowledge is changing, and assessment must address elements of
mathematics power—problem solving, communicating, reasoning, and
making connections.

Second, assessment should *enhance mathematics learning.* It should be
an integral part of the learning process, with opportunities for students to
demonstrate what they know and can do. Assessment must also address
important mathematics.

Third, assessment should have *equity* and give each student opportunities to demonstrate mathematical power. Each child should have access to assessment tasks (Zawojewski, 1996). Honoring students' unique
qualities and experiences, assessors should be open to alternative ideas
and solutions and must listen carefully to explanations.

Fourth, assessment should be an *open process.* Stakeholders in education—students, teachers, parents, and others—should be informed of
expectations, ways performance will be assessed, and the consequences
of assessment.

Fifth, assessment should include *valid inferences.* Evidence from multiple sources helps to capture a broad picture of students' learning. Mathematics assessment should include evidence from observations, interviews, problem-solving situations, and portfolios. It may also include information from more traditional instruments such as objective tests.

Sixth, assessment should have *coherence.* The assessment process should form a coherent whole with phases that fit together with the curriculum and instruction. Assessment should be valid, matching the purposes for which it is intended.

The *Assessment Standards* (NCTM, 1995) outline four purposes for assessment. First, *monitoring and documenting student progress* in the classroom through formal and informal means helps teachers decide where students are in their learning of mathematics. Second, assessment should help teachers make *instructional decisions* to link teaching and learning. Teachers can use three basic kinds of data when assessing: observation, questioning, and student products—written work, projects, and tests.

Evaluating and reporting student achievement is a third purpose of assessment; it involves gathering data to show a broad picture of student progress over a period of time. Portfolios are one way of accomplishing this purpose, and they offer a basis for communication with parents. Communicating to the public information about student progress on important mathematics is another aspect of reporting evaluative data.

Evaluating programs is a last assessment purpose. Used to indicate quality and effectiveness of programs, evaluation documents program strengths and weaknesses and makes recommendations for improvement. Educators should look critically at programs at various time intervals and levels. In program evaluation, educators consider broad issues: the scope of the entire preschool mathematics program, the relationship of the mathematics program to the rest of the curriculum, goals for the entire elementary math program, and ways of informing citizens about the changing nature of mathematics for children.

The authors of the *Professional Standards for Teaching Mathematics* (NCTM, 1991) present the idea that evaluation and assessment also let educators examine their own work with the purpose of professional improvement. For example, they point out that teachers must be participants in a cyclical process of evaluation beginning with examination of current practice. It might involve something as simple as a teacher reflecting back and reviewing a single day's math lesson or it can be other more complex techniques—videotaping and using a checklist to analyze a series of lessons.

TECHNIQUES FOR FORMATIVE ASSESSMENT AND EVALUATION OF CHILDREN'S WORK

Informal, ongoing, routine methods of assessment and evaluation are many and varied. These formative assessments are natural parts of classroom work that most educators perform without much conscious thought. Intended to help educators make decisions and guide children, formative techniques also help educators determine more about children's thought processes.

Educators can use many formative techniques for gathering information about children and for making judgments about that information. Observation—casual and routine or guided with checklists—questioning and discussion; interviews; examining children's drawings, writing, and other products; and looking at problem-solving situations or performances are some of the choices educators have for formative assessment and evaluation.

Observation

As teachers involve children in worthwhile group and individual work, they have more time to be "kidwatchers" (Goodman, 1982, p. 120) who use informal observation to understand and document children's growth and progress. Observations help teachers make decisions and judgments, determining which children need support and which ones may profit from more challenge.

As they observe, teachers should focus on a limited number of aspects rather than trying to gain a global picture of all that is happening (Stenmark, 1991). They may focus on children's ability to estimate and talk about their reasoning processes, or on expertise in recording data from a probability experience.

Teachers may also focus on attitudinal aspects or social behaviors in their observations: showing persistence, asking probing questions, sharing materials, or reviewing their results may be noted. Teachers may be able to observe cooperative work, sharing of ideas and materials, and interest (Stenmark, 1991).

Teachers can construct observational checklists including items reflecting content and attitudes. As kindergartners work with geometry, these checklist items, with the flexible "other" category, might be used:

- Classifies figures on a number of bases
- Describes figures, noting relevant features
- Recognizes geometric figures and properties in everyday life
- Models and draws figures
- Names figures
- Works with spatial relationships
- Shows interest in geometry
- Cares for geometric manipulatives and materials
- Shares ideas and materials

◆ Works cooperatively

◆ Works persistently

◆ Other

Beyer (1993) suggests using performance indicators for daily observations. She recommends choosing a limited number of important outcomes, then generating indicators at three levels. Beyer's examples for aspects of communicating mathematically and working with data are shown in Table 5.1 (Beyer, 1993, p. 116–117).

Questioning and Discussion

Questioning and discussion are routine parts of classroom life. Children's responses to questions and commands offer much assessment information, telling the teacher whether children are "with her" and understand the content. Questions can reveal which children are confident and eager to respond and which are more hesitant, or whether some children respond better in small groups than large groups.

Discussions are opportunities for exchange of information, allowing many participants to share their views. Young children are often more able to participate in a discussion if it is based on a recent and common experience—a math activity using calculators or taking a walk to find shapes in the neighborhood. Pictures and manipulatives often stimulate discussion. To make good use of discussions to assess and evaluate children's learning, educators can use these guidelines:

Distribute questions widely among the group and encourage all to participate. Be sure to call on different children as well as let volunteers talk. Make plans to include children who do not often participate.

TABLE 5.1

Not Understanding	Developing	Understanding and Applying
	Mathematical Communication	
• Has difficulty communicating ideas	• Expresses ideas in rudimentary form	• Communicates clearly and effectively
• Withdraws from discussions	• Can support simple explanations with models, drawings, etc.	• Explains thinking process well
• Cannot bring thinking to conscious level writing,		• Can communicate ideas in several forms (orally, in drawings, graphs)
• Does not use, or misuses, terms	• May need some assistance or prompts in refining skills	
• Offers unrelated information	• Uses some terms appropriately	

Use higher-level, open-ended questions to assess and stimulate children's thinking. Even young children are capable of higher-level thinking, so teachers should use questions that require elaborate and creative thinking, problem solving, reasoning, and analysis. The chart contrasts the two types of questions.

Lower-level Questions	Higher-level Questions
What shape is this?	Tell me some things about this shape.
What category got the most votes?	What does the graph tell us?
What's the sum of 5 and 3?	What are some numbers with a sum of 8?

Ask several children for responses to the same question. When educators ask several children to explain their thinking, they gain information for tailoring instruction to children's needs. They also present and reinforce the idea that there are many good ways to think about problems; people can learn from others' thinking.

Encourage children to add to and build on each others' responses. Quality cycles of discussion are not dominated by the teacher, rather they involve children reacting to each others' responses. Prompts such as, "Demetrius, what can you add to Felicia's answer?" or "What do you think about La-Toya's solution?" invite children to comment on others' responses. Allow time for such responses; they build a higher level of dialogue than a cycle of teacher-question, single-answer, teacher-question, single-answer.

Model the thinking processes for children. If children are silent when you ask open-ended questions, model some answers. After you suggest an answer or two, ask the children for more responses.

Encourage children to listen carefully to each other. Help the children "tune in" to others' comments by asking them to listen carefully. You might occasionally ask one child to confirm what another has said: "Josh, tell us in your own words the idea that Rhonda just presented." Questions such as, "What do you think of that idea?" or "What can you add to that?" help children attend to each others' responses. Watch for signs of inattentiveness. Refocus children's attention, revitalize the discussion, or move to another activity when attention wanders.

Plan ways for many children to participate in discussions. Pose a topic, then let the children talk with partners. After a brief period, each pair can share ideas with another pair. Or seat children in small groups, pose a question, let each group discuss it, then take turns reporting to the larger group.

Record the children's responses often; help them record ideas. As children respond, write on a large pad or chalkboard, providing ideas to reread, and add to later in the discussion or unit. Children as young as

WHAT DO *YOU* THINK?

Think about the techniques you use as you talk with young children. Which are most valuable? How do your techniques compare with the ones in this section? What ideas might you apply as you work with children?

four can occasionally record their own ideas in journals or on erasable writing boards.

Anecdotal Records

As teachers observe, anecdotal records help them gain a clear picture of children's work habits and mathematical knowledge. Such records, which are typically brief, dated notes, reflect progress over time. Some teachers keep note cards handy for jotting down observations to be filed in children's anecdotal records. Others use self-adhesive notes with the children's names, make notes, and stick them to the children's files after completion. Still other teachers sit down once a week to write notes about what they remember of children's progress and problems. They do not try to make notes for each child each time, rather they focus on unusual or important occurrences. Some examples are shown in Figure 5.2.

Brief anecdotal records can be made on a checklist with large spaces. Figure 5.3 concerns problem-solving attitudes (modified from *Curriculum Standards* [NCTM, 1989, p. 235]).

Marking a checklist as children work helps a teacher capture a picture of children's abilities and interests.

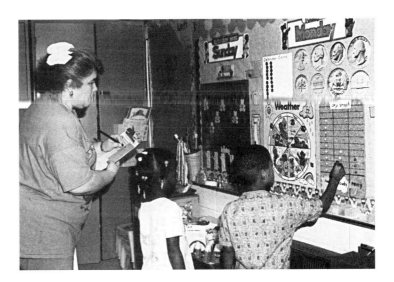

Figure 5.2 *Examples of anecdotal records.*

10-17
Dave was interested
in working with
spinners. He wanted
to get 100 trials and
carefully recorded
results. How can I
foster this interest?

10-18
Vicki got very
excited about our
"after school" graph.
She had comments
and brought in
data from her sister
today.

10-20
Mandy loves working
with paper shapes
and sorting them
many ways. She
helped Joe tactfully
with vocabulary.

10-20
Kate was confused
with subtraction
regrouping. She
knows basic facts,
but not place value.
Could P. J. help her?

Interviews

In an interview, another formative assessment technique, a teacher talks with an individual child or small group of children and attempts to probe their thinking. Interviews can supplement traditional written work and tests where educators see children's answers but cannot tell much about their understanding and thinking (Sammons et al., 1992).

Huinker (1993) describes several decisions about interviews: (1) How will results be recorded? Teachers might use checklists, make notes, or tape record interviews. (2) Who will you interview? If a teacher decides to interview the entire class, she can talk to several each day or interview selected children on different topics, spacing the interviews throughout the school year. (3) When and where will you conduct the interviews? Children might be called aside as others work, or the teacher might stop by individual's tables for brief conversations. During interviews, Huinker recommends asking children to "think out loud" about tasks.

Making students feel comfortable at the start of an interview is important. Stenmark (1989) suggests establishing rapport by finding a level where the student is comfortable. For example, a teacher might provide base-ten blocks and invite a pair of second graders to handle the blocks

	Andy	Tara	Mei Lei	Anita	Billy
Shows Confidence		10-22 Proudly shared new family calculator.	10-22 Wrote in math journal she was proud of work.		10-22 Worked all problems—asked for more.
Helps Others	10-21 Volunteered to help Frank with basic facts.	10-21 Helped group members find needed information.			
Perseveres		10-23 Returned to yesterday's problem and kept working.		10-20 Worked in free time on ice cream problem.	10-21 Worked on coin problem and found many solutions.
Solves Problems More Than One Way	10-21 Used chart and found pattern for same problem.		10-20 Found all six ways to do ice cream problem.		
Other	10-24 Shared graphs from newspaper.			10-23 Seems to enjoy spatial problems.	10-24 Loved the building activity.

Figure 5.3 *Checklist style of anecdotal recording.*

and tell some things they know about them. She might ask them to show numbers such as 78 or 146. The teacher might probe the children's thinking by asking general questions such as, "Talk me through what you're doing," then proceed to specific questions such as, "What do these blocks (the tens) show?" or "How do the blocks show the larger number?" The teacher may also ask, "Where are you having trouble? Try to show me."

Interviewing is time consuming and requires interviewers to choose questions carefully, but the process provides valuable information to supplement more casual observations. It allows the educator to explore children's thinking and to gather detailed information on what the children are doing (Lester, Charles, Lester, O'Daffer, 1986). Not every child needs to be interviewed on every topic. Candidates for interviews can be carefully selected to both provide information for assessment and to give individual attention.

Written Work and Drawings

Even young children can write in a journal or learning log on a regular basis. Teachers should set the stage for writing in mathematics as a way of expressing and organizing ideas by regularly engaging children in writing group compositions or experience stories. As they help children read back what they have dictated, and include additional ideas, educators illustrate the process and value of writing. Writing can take many

Figure 5.4 *Labeled pictures and webs offer insight into children's thinking.*

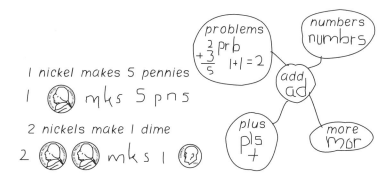

forms. Children can write stories, sequential narratives, lists, charts, and concept diagrams or webs such as in Figure 5.4.

Children who write laboriously can dictate their thoughts or make audiotapes of their ideas. Such tapes are easy to share with parents or file in children's portfolios. Some children respond well to typing on the computer; others are motivated when asked to act out their ideas before writing. Some children react well to having generous periods of writing time, or to writing while soft music is played.

Teachers should take time to talk with each child about his/her writing, though short writing conferences need not be held with each child each day or even each week. Individual attention indicates that adults value attempts at writing; it helps the child orally review and communicate ideas from a written product in conversational form. Besides talking about what the child has written, the teacher can encourage more writing or adding details to pictures. She might ask the child if he wants "adult spellings" added to his invented spelling (Figure 5.5).

Perusing children's written work and drawings can give educators insight into a variety of children's ideas, abilities, and attitudes. As five- and six-year-old children work with numbers 5 through 9, they might draw several pictures of things to represent each number in their journals, then add words about their work with the numbers. From looking at their pictures, the teacher can gain insights about which children are able to match pictures and numbers and make several representations of each

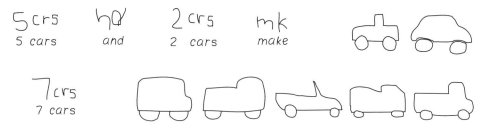

Figure 5.5 *Adult spellings can be added to a child's invented spelling.*

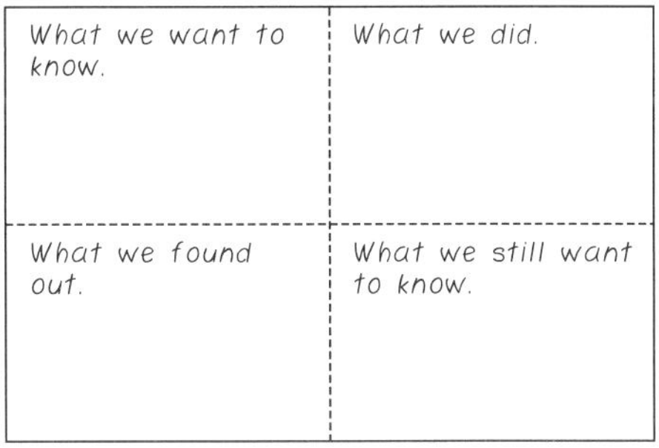

Figure 5.6 *Using charts that clarify categories help children focus on thinking.*

What we want to know.	What we did.
What we found out.	What we still want to know.

number. If a teacher asks kindergarten or primary children to draw and write about their favorite parts of a unit, the teacher can see their interests and their ability to recall learning activities.

A useful format for children's writing and drawing uses four parts: what we want to know, what we did, what we learned, and what we still want to know. Recalling the parts helps children reflect on the learning process in which they have been engaged and will continue to be engaged. Children might work on a piece of paper folded in quarters to organize the four parts (Figure 5.6).

Most educators do not grade children's drawing and writing, but view the work as evidence of their thinking and communication abilities. They expect that some children will be more advanced than others; however, they expect each child to progress. Each child can date writing and drawing samples and keep them in a notebook or folder. Children, educators, and parents can then review the work and see evidence of growth and progress.

Performances and Problem Solving

When children complete mathematical tasks individually or in groups, they often solve problems. Math tasks involve the actual doing and using of mathematics. Using performance tasks lets children display a range of mathematical abilities—not just speed, accuracy, and the ability to choose from prestated answers and bubble in responses (Stenmark, 1991, p. 19)—and lets children work in engaging contexts with "real" materials and problems.

What might mathematical performances or problem solving look like in a classroom with young children? First-grade children might be asked to work with grid paper and find all the arrangements they can for five squares. They might then predict whether each arrangement, if cut out, could be folded into a box. The same sort of task might be assessed as four-year-olds use sets of four cubes and arrange the cubes in many different ways, describing and comparing the arrangements they make.

Stenmark (1991) suggests that tasks and problem-solving situations be devised to represent big ideas from the curriculum. Often good tasks will be thought provoking and open ended, with several possible solutions or several possible approaches. Problem tasks should be pertinent and engaging for children. Problems about current events, seasons, and favorite books are often appealing to children. Activities such as field trips and cooking can form a realistic context for problem solving.

Once problem-solving tasks are selected, educators must consider response formats: Will children make drawings or written reports? Might they report their results orally? Could they create a bulletin board or booklet? Perhaps they could present a play or "panel discussion"? (adapted from Stenmark, 1991). Educators will also need to decide on ways to assess the results. Stenmark (1991) suggests that educators observe children as they work, noting mathematical and social skills. Educators might mark checklists to record how children use mathematical thinking skills such as understanding and defining problems, making plans and using organized approaches to solving problems and completing projects, collecting information, explaining their thinking, and producing reports on their work. They might also note whether children exhibit creativity in their thinking, show initiative, and are persistent and thorough.

For teachers who want to evaluate primary children's written explanations and drawings for problem-solving situations, Austin (1995) suggests the following simple scoring rubric:

◆ 2 Correct answer and explanation are given
◆ 1 Correct answer without thorough explanation
◆ 0 Other

The rubric might be modified for use with younger children who offer verbal explanations for problem-solving situations.

Children's Self-Assessment and Evaluation

Self-assessment and evaluation are parts of becoming an independent learner. Teachers can prompt children's thinking about their own work by initially listing items. For instance, before her first-grade children started a group activity, Ms. Smith asked them, "How will you know you have done a good job?" The children offered a variety of responses such as, "We'll get answers," "We have to show our work," "We will work quietly," and "Share the materials." As the children offered ideas, Ms. Smith wrote them on a pad. She prompted the children to add others, including the ideas that all should participate and that the children should talk in their groups about how well they cooperated.

As the children worked, Ms. Smith walked around and observed. She focused on one group, made notes, then sat down with the group and shared her notes. As they listened, the children seemed delighted at the specificity of the things she noticed ("Kenny got the materials and passed them out quietly. Gracie thanked him. You all used the materials to work on the problems, but Josie quickly got everyone together and asked others to share their ideas.") and at the individualization of some of her comments. Ms. Smith planned to work with another group the next day and share specific comments with them. She reviewed the list of group behaviors to refer to and invited the children to add items to it. On subsequent days Ms. Smith talked to groups of children as they worked, asking open-ended questions: "How did you do today?" "What are some ways you helped each other with the problems?" "How did you show respect for others' ideas?" and "What do you still need to work on in your group?"

Stenmark (1989, p. 26) offers additional suggestions for questions to prompt young children's thinking about their own work: "What mathematics did you learn?" "What could you have done to make your group work better?" "What new questions did you raise?" She further suggests that children write in their journals responding to prompts such as, "Today in mathematics I learned _____," "My plan for what I will do tomorrow is _____," "What I don't understand is _____," or "When I find an answer I feel _____."

Teachers might conference with individuals or small groups and encourage the children to reflect on their work. Such conferences can be helpful toward the end of a unit of work. The teacher might try to get the children to talk about their work, starting the conversation with questions such as, "What did you do here?" "What was easiest? Hardest?" "What different ways did you try?" "What did you learn to help you do some things differently the next time?" "What work are you proud of? Why?"

During reflective conferences, the teacher should encourage the children to talk as much as possible. The teacher might use criteria such as the following to gain a picture of the children's abilities to reflect and self-evaluate:

◆ Seems to give thought to the process
◆ Is able to comment on strengths and weaknesses of work
◆ Seems to see self and work objectively
◆ Offers elaborated answers
◆ Comments on feelings about work

Developing skill at self-evaluation takes time and practice, even for adults. Most children will build self-evaluation skills only if they are asked to. The self-evaluation skills suggested in this section need not be implemented all at one time; phasing in the process of engaging children in self-evaluation can be gradual.

TECHNIQUES FOR SUMMATIVE ASSESSMENT AND EVALUATION OF CHILDREN'S WORK

Educators must use more formal, summative techniques for assessing and evaluating children's work. These techniques are often used after a period of study and work, and are intended to present a picture of long-term achievement and progress. To gather summative data teachers may examine children's projects and products. Another powerful technique is having children compile portfolios to present as evidence of understanding, skills, and positive attitude. Other summative techniques include using tests and written work prepared by learners.

Projects and Products

When children work independently on an idea for a period of time, or when they produce something such as a poster, an elaborate picture, a bulletin board, a lengthy report, a model, or a geometric design, they have worked with a project and have ended up with a product. Often children show considerable thought, independence, creativity, and initiative when preparing projects and products. They may feel like experts on a segment of content, and they have something to share with others. Examples of projects and products are making life-size pictures of animals; collecting, grouping, and displaying sets of 100 small objects; or making a playground map.

Evaluating projects and products includes elements of both formative and summative evaluation. As they look at projects and products, teachers might set up flexible criteria using items such as: having mathematical purpose and value, clarity, individual or group initiative, conveying information, and creativity. They might use these criteria in talking with children about their work or for writing narratives.

The same criteria might be used to help children self-evaluate their own work while it is in progress or when it is completed. For instance, a teacher might ask questions such as these of a group of children working on a map: "What are you trying to show on your map?" "Could others tell that this part of your map is our bookshelves?" The teacher might also ask, "What were some ways you used materials creatively as you worked?" "What problems did you solve as you made your map?" or "Are you proud of your work? Why?" "What might you change if you did it again?"

Projects and products might be displayed at a parents' night or math fair. Parents and other community members might view them and comment on the work or write brief narratives about stronger and weaker points of the projects and products.

To document children's work, teachers might take photographs of finished projects for display, to show to parents, or to file in the children's or the teachers' portfolios. Teachers can also help the children videotape their work, view the tapes, then use them as portfolio entries. The teacher might have children keep a log of their progress on a long-term project, adding to calendar forms or writing narratives about their project work in their math journals. The teacher might also make brief annotations about the children's work as it progresses.

Portfolios

"A portfolio is a showcase for student work, a place where many types of assignments, projects, reports, and writings can be collected. Progress in, attitudes towards, and understanding of mathematics can be seen in a comprehensive way. The collection . . . will show much more than will a single test" (Stenmark, 1991, p. 35). "Portfolio assessment builds a textured, multilayered, focused measure. . . go[ing] beyond traditional testing . . . to show progress as well as identify areas where . . . help may be needed. . . . Portfolios show the breadth and depth of a school's math curriculum. They help to improve teaching and learning [and can] be used to achieve a common standard of excellence" (Vermont Mathematics Portfolio Committee, 1990, p. 3).

Although using portfolios can be time consuming and intimidating to teachers unfamiliar with it, it is a powerful assessment and evaluation technique that offers many benefits. Intended to show development, growth, and achievement in its rich variety, portfolios are compilations or collections of student work. Portfolios should contain items that are considered evidence of children's abilities to understand mathematics, to communicate, and to problem solve: reports, problem solutions, graphs, and photos or videotapes of projects. Primary children's portfolios might include math autobiographies (Shaw & Chessin, 1996) in which children periodically describe the concepts they are learning and describe their experiences with mathematics.

When teachers discuss portfolios with children or parents, or when children take home their portfolios, much productive conversation can ensue. As children and their family members examine the work and talk about it, parents may be able to see the breadth and creativity of the child's work. The child can comment on the work and address questions by family members. Asking open-ended questions such as, "Tell me about this work," or "How did you feel about this?" may solicit many comments from the child and show much about the child's learning.

Portfolio selections may include examples of dealing with many aspects of subject matter, as well as evidence of attitudes toward mathematics. Stenmark (1991) offers examples of portfolio selections for children to show positive attitudes such as perseverance and flexibility: a log of project work, a paper with several solutions to an open-ended problem, a photo of a multiday activity, or an audiotape of the child narrating all the steps that were involved in solving a problem.

A child takes an active role in presenting work from his portfolio to his teacher and mother.

 WHAT DO *YOU* THINK?

Suppose you had to include in your own portfolio evidence of your attitudes toward mathematics. What materials would you include? How might you address developing positive attitudes in children's portfolios?

How can educators help children compile portfolios? Stenmark (1991) suggests helping children keep two portfolios, a work portfolio for work over a short period and an assessment portfolio for work chosen by the child to represent his/her best work. At the end of a unit, grading period, or month, each child can examine the material in their work portfolio, revise it as warranted, and pick the papers that reflect growth, change, or understanding of the topics studied for inclusion in the assessment portfolio. Each child can then write a "cover letter" or summary about the work that is included. Each student could pick a favorite piece of work, label it, and explain why it was chosen. This process is valuable, demanding higher-level thinking and allowing children to have a part in determining part of the work offered for evaluation.

Evaluating Portfolios
After assessment portfolios are compiled, educators can scrutinize the included material. To evaluate portfolios, educators should set up criteria, perhaps paralleling the goals for a particular unit. If a unit's goals include problem solving, organizing and interpreting data, relating math to other subjects, and increasing children's confidence, educators should look for evidence of progress toward each goal. They might write a brief

narrative about each goal or use a rating scale with indicators from excellent to poor.

An example of using such a rating system for one child's portfolio follows. For the portfolio, seven-year-old Karen selected items to show her best work from a month-long unit about nutrition. Since she liked peanut butter, Karen investigated peanut butter prices as one of her independent tasks. She not only made a graph of peanut butter prices at local stores, but she researched the prices of bread and jelly and calculated the price of a peanut butter sandwich. She also polled classmates about their favorite sandwiches and asked questions about her graph.

◆ Problem Solving: Exceptional—Included problems with many different solutions, posed and answered questions based on a graph, included two questions that required two steps to answer.

◆ Reasoning: Good—Explained thinking, discussed how she reached answers in three out of five examples. The peanut butter price graph gave prices for two different stores and three brands, but Karen did not make conclusions based on this data.

◆ Relates math to everyday life: Excellent—Chose home and store for settings for data gathering. Used math operations in answering questions on graphs.

◆ Organizing and interpreting data: Acceptable—All graphs were of same type. Although Karen apparently understood the material in her graphs and used it in problem solving, she did not label them with titles and category names. Two of the three graphs were messy and confusing.

◆ Displays confidence: Excellent—Cover letter showed pride and enthusiasm; told importance of information. Displayed initiative in posing peanut butter price question and answering it. The photo of Karen's group presenting their survey results makes me recall her confidence as she reported.

To increase their confidence in examining portfolios, teachers might work together to review portfolios. To focus their work, educators might decide on a small number of factors or criteria to review at one time. The teachers should try to develop a working understanding of what the criteria mean and how the students' work might show evidence of progress or achievement in the criteria. For instance, if the teachers are looking for evidence of creativity in mathematics, they will need to discuss what "creativity" means and what evidence of it might be present.

Program Assessment and Evaluation
Portfolio evaluation can also give teachers, supervisors, and administrators data for making judgments about mathematics programs. The

teachers can examine student portfolios and sort them into several groups. Using criteria such as evidence of broad curriculum, problem solving, reasoning, and connecting mathematics to other subjects, they might look for evidence of thought and effort as shown in student writing and videotapes of group projects and products.

In examining portfolios to determine program quality educators might also use a scoring rubric with qualities such as these extracted from Stenmark (1991, p. 44):

♦ Level 4. Portfolios from this top level are exciting to look at and show clarity of communication, creative work, and enthusiasm. They reflect use of many resources, a broad curriculum, student involvement in activities and investigations, problem solving, and reasoning.

♦ Level 3. This level portfolio shows evidence of a solid math program. Students are able to explain their work fairly well. Factors such as evidence of student enthusiasm or self-assessment may be missing.

♦ Level 2. Portfolios show an adequate program, somewhat bound by textbook requirements. There is little evidence of original student thinking or a broad curriculum.

♦ Level 1. Portfolios show almost no creative or thought-provoking work and no evidence that students are discussing mathematical ideas and explaining their reasoning.

Tests

Tests are a traditional part of education at all levels. Recently however, testing of young children has been questioned by a number of authorities and professional groups. For example, the National Association for the Education of Young Children (NAEYC) issued a position statement in 1988 describing some of the harmful effects of standardized testing of young children: narrowing of the curriculum to easily tested cognitive material, ignoring development of self-esteem and social competence in a desire to improve test scores, focus on memorization of material rather than problem solving and creative thinking, and stress placed on young children during tests. The position statement further describes the harm done to children when they are "labeled" or denied access to programs because of test results.

Most standardized achievement tests are designed to give information about the skills and knowledge children have acquired. However, the number of items on each skill or knowledge area may be very small, and thus may not reflect the many things children know about the topic. Young children are typically not good test takers. Scores may be influenced by factors such as ability to sit still, be quiet, make appropriate marks (NAEYC, 1988), interpret examples pertinent to other cultures, and maintain motivation for an adult-imposed task. Tests may not show aspects such as variety of interests, effort, attitudes, or progress.

Where tests are mandated, conscientious educators must work with children to prepare for the tests. At the same time they can work with parents and administrators to balance the weight given to test results in decision making with other data such as teacher observation, information from parents, and portfolio assessment. They look at aspects such as persistence and creativity in children's work. They include data on social skills and personal growth when making judgments, and work to eliminate the use of standardized test scores as the sole basis for judgments of program quality or for placement of children.

Teacher-made tests may be a source of data about primary children's progress. Such tests can be constructed to reflect learning activities; results of such tests can be used to guide subsequent instruction. If they prepare tests, educators should remember to try to measure skills and knowledge that are "worth learning" (Mathematical Sciences Review Board, 1993; NCTM, 1995). As with standardized tests, teacher-made tests should be only one source of data about young children's learning. Any test can provide only a sample of what children know; tests are poor indicators of affective growth and results must be balanced with other aspects of assessment.

Teacher-made tests should be appropriate for primary children, including a variety of tasks such as drawing, writing, and explaining. Some test items might allow children to work with manipulatives and record their results; others can include the use of calculators. Test items should provide opportunities for open-ended problem solving and for students to explain how they reached their answers and how they know they are right. True-false and multiple choice items tend to confuse young children and should be avoided. The value placed on test results determining young children's grades should be small. Judgments made from tests must be balanced with observational and performance data.

CHANGING ASSESSMENT AND EVALUATION TECHNIQUES

Many teachers—parents too—are concerned about the many assessment and evaluation options offered them. Although traditional tests and grades are "easy" to understand and interpret, they actually tell little about the depth and breadth of children's work. Changing to new options is exciting, but it takes effort; the unknown or untried is often scary.

If grades are given, evaluations on projects and performances should be included as well as data from worksheets and tests. Comments on children's progress, observed strengths and weaknesses, and attitudes might accompany reporting of letter or number grades. In addition to grades, teachers might offer portfolios for examination by children's families.

Stenmark (1991, p. 1) offers suggestions to ease the transition from traditional testing and grading to multifaceted, authentic assessment: (1) Don't try it all at once. Rather, focus on one new assessment idea to try out. Revise and refine the idea trying to use one new technique per lesson. (2) Get support for your efforts. Work with a group of colleagues. Enlist parental and administrator understanding and support. (3) Get involved in a math network such as a national, state, regional, or local NCTM affiliate group or mathematics education organization.

SUMMARY

Assessment and evaluation are necessary to "inform practice." These processes help educators make changes based on children's responses. Assessment and evaluation also help educators gauge children's progress and decide whether programs are broad and effective. A variety of formative, ongoing evaluation techniques—observing and questioning children, using checklists and notes, interviewing children, and making judgments about children's problem-solving abilities—can be informal and routine aspects of classroom life. Children's self-evaluation complements adults' efforts to understand children's mathematical knowledge, attitudes, and thinking processes.

More formal, summative means of assessment and evaluation are also necessary. Examining children's projects and products provides data about children's longer-term progress. Portfolio compilation and assessment provide much data about individual children's progress, as well as the breadth and depth of programs. Information gathered from assessment and evaluation guides many decision-making processes and helps educators improve mathematics education opportunities for children.

◆ *APPLICATIONS: THINKING AND COLLABORATING*

Use some of the following exercises to synthesize some of the chapter's ideas and apply in your teaching.

1. Choose a single goal or topic that you think is especially important in teaching and learning mathematics. Devise a checklist you could use in observing children and gathering information about their knowledge, skills, and attitudes. Try out the checklist, refine it, and share it with colleagues.

2. Compile a list of important attitudes as children learn and use mathematics. Decide how you will gather data and make judgments about some of the attitudes. Could you observe or interview children to gather evidence of their attitudes? Can the children mark an attitude scale? Might they write something that will give indications of

their attitudes? Make some decisions and then try out some ideas as you work with children.

3. Choose an assessment and evaluation topic and read more about it. Write a summary of your findings; react to them in terms of applicability, usefulness, or pertinence. Share your findings with classmates, a colleague, or an administrator.

4. Audio- or videotape a lesson with a group of children. Evaluate your discussion techniques: Did you involve all the children? Did you ask open-ended or higher-level thinking questions? Did you encourage children to build on others' responses? What might you change about the ways you conducted the discussion? What other decisions might you make based on the tape?

5. Suppose you were implementing or enhancing portfolio assessment. What might you ask children to include in a math portfolio for a given unit, semester, or year? How can children have input into deciding the portfolio's content? Evaluate your plans using criteria such as these: Would the portfolio include materials to show a broad curriculum? Would it include evidence of children's work in problem solving, communicating, and reasoning? How might the portfolio address affective areas of learning mathematics?

6. You may have started a file of problem-solving and reasoning ideas in Chapter 1. Implement a selection from the file with a young child. Study the child's work and make judgments about his/her strengths and weaknesses after evaluating the work.

7. You may have started a mathematics autobiography in Chapter 1. If so, add to the autobiography, recalling some of the ways you have been assessed and evaluated as a student and teacher. Add reflections about current views of assessment and evaluation.

◆ REFERENCES

Austin, G. R. (1995). Implementation of the Maryland performance assessment program. *Assessment in Practice*, 2(1), 1, 5.

Boyor, J. (1993). Assessing students' performance using observations, reflections, and other methods. In Norman L. Webb (Ed.), *Assessment in the mathematics classroom, 1993 yearbook*. Reston, VA: National Council of Teachers of Mathematics.

Charles, R., Lester, F., & O'Daffer, P. (1986). *How to evaluate progress in problem solving*. Reston, VA: National Council of Teachers of Mathematics.

Goodman, Y. (1982). Kidwatching: Evaluating written language development. *Australian Journal of Reading*, 5(3), 120–128.

Huinker, D. M. (1993). Interviews: a window to students' conceptual knowledge of the operations. In Norman L. Webb (Ed.), *Assessment in the mathematics classroom, 1993 yearbook*. Reston, VA: National Council of Teachers of Mathematics.

Kroll, D. L., Masingila, J. O., & Mau, S. T. (1992). Cooperative problem solving: but what about grading? *Arithmetic Teacher, 39*(6):17–23.

Mathematical Sciences Review Board. (1993). *Measuring up: prototypes for mathematics assessment.* Washington, DC: National Research Council.

National Association for the Education of Young Children. (1988). Position statement on standardized testing of young children 3 through 8 years old. *Young Children, 43*(3), 42–47.

National Council of Teachers of Mathematics. (1989). *Curriculum and Evaluation Standards for School Mathematics.* Reston, VA: Author.

National Council of Teachers of Mathematics. (1991). *Professional Standards for Teaching Mathematics.* Reston, VA: Author.

National Council of Teachers of Mathematics. (1995). *Assessment Standards for School Mathematics.* Reston, VA: Author.

Routman, R. (1991). *Invitations: changing as teachers and learners K–12.* Portsmouth, NH: Heinemann.

Sammons, K., Kobett, B., Heiss, J., & Fennell, F. (1992). Linking instruction and assessment in the mathematics classroom. *Arithmetic Teacher, 39*(6), 11–16.

Shaw, J. M., & Chessin, D. A. (1996). Using preservice teachers' mathematics autobiographies to promote learning. *Teaching Children Mathematics, 2*(8), 486–490.

Stenmark, J. K. (1989). *Alternative assessments in mathematics.* Berkeley, CA: EQUALS.

Stenmark, J. K. (1991). *Mathematics assessment: myths, models, good questions, and practical suggestions.* Reston, VA: National Council of Teachers of Mathematics.

Vermont Mathematics Portfolio Committee. (1990). *The Vermont mathematics portfolio: what it is, how to use it.* Montpelier, VT: Montpelier Department of Education.

Webb, N. L. (1993). Assessment for the mathematics classroom. In Norman L. Webb (Ed.), *Assessment in the mathematics classroom, 1993 yearbook.* Reston, VA: National Council of Teachers of Mathematics.

Webb, N. L. (1992). Assessment of students' knowledge of mathematics: steps toward a theory. In Douglas A. Grouws (Ed.), *Handbook of research on mathematics teaching and learning,* pp. 661–686, New York: Macmillan.

Zawojewski, J. S. (1996). Polishing a data task: seeking better assessment. *Teaching Children Mathematics, 2*(6); 372–377.

Problem Solving
and Reasoning

6

◆◆

Linda, a five-year-old, is working with attribute blocks. She tells her teacher that she has made two patterns in one. "See, there's triangle, triangle, circle, circle, square, and square. That's one pattern. Then there's small, large, small, large, small, and large." Linda is using a type of reasoning to recognize the relationships within patterning. As she explains her thinking, she notices a third pattern. "Look, there's another one—thin, thick, thin, thick, thin, and thick." Reasoning and problem-solving thought processes play an important role in mathematical thinking.

111

Every day each of us solves problems in a variety of situations. Events that require solutions occur for all people in all professions every day. Not all problems are mathematical in nature, but the thought process behind solving problems is similar in all situations. Problem solving requires different approaches and a flexible means of approaching problems.

Well-known educator John Dewey laid the ground work for use of a problem-solving approach in education. He advocated the project approach to teaching and learning in which children actively engage in activities that are designed to encourage problem solving. Dewey (1916) characterized concepts in the mind and experiences in life as having an interactive nature—one constantly modifying the other: good teaching ideas are those that enhance the learners' experiences and good experiences are those that encourage a person to think through and test ideas. Dewey (1938, p. 88) further wrote that this approach is "the only authentic means at our command for getting at the significance of our everyday experiences of the world in which we live."

In the current climate of school reform, there are clear calls for teaching problem solving in all curriculum areas (Evertson and Randolph, 1995). This movement places new demands on educators—teaching a new broad range of cognitive skills rather than a narrow development of basic skills. Use of behavioral objectives would no longer be the primary instructional focus, practice would be guided by goals or general objectives or by problem-solving objectives. Problem-solving objectives such as how the school community feels about different topics allow for greater diversity in what is learned by students (Klein, 1995).

The National Council of Teachers of Mathematics (NCTM) recommends that problem solving be the central focus of the mathematics curriculum. The *Curriculum and Evaluation Standards for School Mathemetics* (NCTM, 1989, p. 23) state:

> In grades K–4, the study of mathematics should emphasize problem solving so that students can
>
> ◆ use problem-solving approaches to investigate and understand mathematical content;
> ◆ formulate problems from everyday and mathematical situations;
> ◆ develop and apply strategies to solve a wide variety of problems;
> ◆ verify and interpret results with respect to the original problem;
> ◆ acquire confidence in using mathematics meaningfully.

Young children need to use problem-solving approaches to investigate and understand mathematical content (Krogh, 1995). While young children may not think logically in an adult sense, they can still develop a trial-and-error thought process that lays the foundation for later problem solving or logical thinking. Children need to be comfortable formulating problems from everyday and mathematical situations. The way in which people originally learn mathematics plays an important role in determining whether they are able and willing to use it to help them understand the world around them and solve problems (Willoughby, 1990).

Mr. Erives works with three- and four-year-old children. He wants his children to learn to love mathematics. He always plans activities that are fun yet are important for enhancing mathematics. Some days he uses snack time to develop mathematical thinking. One day his class ate animal cookies for snack. "What animal cookie did you choose?" When the children answer, Mr. Erives places the same kind of cookie on a simple graph he has made from shelf paper. He arranges the cookies in straight rows and then discusses the relationships with the children. "Which type of animal cookie was the favorite?" "How do you know that?" These types of questions help the children begin to think about mathematical relationships.

WHAT DO *YOU* THINK?

This problem is used throughout the country and has been used with a variety of age levels. See what solutions you come up with. Cori the camel carries bananas to a market that is exactly 1000 miles from her home. Cori can carry 1000 bananas at one time, but she has to eat one banana every mile she walks in order to maintain her pace. What is the greatest number of bananas that Cori can arrive with at the market if the number she arrives with at the market is more than 10. Work and explain your answer to this problem. Compare your answer with peers and see how many different approaches and answers you come up with.

WHAT IS PROBLEM SOLVING?

Before problem solving can be defined it is important to establish what a problem might be. There are many possible definitions for what a problem could be; therefore, recognizing a problem may not always be a clearly defined task. Willoughby (1990, p. 5) uses the following example to illustrate how complex the process of problem identification might be.

A hunter started at camp and walked one mile south. Then she walked one mile west. There she shot a bear. The bear was heavy, so instead of retracing her steps, she walked one mile straight back to camp, dragging the bear behind her. What color was the bear?

Analyze this paragraph and decide if this is a problem or not. If you are familiar with this story, then it is an exercise in memory and not a problem. If you have never seen this story before, you may see no relationship between the facts and a solution. If you are direction conscious you might find a clue in the facts presented. Problems are relative to an individual's experiences, background knowledge, and the situation in which the problem is presented. The term *problem* can be defined in different ways.

Traditional mathematics curriculum has often labeled problem solving as addition, subtraction, multiplication, and division operations with little or no emphasis on the thought process behind these actions. But mathematical operations do not require children to use reasoning and problem-solving skills, and so they should not be considered the only important element in problem solving. Problems should actually involve children in active exploration.

The foundation of the problem-solving thought process begins during children's early years. Piaget stated that problem solving begins during the sensory-motor stage of development. As children grow and develop, the ability to solve more complex problems depends on integration of skills such as object permanence, means-ends behavior, and spatial understanding. Problem solving for very young children integrates key developmental skills.

Young children are capable of microthinking or small step processes necessary for performing all thinking processes (Hester, 1994). These thinking skills are necessary for mastering basic subject-related skills and are characterized by perception and organization abilities, skills necessary for inferential thinking, predicting, and problem-solving operations. These thinking skills precede and form the basis for reasoning, a key element in problem solving.

WHAT IS REASONING?

Before reasoning can be clarified it is important to define what the word "reason" means. Of the several definitions the *American Heritage Dictionary's* (1994, on disc)—the "capacity for logical, rational, and analytical thought"—is probably most appropriate for mathematical purposes. Reasoning relates to how one thinks and the thought process behind problem analysis. Reasoning is the act of using reason or critical thinking to form conclusions, inferences, or judgments. Consider the following problem. Is reasoning needed to solve it?

 ## THE ATHLETIC SHOES

Change the content of this problem depending on the children's interests. Some children may be interested in sports teams, paintings, or books.

Focus: Problem solving.

What To Do: Have primary children work in small groups. Give them play money—

100, 50, 10, and 5 dollar bills. Have the children try to solve the following problem first without money and then let them use money.

Michael Jordon bought a new pair of athletic shoes for $100. He decided he didn't like the color so he sold them to Scotty Pippin for $150. Scotty had to sell the shoes to get money to pay off an NBA fine, so Michael bought them back for $160. But Michael convinced Charles Barkley to buy them for $170. Did Michael gain, lose, or come out even after the transactions? If he lost or gained, how much?

Adjustments: Have the children make up problems concerning something they themselves own or would like to own.

Ongoing Assessment: Observe children to see what procedure they use to solve this problem. Do they use pencil and paper or do it in their head? Do they need to use the play money and act out the problem?

Mathematics is reasoning; one cannot do mathematics without reasoning (NCTM, 1989). The NCTM supports reasoning as a vital element in mathematical thinking. The NCTM *Curriculum Standards* (1989) recommend that critical thinking be at the heart of mathematics instruction. It is important for even very young children to learn to explain and justify how problems are solved. Teachers should ask questions like, "Why do you think that is a good answer?" or "Do you think you would get the same answer if you used these other materials?" Children should be provided opportunities to justify their solutions, thinking processes, and conjectures in a variety of ways.

The mathematics as reasoning standard states:

In grades K–4, the study of mathematics should emphasize reasoning so that students can

◆ draw logical conclusions about mathematics;

◆ use models, known facts, properties, and relationships to explain their thinking;

◆ justify their answers and solution processes;

◆ use patterns and relationships to analyze mathematical situations;

◆ believe that mathematics makes sense. (NCTM, 1989, p. 29)

The reasoning standard emphasizes the importance of reasoning but does not demand that formal reasoning be taught to young children. It is recommended that reasoning at this level involve informal thinking, conjecturing, and validating that helps young children see that mathematics has meaning. Children should be provided a variety of manipulative materials so they can work through and illustrate their thinking. Reasoning cannot develop in isolation. The ability to reason is a process that grows out of many experiences that convince children that mathematics makes sense (NCTM, 1989).

Reasoning should be used constantly as children learn mathematics. Educators encourage children to explain the reasoning processes behind conclusions and justify why their particular approaches to problem solving are appropriate. The main goal of emphasizing reasoning is to empower students to reach conclusions. Children must learn to justify statements on their own rather than relying on the authority of a text or the teacher.

WHAT DO *YOU* THINK?

Here is an exercise in reasoning. Explain and illustrate your solution.

Ten pennies are arranged in the form of a triangle. What is the fewest number of moves it would take to turn the triangle upside down? Only one penny may be moved per turn.

Try cases with triangles made of 3, 6, 15, and 21 pennies. Share your data with a partner and look for a pattern in your results.

Types of Reasoning

Mathematical inquiry often begins with a conclusion drawn from intuitive or inductive reasoning called a conjecture. Even very young children are capable of intuitive and inductive reasoning and making conjectures. As children work with the meanings of mathematics operations, or the thinking behind mathematical problem solving, they use reasoning skills. Let's examine what researchers consider the three major types of reasoning.

Figure 6.1 *Which line is longer? Measure and find out.*

A. $\longleftrightarrow$

B. $\succ\!\!-\!\!-\!\!\prec$

Intuitive Reasoning

Intuitive reasoning plays an important role in problem solving and has been the basis for many advancements in mathematics and science. This type of reasoning is based on appearances or assumptions. Intuitive reasoning entails insight or playing a hunch relating to mathematical learning. For example, look at the lines in Figure 6.1 and decide which line is longer. Based on appearances, line B looks longer. In actuality both lines are the same length. Intuitive reasoning may be misleading because all the information may not be evident or available. It is important to encourage young children to use this type of reasoning, but emphasize the "why" and "how" aspects. Educators should ask questions like, How did you decide which line was longer? or Why is that line longer? Conclusions drawn from intuitive reasoning need to be substantiated by collecting data or deductive logic.

Inductive Reasoning

Inductive reasoning involves perceptions of regularity (Baroody, 1993). When children use this type of reasoning, they are looking for a pattern or finding a commonalty among a group of things. See Figure 6.2 for an example. Look at the figures in Figure 6.2 and determine the definition of a dodecagon.

What characteristics did you discover the figures had in common? You were using inductive reasoning as you analyzed the figures; however, inductive reasoning alone cannot prove a conclusion true because it may not generalize to include all aspects of a concept. Inductive reasoning may produce a conclusion true to specific examples studied, like the figures pictured, but there is no guarantee that the conclusion will fit all situations.

Searching for patterns, relationships, and order is the heart of mathematics (Baroody, 1993). But in order for inductive reasoning to prove a mathematics rule, it must fit all examples or be tested against a wide range of problems, situations, and samples. Try to find different patterns while working through the following problems.

Figure 6.2 *Closely examine these figures. Make a list of the characteristics they have in common. What is a dodecagon?*

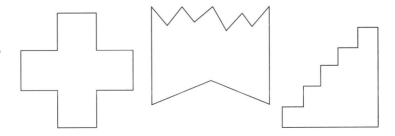

THREE BEAN SALAD

Use dry beans, an inexpensive and readily available manipulative. Primary children work on problems such as these.

Focus: Reasoning, problem solving, communication.

What To Do: Provide a data sheet like the one illustrated below. Give or read the following problems to the children and allow them to use real beans to find the solutions. Each salad contains red beans, lima beans, and black-eyed peas.

	Lima Beans	Red Beans	Black-Eyed Peas
1.			
2.			
3.			
4.			
5.			
6.			
7.			
8.			

1. This salad contains 2 lima beans, twice as many red beans as lima beans, 10 beans in all.
2. This salad contains 4 red beans, 1/2 as many black-eyed peas as red beans, 10 beans in all.
3. Lima beans make up 1/2 of this salad. The salad has exactly 2 red beans. The number of lima beans is twice the number of red beans.
4. This salad contains the same number of red beans as lima beans, 3 more black-eyed peas than red beans, a total of 18 beans.
5. This salad contains 9 beans, 1/2 of the beans are red, and lima beans make up 1/4 of the salad.
6. This salad contains at least 12 beans. It has 1 more lima bean than red bean. It has 1 more red bean than black-eyed peas.
7. This salad contains 3 times as many red beans as black-eyed peas, one more lima bean than red beans, 8 beans in all.

8. This salad contains an equal number of red beans and black-eyed peas, 5 more lima beans than red beans, no more than 20 beans.

Adjustments: Make up a different salad and a problem to go with it. Increase or decrease the number of beans to fit the developmental level of the children. Have the children make up salad problems to use with friends.

Ongoing Assessment: Have the children write in their math journals or dictate into a tape recorder their reasoning as they tried to solve the salad problems.

Deductive Reasoning

Deductive reasoning refers to drawing a conclusion from what we know over a period of time or after much data collection. One example might be the fact that we know that we can always add one to any number. Based on this we can conclude that there is no largest number because the list of numbers extends to infinity. In order to determine if deductive reasoning is sound there are two important premises to remember. A conclusion is true if

♦ the premises of the argument are true
♦ the argument is valid

When using deductive reasoning remember to carefully analyze the factors that influence this type of thinking.

 WHAT DO *YOU* THINK?

Find the solution to the following problem. If toothpicks are arranged as a row of triangles as shown below, how many toothpicks will be needed to make a row of 100 triangles?

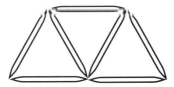

As you reason, you might examine simpler cases of the problem. Communicate your data to colleagues and look for a pattern. Compare your answers with your peers.

Reasoning and Young Children

Inhelder and Piaget (1964) believed that children's ability to reason logically changed dramatically with age. He presumed they could reason about the concrete, but not theoretical propositions. Piaget also found that concrete operational children could not systematically consider all logical possibilities until children had reached a mature developmental level. He pointed out that young children had difficulty with tasks requiring ordering and classifying skills.

Research suggests that Piaget underestimated children's logical abilities (Baroody, 1993). When young children are helped to remember original relationships they are capable of transitive reasoning (Bryant and Trabasso, 1971). Transitive reasoning allows children to transfer observations or concepts from one situation to another. Therefore even very young children are capable of deductive reasoning. This is often referred to as "if-then" thinking or "eliminating cases."

 ## WEIGHT TRANSFERENCE

In order to use "if-then" reasoning children must experience many different types of activities that promote such thinking. The activity listed below helps children to think about weight transference and the concept of equal weight may not mean equal size.

Focus: Problem solving and reasoning.

What To Do: Provide children with several blocks, interlocking cubes, rocks, paper clips, a balance scale, a spring scale, boxes, yarn, and other measurement devices. Explain the idea of "equal" or "same as" to children. Ask the children, "How many blocks will it take to equal the weight of one rock?"

Allow the children to determine their own strategy to solve this problem. As the children work ask them, "What if I add three more blocks to this side of the scale, what will happen?" Repeat the activity with paper clips and other materials. Help the children to group the number of paper clips, blocks, and cubes that were equal to the weight of the rock. Ask the children, "If this many paper clips equal the weight of one rock, how many paper clips will equal the blocks?"

Adjustments: Add different materials to the experiment. Encourage more mature children to include standard measurement.

Ongoing Assessment: Keep short notes on which children can and cannot construct equal groups and transfer to other materials.

SORTING AND CLASSIFYING

Sorting and classifying are two important types of activities that encourage deductive reasoning. These activities foster the language of logic and build the base for more mature thinking. Discrimination, or the ability to distinguish between sensations, can be seen very early in children (Linder, 1993). From 9 to 12 months of age children are capable of seeing easy relationships between objects and to combine objects, such as a shovel and a pail. By two years of age, a child can place a circle or square into a puzzle and by age three the child can discriminate a triangle from other shapes. Combining these increasing representational skills, spatial understanding, and problem-solving skills, the four- to five-year-old child is capable of simple classification (Linder, 1993).

Baroody (1993) recommends that children begin sorting and classification activities as soon as they enter school. Baroody identifies some key words associated with reasoning and important for the sorting process. These words are "all," "some," "not," "and," "or," and "if." Each of these words help children think about attributes for classification purposes. Educators should provide concrete materials so that children can construct meanings for descriptive words in a natural environment.

 ## ATTRIBUTE BLOCK TRAINS

Attribute or logic blocks are designed to ensure that children explore fundamental concepts of sorting and relationships of order, equivalence, and difference.

Focus: Reasoning—classification, sorting, communicating.

What To Do: Have small groups of children explore and discuss differences in attribute blocks. As the children identify specific attributes such as size, thickness, or color, write their ideas on the board. Have one child from each group select an attribute block from his/her set to start a train. The next child finds another block that differs by one attribute and places it next to the first block. Continue this process until the children can no longer place a block on the train. Another type of attribute train is a two-attribute train where children find blocks that differ by two attributes and so on.

Adjustments: Continue to change the number of attributes. Use a Venn diagram and allow the children to identify criteria for sorting. Use the attribute blocks like a domino game where children match attributes and the first child out of blocks wins. Invite the children to make up other games using classification.

Ongoing Assessment: Encourage the children to write or dictate their reasons for adding blocks to the train. Check the thought process to determine if they are following a logical sequence.

Venn diagrams are useful tools when helping children learn to sort and classify. In Venn diagrams the positions of circles indicate the relationships of sets. To work with Venn diagrams young children might start with loops of yarn or large embroidery hoops. After children have been introduced to

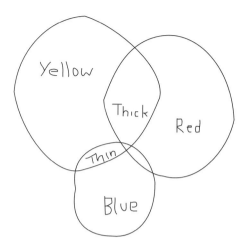

Figure 6.3   *Children at Cravens Elementary use Venn diagrams as they classify and reason.*

the various ways Venn diagrams can be used, they can make their own diagrams. It is helpful to discuss how to set up each Venn diagram until children have gained enough confidence and experience to design their own. See Figure 6.3 for one example used by children in a multiage classroom at Cravens Elementary. These children ranged in age from five to seven. Sorting and classifying are important steps in developing deductive reasoning. Young children should be allowed a variety of opportunities to engage in deductive reasoning activities. One major goal of mathematics instruction is to help children develop the belief that they can do mathematics and that they have control over their mathematical success or failure. This independence develops as children gain confidence in their ability to reason and justify their thinking. A classroom that values reasoning also values communication and problem solving, which integrates with the broad goals of the NCTM.

WOULD YOU RATHER HAVE A KILOGRAM OF NICKELS OR DIMES?

This activity allows primary children to integrate mathematics areas and work with measurement.

Focus: Problem solving, reasoning, communicating, measurement—weight, metric system, money.

What To Do: For each small group of children provide a nickel, a dime, other coins, a balance scale, calculators, and gram weights. Ask the children how many grams a nickel weighs; write estimates on the board. Repeat with a dime. Weigh one nickel in grams. Ask the children how much money one kilogram of nickels would be. Let the groups discuss how to solve this problem. Have one person in each group write or dictate the group's strategies.

Weigh the dime in grams. Repeat the above procedure. Have the children determine whether they would rather have a kilogram of nickels or dimes and explain their answers.

Adjustments: Weigh other coins and have each group report. Add paper money to the groups to see which they would rather have. Which is the heaviest?

Ongoing Assessment: Keep the reports from each group regarding their strategies for solving the problem. Is there clear evidence of problem-solving strategies being used? Did the group try more than one strategy?

DEVELOPING PROBLEM-SOLVING STRATEGIES

Most researchers agree on common, basic strategies for problem solving. As we discuss each strategy, think about each approach and ways you may have used each when working through mathematics problems.

Guess and check. Young children use this approach to solving problems long before they enter school. This approach requires the use of estimation or intuitive reasoning and often children make random guesses.

Draw a picture, act it out, use models. Even very young children engage in this type of problem-solving activity during playtime. When children build with blocks or construct sand pile roads and tunnels, they are using informal problem-solving models. These activities reinforce and extend problem-solving skills. Acting out, drawing, or constructing models represent problems giving children something to experiment with and reflect on. Drawing a picture is a strategy that permeates mathematical thinking, not just the solution of process problems or in connection with other strategies (Van de Walle, 1994). Children can self-correct and adjust their solutions as they work.

Ms. Villagrana has placed several plastic containers of varying size in her water center. Ms. Villagrana works in a center with children from age

Working together to solve the problem of where the shapes belong enhances children's self-confidence and lets them share their reasoning about the solution.

three to five. She notices Kendrick is experimenting with the containers and sits beside him. She fills a small container with water and then asks Kendrick how many of that size container it would take to fill the quart jar with water. Kendrick says, "at least fifty." Ms. Villagrana responds, "Fifty, why do you think it would take so many?" Kendrick tells Ms. Villagrana that his container is very little and the quart is very tall. Ms. Villagrana pours one small container of water into the quart and lets Kendrick see how much space the water fills. She then asks Kendrick, "Do you still think it will take fifty?" Kendrick looks at both containers and says, "No, but it will take a lot." Ms. Villagrana says, "You count while I pour and we'll see exactly how many it takes."

Ms. Villagrana suggests that Susie get a crayon and a piece of paper and make a mark every time Kendrick adds a container of water to the quart jar. The final tally was 15. Ms. Villagrana continues the discussion and draws 50 marks so the children can see the difference between the guess and the actual number of containers. Kendrick pours the water from the quart jar into a gallon jar and continues to add small containers of water while Susie tallies.

Ms. Villagrana is allowing her children to use a combination of the guess-and-check, act-it-out, and use-a-model strategies of problem solving. She guided the children in the process so that next time they will be able to try these approaches on their own. As the children work, they gain confidence in their abilities to solve problems and think through strategies.

Look for a pattern. Young children recognize a pattern when stringing beads, clapping rhythms, or when counting by twos, fives, or tens. With practice, young children can learn to expect patterns to exist in certain situations. The educator plans activities where patterns are easily discernible at first to help children learn how to identify patterns. When children seem to understand patterning, introduce more subtle patterns and help them discover generalizations.

Make a table, chart, or original list. Often children will encounter a series of numbers when thinking through a problem. The solution may be found

WHAT DO *YOU* THINK?

The following problems lend themselves to making tables or charts. Work these two problems, recording your work as you go and comparing your work with your peers.

◆ Can you make change for a quarter using exactly 9 coins? exactly 17? exactly 6? How many ways can you make change for a quarter?
◆ How many ancestors have you had in the last 200 years?

How many different types of tables and charts did your class devise? Were they alike or different? Communicate your data on a chart.

through a list of numbers organized in a way that allows children to easily see the answer. Placing symbols into a format organizes data and can aid problem solving and facilitate looking for patterns. Charts or tables usually consist of rows or columns that list important elements of the problem.

Account for all possibilities. Included in this strategy is making an organized list or systematic counting. This strategy is useful for problems that require some method of counting things or making certain that every possibility is covered. Sometimes it is easier to solve a problem by trying out all solutions.

Work backwards. Some problems are presented in a manner such that the final conditions of an action are given and the questions deal with prior actions. Problem solvers know the result but need to determine the starting condition. If the events are arithmetic operations, the task is to reverse these operations. Other problems present a series of unknown events in some condition and the task is to determine the sequence of events.

Try a simpler problem. Some problems are made difficult by large numbers or complicated patterns, so the solution may be unclear. For such problems it may help to make an analogy that is simpler to help the students find the solution. Working the easier problem may help students see a way to solve the original problem, or starting with a series of simpler problems may lead to a pattern or generalization that will solve the original problem.

Children often fail to recognize the need to answer one question before another can be answered. Many kinds of problems are interrelated, and knowing how to solve one problem may lead to the solution of another. One classic example that illustrates such a strategy follows.

 WHAT DO *YOU* THINK?

Write the numerals 1 to 19 in the 19 spaces below so that any three numbers in a row have the same sum. Solve a simpler problem (perhaps filling in a five-space version with the numbers 1 to 5) and look for a pattern.

Number patterns offer fun and problem solving.

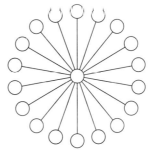

Write an equation or open sentence. This strategy is the traditional mathematics approach to problem solving found in many textbooks. Once primary children write the open sentence, they probably can solve the problem; the hard part is writing the sentence. Children must be able to perceive the relationship between given and sought after information in order to write the sentence. Young children may use boxes or triangles to represent unknown numbers in their equations. Such equations are referred to as open sentences since an unknown is present. These provide the children with a blueprint or "map" of procedures to be used. Calculator use will help children until they have developed their confidence.

Logical reasoning. This method is sometimes called the "if-then" approach to problem solving. This is appropriate when establishing connections or relationships and helps narrow the number of relationships involved or in some way moves us closer to the solution.

Whatever strategy is used, the purpose is to help children put the problem into perspective and get them thinking at each stage. Using strategies provides children with a plan for problem solving when a solution does not seem evident. Problem-solving strategies help children focus on the process and which strategies work for them.

When children think about how they solve problems, it helps them transfer their thinking process to other problems. The reflective process helps individuals develop a greater awareness of strategies that enable them to approach a task more successfully.

Educators can use questions such as the following to help children learn to be aware of their own approaches to thinking.

◆ How would you describe this problem using your own words?

◆ Where did you find the information you needed to work this problem?

"How are you solving it?" Children share ideas about problem-solving strategies.

♦ Why do you think this approach did or did not work?

♦ Can you demonstrate with manipulatives how you solved that problem?

♦ Did drawing help you think about that problem?

♦ Did you have a system or plan for solving that problem? What was it?

♦ Describe what you have learned from this activity.

♦ How does this situation relate to what you have learned before?

♦ What questions do you have now?

♦ What would you change if you were to work this problem again?

Questions like the ones listed above should help children think about what they have done to solve problems and how they approach their work. Another way to help children become reflective is to have them talk out loud as they go about determining how to tackle a problem. The teacher should offer feedback information to the children based on what they have communicated as they talk about their plans. The more aware children become of thinking about thinking, the more they can use higher function ordering (Charbonneau & Reider, 1995).

DEVELOPING PROBLEM-SOLVING AND REASONING SITUATIONS

Now that elements of problem solving have been discussed, it's time to think about how to develop situations that will enhance problem solving and reasoning. Problem solving should be the central focus of the mathematics curriculum (NCTM, 1989). "Classrooms with a problem-solving orientation are permeated by thought-provoking questions, speculations, investigations, and explorations; in this environment, the teacher's primary goal is to promote a problem-solving approach to the learning of all mathematics content" (NCTM, 1989, p. 23).

If students do not demonstrate a willingness and interest in problem solving, it is difficult to teach them problem-solving processes. Willingness to solve problems, even enjoyment, should be one of the highest priorities in a problem-solving program (Van de Walle, 1994). Mathematics activities should be engaging.

Plan for Success

Almost everyday students and adults alike are faced with making decisions that are directly related to their skill or confidence levels in one way or another. Children base their decisions on past experiences, or how successful they feel they will be making one decision or another. To build success educators can plan a variety of problems on different levels and start the year with problems that students can solve. The success should be genuine rather than a false success that depends on the educator to lead the children to the answer. Problems should be solved through the children's own efforts. All children will not progress at the same rate or develop the same problem-solving abilities. Children who are slower need success as much, if not more, than more confident students, so teachers should plan to involve these students in small groups with strong, supportive students. Children need a variety of problems, especially problems that can be solved in more than one way. Some examples follow.

PROBLEMS FOR SUCCESS

These problems are open-ended, their answers can vary, and they can be used to encourage self-confidence. Children can work alone or in small groups to find solutions. Children of different ages can work these problems.

Focus: Problem solving.

What To Do:

1. Cut out newspaper ads for five different items. Arrange them according to price, from greatest to least. What two items can you buy for $5? Can you buy three different items for $4?
2. With 1 quarter, 2 dimes, 5 nickels, and 25 pennies, how many different ways can you make 25 cents?
3. Are there more blue, brown, or other eye colors in your classroom? Compare the eye colors in your room with another room. Decide on approaches to collect and display this data.
4. Write the phone numbers of three of your friends. Compare them. Find three ways they are alike. Find three ways they are different.

Adjustments: Increase or decrease the amount of information.

Ongoing Assessment: Allow children to share problems and solutions. Listen and make short notes concerning the interaction and thinking.

Praise Risk-Taking

Often adults are afraid to try new approaches or ideas, and certainly children do not want to "fail" in front of their peers. Children need to know that it is all right to make mistakes, as long as they try again. The more the children are encouraged, the more effort they will make to receive praise. When students volunteer ideas, teachers should listen carefully and give credit for their thinking and for speaking up about what they think. If children's ideas are put down or ignored, sooner or later the children will quit sharing ideas.

Use Nonjudgmental Responses

Think about responses you can use when the children share ideas that will not make any student feel their answer was weak or a "bad idea." Compliment the process of thinking rather than attacking the idea. Things like, "That's a good point" or "I can see you are really thinking about this problem" are acceptable responses. Encourage the children to talk, and always respond when one of them shares a thought about how to approach a problem. Other appropriate responses might include things like, "I really like the way you are thinking, who else has an idea?" and "That's really an unusual way to approach this problem, how are you going to develop that idea?"

BIGGER AND BIGGER SHAPES

Allowing children to talk and encouraging them to express themselves in a creative manner helps children develop problem-solving skills. The following exercise allows children to work together and think about shapes.

Focus: Problem solving, reasoning, communication—geometry.

What To Do: Use pattern, parquet blocks, or geometric shapes cut from posterboard. Ask the children if they can build large figures of the same shapes as the initial ones. For example, a child might start with an equilateral triangle and make an equilateral triangle that is still larger. Can children start with one square and then make larger squares?

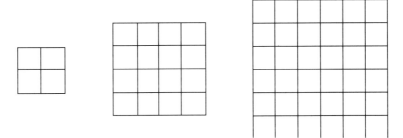

How many more tiles does it take if you double the size of each side of the original square? Triple the length of the side? Children can count the blocks they use in each figure.

Adjustments: Older children can look for patterns in the numbers used to increase the size of the shapes. Perimeter problems can be added for more mature children.

Ongoing Assessment: Observe the children to determine if they can enlarge the shapes and predict the number of needed shapes to complete construction.

Small-Group Cooperative Work

Problem-solving practice usually improves when other children are involved. Sharing ideas helps children think of new approaches and allows them to analyze their thinking in a nonthreatening atmosphere. Cooperative learning enhances problem solving. This teaching method decreases math anxiety because a group is talking and working through the solution rather than one person being on the spot. Children share ideas, so new thoughts emerge; children build on others' responses. Cooperative learning also encourages socialization by allowing children to work together toward a common goal.

 ELIMINATION PROBLEMS

Helping children think about what numbers are sensible answers to problems requires reasoning. The following problem helps children eliminate incorrect numbers as well as develop reasoning skills.

Focus: Problem solving, reasoning, communication.

What To Do: Allow primary children to work in small groups. Give each group a 100 chart and one-inch manipulatives such as interlocking cubes. Each group will have a series of word clues to read or listen to, and they will use the manipulatives to mark any numbers that are eliminated. Each clue should be written on a separate piece of paper. Following are examples of appropriate clues.

Candice's number:

1. You get Candice's number if you count by threes.
2. Candice's number is a multiple of 5.
3. If you add the digits of Candice's number, you get an odd number.
4. Candice's number is near the center of the chart.
5. If you multiply the digits of Candice's number together, you get an even number.
6. Candice's number is odd. Help your group find Candice's number on the 100 chart.

Ava's number:

1. Ava's number is a multiple of 7.
2. Both digits of Ava's number are even.
3. The first digit of Ava's number is larger than the second.
4. The difference between the two digits of Ava's number is greater than 3.
5. Ava's number is not odd.
6. The sum of the digits of Ava's number is greater than 10.

Adjustments: Adjust the numbers chart to fit the maturity of the children, for example, a chart of 1–10 or 1–20 can be used. Adjust the complexity of the problem clues to fit the developmental level of the children.

Ongoing Assessment: Observe the children to determine if they work well together and if they can reason through the clues to eliminate incorrect answers.

The NCTM *Curriculum Standards* (1991) recommend that teachers engage students in mathematical discourse about problem solving. Students should be encouraged to try different approaches to problems and explain their thinking. Teaching mathematics as reasoning should be commonplace in the classroom. Students need frequent opportunities to engage in mathematical discussions in which reasoning is valued.

Mr. Cortez applies this idea in his daily activities to encourage problem solving and reasoning. He knows that the children will engage in more substantive problem solving if they see a reason for finding solutions. Throughout the day he says things like, "There are 20 children in our class. Two are absent and three are in the library. How many children are in the room right now?" During art Mr. Cortez says, "We want to wrap paper around these half-gallon milk cartons to make our art project, what size paper do we need?" or "Each child will need five pieces of paper to make this book, how many pieces of paper do we need?" He encourages the children to try different approaches to solving daily problems. "How can we find out how much paper we need for this book?" Mr. Cortez constantly poses problems for the children to solve. When the children work through his daily problems, he has them talk to him or each other and uses manipulatives and other materials to support their thinking.

Mr. Cortez presents questions that engage the students in mathematical reasoning and communication. He often thinks about his ability to question the children and adjusts his questions to the different developmental levels of the children. Mr. Cortez continually poses questions to extend his students' capacity for reasoning.

Using everyday activities to teach problem solving helps children make connections to their lives and see that there are many reasons to use mathematics. Often teachers can construct their lessons on the basis of their student's previous experiences. When selecting any task always consider the potential for fostering mathematical reasoning and problem solving.

 ## FINDING MEASUREMENTS

Allowing preschool children to solve simple measuring problems using nonstandard measurement allows them a chance to actively engage in meaningful activities relative to themselves.

Focus: Measurement—comparing.

What To Do: Give each child a piece of yarn. Have the children find something on their bodies that is the same length as their piece of yarn or something that is longer and shorter than their piece of yarn. Have the children find something in the room, outside, and at home that is the same length, longer, and shorter than their yarn.

Adjustments: Allow children to use other material to measure with and then make a chart that illustrates a comparison of materials. For example, 7 interlocking cubes equals 12 paper clips, and so on.

Ongoing Assessment: Make short notes for the children's anecdotal records as to whether they accurately find comparative measurements.

SUMMARY

A problem only exists if it challenges children. Participation in project problems allows children to acquire confidence in their problem-solving ability. In working with others they realize their own self worth. Problems are constructivist in nature, depending on an individual's background, experience, and exposure to mathematics.

Problem solving is influenced by many factors. Affective influences include willingness to work, self-confidence, stress and anxiety, tolerance for ambiguity, perseverance, and interest or relevance to real life. Experiences that influence problem solving include age and exposure to the context of the particular problem and to prior use of specific problem-solving strategies. Cognitive influences relate to specific mathematics content, the ability to reason in a logical manner, short- and long-term memory capacity, and computation skills.

Metacognition is literally "thinking about thinking." Reflection on how one has approached and either solved or failed to solve a problem helps children become better thinkers and problem solvers.

Problem-solving strategies are available to assist children in approaching problems. Recommended approaches to problem solving are guess and check, draw a picture, act it out, use a model, and look for patterns. Others include make a chart or table, work backwards, eliminate all possibilities, try simpler problems, and write an equation or open sentence. Logical reasoning requires deductive reasoning and is recommended for mature children.

To develop children's problem solving and reasoning requires a classroom permeated by thought-provoking questions, speculations, investigations, and explorations. In this type of environment, the teacher's main goal is to promote a problem-solving approach to learning all mathematics content. Communication and reasoning are a vital part of problem solving. Children must be allowed to openly discuss and defend their mathematical thinking.

◆ *APPLICATIONS: THINKING AND COLLABORATING*

To help you further assimilate the ideas presented on problem solving and reasoning in this chapter, here are some suggestions for exploration. Choose and carry out one or more of them that fit your interests and needs.

1. Plan a mathematics day for your school. The children, in small groups, are to design problem-solving activities to be completed by children in other classes. Each group will supply the necessary materials and monitor the activities.

2. Interview 10 colleagues concerning how they solve problems. Compare their methods and see if you find a pattern.

3. Write down the figure 1089. Ask a friend to write down any three-digit number, with the number's first and last digits being different. Ask your friend to reverse the number and subtract the lesser from the greater. For example, if 123 is chosen, the reverse will be 321 and the subtraction is: 321 - 123 = 198. Now reverse the new number. Add the new number and its reverse: 198 + 891 = 1089. Try this with several different numbers. What can you discover?

4. Choose one problem from this chapter. Observe different-age children working this problem. Record each child's approach. How many different approaches did you see? Can you make any analysis of the children's developmental levels from your experiment? Compare with a peer and see how many different approaches you can find between you. What about other colleagues?

5. The formation of magic squares dates back at least 2000 years to ancient India. The magic lies in the fact that whichever way you add the numbers in the square, you always arrive at the same sum. Design a magic square of your own working with a partner. How did you decide to approach this problem?

◆ REFERENCES

Baroody, A. (1993). *Problem solving, reasoning, and communicating, K–8.* New York: Merrill.

Bryant, P., & Trabasso, T. (1971). Transitive inferences and memory in young children. *Nature, 232,* 456–458.

Charbonneau, M. & Reider, B. (1995). *The integrated elementary classroom.* Needham Heights, MA: Allyn and Bacon.

Dewey, J. (1916). *Democracy and education.* New York. Vintage/Random House.

Dewey, J. (1938). *Experience and education.* The Kappa Delta Pi Lecture Series. New York: Collier/Macmillan.

Evertson, C., & Randolph, C. (1995). Classroom management in the learning-centered classroom. In A. C. Ornstein (Ed.), *Teaching theory into practice.* Needham Heights, MA: Allyn and Bacon.

Inhelder, B., & Piaget, J. (1964). *The growth of logical thinking.* New York: Thorton.

Klein, F. (1995). Alternative curriculum conceptions and designs. In A. Ornstein and L. Behar (Eds.), *Contemporary issues in curriculum.* Needham Heights, MA: Allyn and Bacon.

Krogh, S. (1995). *The integrated early childhood curriculum.* New York: McGraw-Hill.

Linder T. (1993). *Transdisciplinary play-based assessment.* Baltimore, MD: Paul Brooks.

National Council of Teachers of Mathematics. (1989). *Curriculum and evaluation standards for school mathematics, K-12.* Reston, VA: Author.

Van de Walle, J. A. (1994). *Elementary school mathematics, teaching developmentally.* White Plains, NY: Longman.

Willoughby, S. (1990). *Mathematics education for a changing world.* Alexandria, VA: ASCD.

◆ SELECTED CHILDREN'S BOOKS

Ashley, Bernard. (1991). *Cleversticks.* Topeka, KS: A.E.S. This story is realistically illustrated and evokes the atmosphere of an interracial classroom where Ling Sung feels the pangs of being a nonachiever. See how Ling Sung solves this real-life problem.

Brett, Jan. (1992). *Trouble With Trolls.* New York: G. P. Putnam's Sons. This colorful book may be used to stimulate students' imagination and enhance their data and problem-solving skills. Students may use problem-solving skills as they travel along with Treva and help her outwit the trolls.

Gibbons, Gail. (1994). *Country Fair.* Boston: Little, Brown. Through this brightly illustrated account of a county fair, children may become involved in counting, data collection, and problem-solving activities.

Gretz, Susanna. (1991). *Frog in the Middle.* New York: Four Winds. This attractive book can be an excellent source of problem-solving and reasoning activities. Through the author's colorful illustrations and story, children delight in helping Frog solve his problems.

Maestro, Betsy. (1994). *Why Do Leaves Change Colors?* New York: Harper Collins. Through the brightly colored pictures in this book, children engage in problem-solving and geometric activities as they explore the wonders of fall.

Zimmerman, Andrea, and Clemesha, David. (1993). *The Cow Buzzed.* New York: Harper Collins. This fun story may be used to enhance children's data and problem-solving skills. Using the wonderful illustrations and story, children can record data about each of the animals and help the farmer solve many problems.

Numeration and Number Sense

7

✓ **Developing Number Ideas and Number Sense**

✓ **Materials for Developing Children's Understandings of Numeration and Number Sense**

✓ **Numeration and Number Sense Topics for Young Children**

Counting

Number concepts and number sense

Comparing sets and numbers

Cardinal and ordinal numbers

Numbers, numerals, and number names

Place value

Fractions and decimals

Estimating with numbers

✓ **Summary**

✓ **Applications: Thinking and Collaborating**

◆◆◆

As she introduces five-year-old Brian to you on the first day of kindergarten, Brian's mom brags that he can already count to 50. Brian demonstrates by rattling off number names in rapid-fire order: "1, 2, 3, 4, 5, 8, 10, 11, 17, 35, 45, 50!" He's obviously pleased with his ability to count and so is his mom. As you work with Brian, what can you do to preserve his pride in his counting ability, while filling in the gaps? Does Brian have well-developed concepts of number meanings to accompany his counting ability? How can you find out? What can you do to develop his abilities and number sense further?

Work with numbers is the first thing that occurs to most people when the word "mathematics" is mentioned. Mathematics deals with the quantitative world; numbers are its tools and symbols. People use number concepts and skills as they compare sets and sizes, count, identify locations, measure, and compute. Numbers let people communicate quantitative ideas clearly and precisely.

Preschool and kindergarten children's work with numbers typically includes comparing, counting and using numbers 1 to 5 or 10. As kindergartners work with counting and representing and understanding numbers, they use number symbols to record and communicate. When children play in learning centers such as blocks and home living, opportunities to use numbers in informal situations abound. Work with numbers next extends to numbers in the teens and up to 30 or 31, numbers on the calendar. For numbers 10 and above, educators introduce ideas of place value, first quite informally, then more formally. Primary children extend their knowledge of numbers to hundreds; some explore thousands by the end of the primary grades.

Learning about fractions and decimals is also important to young children. Fraction concepts can be built on children's interest in sharing things evenly. In second or third grade decimals are introduced as special fractions that show parts—tenths or hundredths.

Along with learning about number concepts and the symbols that express quantitative ideas, children also estimate and assess the reasonableness of answers. They develop number sense—a "feel" for number relationships and the relative magnitudes of numbers. For example, a seven-year-old might guess the number of crayons displayed in a box. For a shoe box half-full of crayons, a child with well-developed number sense would realize that a guess of 8 crayons is too small and one of 500 is too large.

Work with numeration and number sense should extend to the home. For example, family members show children numbers they use—phone numbers, addresses on letters, and receipts. Children might record, with the help of family members, uses of numbers at home, and then share the information at school. To build cross-cultural knowledge, family members who use numbers in languages other than English might visit the classroom to demonstrate.

 WHAT DO *YOU* THINK?

Sharing counting in other languages is a way to promote cultural pride and involve families in the classroom. Think of other ways to honor multiculturalism as you help young children learn about numbers.

DEVELOPING NUMBER IDEAS AND NUMBER SENSE

The *Curriculum and Evaluation Standards for School Mathematics* (National Council of Teachers of Mathematics [NTCM],1989) offer guidance for educators concerning a vision for teaching about numbers and for developing number sense. The following excerpts are from the standards for grades K–4, but they apply equally well to prekindergarten children's work with small numbers such as one through five.

The "Number Sense and Numeration" standard (NCTM, 1989, p. 38–40) includes the following:

> In grades K–4 the mathematics curriculum should include whole number concepts and skills so that students can
>
> ◆ construct number meanings through real-world experiences and use of physical materials;
> ◆ understand our numeration system by relating counting, grouping, and place value concepts;
> ◆ develop number sense;
> ◆ interpret the multiple uses of numbers encountered in the real world.

The authors discuss number sense including the ideas that "children with good number sense (1) have well-understood number meanings, (2) have developed multiple relationships among numbers, (3) recognize relative magnitudes of numbers, (4) know the relative effects of operating on numbers, and (5) develop referents for measures of common objects and situations in their environment" (NCTM, 1989, p.38).

The following expectations for students are presented in the "Fractions and Decimals" standard (NCTM, 1989, p. 57):

> In grades K–4, the mathematics curriculum should include fractions and decimals so that students can
>
> ◆ develop concepts of fractions, mixed numbers, and decimals;
> ◆ develop number sense for fractions and decimals;
> ◆ use models to relate fractions to decimals and to find equivalent fractions;
> ◆ use models to explore operations on fractions and decimals;
> ◆ apply fractions and decimals to problem-solving situations.

In their discussion of fractions and decimals the NCTM authors stress the importance of using concrete, everyday situations and a variety of pictorial forms.

One more aspect of children's work with numbers is estimating. The authors address estimation (NCTM, 1989, p. 36):

In grades K–4, the curriculum should include estimation so students can

♦ explore estimation strategies;

♦ recognize when estimates are appropriate;

♦ determine the reasonableness of results;

♦ apply estimation when working with quantities, measurement, computation, and problem solving.

The authors comment that work with estimation helps to impart the idea that mathematics is not always exact; estimation is a legitimate part of working with numbers. For example, in planning the arrival time at a stop on a field trip, an estimate is used; no one can predict an exact time.

Ideas from the NCTM standards are complemented by statements from the National Association for the Education of Young Children's (NAEYC) *Developmentally Appropriate Practice* (Bredekamp, 1993). Stressing the idea that meaningful activities are understood and remembered, Bredekamp points out that children need stimulating, engaging materials and manipulatives to work with as they explore mathematics through projects, learning center activities, and play.

MATERIALS FOR DEVELOPING CHILDREN'S UNDERSTANDINGS OF NUMERATION AND NUMBER SENSE

Educators can use many materials to enhance children's understanding of numbers. Perhaps most important are familiar classroom objects and situations to draw children's attention to the use of numbers. For example, a preschool teacher might show children a stack of books for the next week and lead the children in counting the books. As kindergartners or primary children use the calendar, they might read the numerals, examine patterns in the numbers, and use ordinal numbers to discuss dates. As children play in classroom centers such as blocks or the home living area, they use numbers in many ways.

Classroom supplies can be used for work with numbers. For example, children might use small pieces of paper and hole punchers to make representations of numbers, an engaging, multisensory activity. Children four and older can punch different arrangements of a given number of holes. After the holes are punched, the children can compare arrangements and make number booklets. Classroom drawing and writing materials can be used as children record numbers and write numerals. Besides using crayons, pens, and pencils, children can also form numerals with paints, stamps, or by tracing with their fingertips in shallow trays of cornmeal or salt. Numeral cards can be used for reference. Encouraging children to write lists, "orders," and charts exposes them to the usefulness of numerals.

Educators should provide a variety of counting books and other books that suggest number concepts. The books can be read to the children in large or small groups, enjoyed by individuals in a reading or library center, or checked out for home use. Child-made books can supplement the classroom library collection.

Using counters is essential to developing children's number sense. Counters may be found objects: large smooth stones, acorns, large buttons, or lids from milk jugs. Teachers can also use large dry beans as counters. If beans are spray-painted on one side, they become a valuable resource—two-sided counters. Pom-pom balls, small round magnets, and large beads have much sensory appeal.

A wide variety of counters are also available from educational suppliers. Manufactured as plastic teddy bears, dinosaurs, and people, counters come in different sizes and colors, lending themselves to sorting as well as counting. Wooden and plastic blocks, plastic links, beads, and disks also serve as counters. Interlocking cubes, often called unifix cubes and multi-link cubes, have the advantage of linking together.

For work with numbers greater than 10 and place value, base-10 blocks made of wood, plastic, and a soft, quiet foamlike material called "manipulite" feature unit or "one" blocks that are one cubic centimeter in size. Tens, $1 \times 1 \times 10$ centimeter arrangements, are often called "rods." Hundreds are represented as $1 \times 10 \times 10$ centimeter "flats"; thousands are large $10 \times 10 \times 10$ centimeter cubes. Base-10 blocks are proportional in size and easily handled; using them encourages children to make trades such as ten 10 rods for one 100 flat.

A child-made version of base-10 blocks is bean sticks (Van de Walle, 1994), in which children glue dry beans to tongue depressors or craft sticks. If they are involved in gluing 10 beans per stick, children are encouraged to use their sticks as tens, rather than counting single beans each time they use a stick. They can glue 10 ten-sticks together to make hundreds flats or rafts.

Paper accessories help children organize their thinking about numbers. Ten frames (two by five arrangements of squares or rectangles) provide a place for children to arrange counters; one counter is placed in each section of the 10 frame. Hundreds charts are another visual organizer for primary children. Such charts display numerals 1–100 or 0–99 in rows of 10 numerals each. Children can explore patterns in the rows, columns, or diagonals of hundreds charts.

Other manipulatives for numeration and number sense include real and plastic coins and coin stamps. Children can record their work with money by making coin rubbings or by using coin stamps. Using numeral stamps and picture stamps, children can make displays of different numbers of objects. They might stamp numerals on note cards and matching numbers of pictures on other cards, then shuffle the cards for classmates to match.

NUMERATION AND NUMBER SENSE TOPICS FOR YOUNG CHILDREN

Young children develop number concepts and skills over long periods of time. Their ideas are built based on experiences, reflection about experiences, and communication with others, as well as maturation. A sample of number topics for young children includes counting, representing numbers, number sense, comparing sets, place value, fractions, and estimation. The following sections provide discussions of these topics as well as descriptions of meaningful activities and assessment suggestions.

Counting

Most number skills and understandings are built on counting. One-to-one correspondence is basic to counting; it involves matching items in one set with items in another set to see if each item has a matching item or "partner." For example, three-year-olds could match hats with dolls in the dramatic play center. They might try to match scissors to chairs and see if there are enough scissors for each place at the table. Older children might check different arrangements of the same number and see that when the sets are rearranged, items in one set can be matched one to one with the items in the other set.

Using one-to-one correspondence also lets children reason and solve problems regarding the relationships of sets (Reys, Suydam, & Lindquist, 1995; Taylor, 1995): Is there a game card for each child in a group? One way to find out is to pass out the cards, one per child. If each child has a card, the number of cards and children is the same. With fewer cards than children, at least one child will not get a card; with more cards than children, at least one card will be left over.

Counting is an ability vital to acquiring other number skills. Virtually every child comes to preschool or school able to *count by rote,* saying at least a few number names in sequence. Rote counting can be strengthened and extended by using rhymes, fingerplays, and counting books. For example, children as young as three practice counting as they use the fingerplay "Here's a Circle" or the nursery rhyme "One, Two, Buckle My Shoe." Songbooks and books of fingerplays (e.g., Palmer, 1981, and Raffi, 1980) offer many other suggestions. Teachers can also learn and share pertinent songs and fingerplays in classes, at conferences, or in informal sessions at schools.

Rational counting, where children say or attach just one number name to each object that is to be counted, is also vitally important. That is, children establish one-to-one correspondence between objects and the number names they say. Rational counting takes practice. Having children move or point to objects as they say number names helps many children. Occasionally a child is able to rationally count the number of objects in a set, but is confused when asked how many objects are in the set. Educators should emphasize that the last number named tells the number of objects in the set. A teacher might model: "One, two, three, four . . . four objects are here. That's how many . . . four."

Many experiences contributes to counting abilities. Suggestions are offered in "Counting Books" and "Count and Cook."

COUNTING BOOKS

Using a variety of counting books adds to whole language programs as well as exposing children of any age to numbers.

Focus: Numeration, rote and rational counting, communicating, connecting to language arts.

What To Do: Display counting books as part of your classroom library. Read them to children, encourage them to "read" to each other, and browse through them. Provide materials for children to make their own counting books using thematic or seasonal contexts or featuring pictures of random collections.

Adjustments: Let children use stamps, stickers, or other materials to make counting books. Base numbers to be included in the books on children's abilities and interests.

Ongoing Assessment: As you share books with children, note their interest level; if it wanes, read to smaller groups, use props, or let children act out the books.

COUNT AND COOK

This healthful recipe involves counting during preparation.

Focus: Counting, numeral recognition, connecting to real life.

What To Do: Help children read the picture-word recipe. Encourage counting as each prepares and eats the snack.

Use 1 celery stick. Add 1 spoon peanut butter. Add 4 raisins. Count your frogs, then eat!

Adjustments: As children gain proficiency, use more complex recipes that require children to take turns or use greater numbers. Talk about the sequence of preparing a recipe. Let the children draw pictures of what they did, sequencing the steps and using ordinal numbers.

Ongoing Assessment: Observe the children's work habits. Does each follow directions independently? Do they share? Do they use numbers as needed? Can children use numbers as they work?

 ASSESSMENT SUGGESTION:
Observation, Performance

Routinely watch children as they work. Ask individuals to use manipulatives and count aloud, determining whether each counts by rote and rationally. Which children point to objects as they count or move objects from one pile to another? Ask children to "talk you through" a drawing to represent a number, explaining the counting processes they used. Use the results of individual and group progress to plan subsequent activities.

Computers and calculators can enhance children's counting skills. Many computer programs feature objects to count; some display numerals as children use computer functions to "stamp" or produce pictures on the screen. Others show images of objects for children to count, then ask children to enter matching numerals. The calculator can also serve as a stimulus for counting. For example, children can count and arrange sets of objects or counters, then key numbers that match into the calculator.

Teachers can show five- or six-year-olds how a calculator "counts." Children might start with one block or counter and key 1 into the calculator. They can next add a counter and press + and 1, then press =. They should see 2 on the display as well as two counters. If children add a counter and press = again, the calculator should read 3. Children can continue adding objects and pressing the = key. The calculator thus provides an intriguing stimulus for counting.

As children progress, *skip counting* becomes an important skill. Skip counting is often introduced in kindergarten as counting by twos, then fives or tens. Teachers might begin skip counting by having the children arrange themselves in pairs and count aloud the total number, saying the odd numbers softly and even numbers very distinctly: 1, **2**, 3, **4**, 5, **6**, 7, **8**, ...

Kindergarten and primary children should practice skip counting by fives in realistic situations, using fingers on hands, the value of nickels, or minute intervals on a clock. They might start with a handful of nickels

Using a calculator enhances work with manipulatives and with symbolic representations of number ideas.

and count their value by fives, pushing them from one pile to another. Counting by tens can be introduced using fingers and toes—*both* hands (or feet) are needed for 10. Primary children might work in groups of five or six. A leader can walk around the group, having her groupmates, in turn, raise both hands while everyone counts aloud to indicate the total number of fingers that are held up.

Counting by rote and counting rationally are skills that are acquired through practice. Short, regular periods of practice with many different kinds of objects helps children acquire and refine counting skills. As children's counting skills are developed and refined, symbolic forms such as number lines and hundreds charts may be added. Primary children will be able to notice many patterns in the positions of the numbers.

Counting backwards is also important and useful. Children might count backwards as they keep track of the "countdown" of days before a holiday or an important school event. Children can count pennies and place them in a pile, then practice counting backwards, by moving pennies away and telling the number that is left. Children can make a calculator with a constant feature "count backwards" by keying in a number such as 10, pressing the minus and 1 keys, then repeatedly pressing the = key.

Number Concepts and Number Sense

Number concepts and number sense, like counting skills, are built over a period of time and are enhanced by use in a variety of real and engaging situations (Bredekamp, 1993). As children count sets of people or objects they gain ideas of the relative magnitudes of numbers—4 people is more than 1; 15 cans in a recycling box is far short of a goal of 100. Children gain understanding that a number is a constant value regardless of the objects to which it is attached. That is, five means the same number whether it describes fingers, paintbrushes, or books.

Numbers can be represented many ways. Composing numbers (making them up in various ways) or decomposing them (breaking them into two or more component parts) helps children learn relative magnitudes of numbers. If 7 is composed of 5 and 2, then 7 is more than either of its nonzero parts, 5 or 2. Composing and decomposing numbers also sets an informal but important foundation for place value, addition, and subtraction.

Working with various arrangements for the same number applies to larger numbers too. After children have had considerable experience with place value concepts for example, they might represent a number such as 135 as 1 hundred, 3 tens, and 5 ones. It might also be configured as 12 tens and 15 ones, or represented as 135 ones.

Representing numbers many ways and verifying the representations involves many opportunities for problem solving and reasoning. Working with numbers helps children develop useful quantitative referents. For example, there are usually 20 to 30 children in the classroom. They may be spread out at different learning stations or in desks, crowded together near the door, or seated near the teacher for a story. The teacher can draw attention to the fact that the number of classmates is generally the same from day to day. Usually the classroom is not "crowded," but if another class visits, it looks very different because of the larger number of people.

The following activities include other suggestions for enhancing number sense and assessing children's understanding.

 ## REPRESENTING NUMBERS MANY WAYS

Children represent numbers many ways and with different materials. This encourages them to "really get to know" numbers.

Focus: Number sense, counting, reasoning, communicating.

What To Do: For any number that kindergarten and first-grade children are studying, have them use interlocking cubes and link one or two colors to show the number. For example, 8 might be shown as 8 blue, 2 red and 6 blue, 4 and 4, 7 and 1, and so on. Have children describe and compare their arrangements.

Adjustments: For a challenge, have the children add numerals and words to the designs. Extend the idea to greater numbers too, using materials such as base-ten blocks.

Ongoing Assessment: Have children peer-evaluate their work, explaining to others what they are doing.

ASSESSMENT SUGGESTION:
Audio- and Videotapes

Make recordings of children discussing number-sense situations to document children's understanding and progress over time; audio- or videotapes can become valuable parts of children's portfolios. Have children draw or write about situations where 4 is a "just right" number and where a number like 25 is "small" or "not enough," then have them explain what they have drawn and written. Review the tapes to find evidence of children's understandings or misconceptions. Add to the tapes during the school year.

NUMBER SENSE ABOUT FOODS

Could you eat 58 peanuts? 58 hot dogs? Would 58 corn flakes be a nice bowlful? Children refine number sense as they speculate on answers to such questions.

Focus: Number sense, counting, reasoning, communicating, connecting to science and to everyday life.

What To Do: While studying nutrition, talk to kindergarten or primary children about foods they eat just one of—one bowl of soup or one baked potato. Make a list of the children's comments. Let the children work individually or in small groups to make and share booklets of foods where one is an appropriate serving.

Use another number such as 15 and have the children give examples where 15 might not be enough, 15 would be "just right," and 15 of the food would be too much. For example, 15 pieces of popcorn might not be enough, while 15 potato chips might be "just right," and 15 peanut butter sandwiches would be too many. Let each child pick an example and illustrate it, then bind the pages together to make a number sense book.

Adjustments: Ask the children to notice the numbers of foods they eat at home, then share ideas at school.

Ongoing Assessment: Let each child write about and sketch the activity, then file the papers in the children's portfolios.

Comparing Sets and Numbers

As children work with two or more numbers, they are comparing sets. With two sets, one of three relationships are possible: the sets have equal numbers of members; one set has more than the other; one set has fewer members than the other.

Educators should help children work with comparison situations and with varied materials. For example, a popular activity for Ms. Cain's three-year-olds involves working with bowls and large cooking spoons. Ms. Cain encourages the children to compare numbers of plastic blocks that they stir in their bowls. She prompts them to work with comparison and number concepts, offering suggestions such as, "Sarah, can you lift out just one with your spoon?" "Charles, can you lift out more than one?" or "Everybody, take a spoonful. Let's line them up and see how the numbers compare."

Older children can compare numbers, record their results, and draw conclusions. They can work from a shared container of crayons, each taking a handful. As they count their crayons, someone can record the numbers. The children can look at their sets and numerals and decide whether any of them have the same number. They can compare their numbers and tell each other how they know that one set has more crayons or fewer than another. After many trials they might be able to look at their results and tell what would be a "typical handful"—perhaps 12 to 15 crayons, with a handful of 6 or 23 being fairly unusual.

Comparisons with fractions should begin with real or pictorial situations. For example, the children can draw pizzas using equal-size circles, then fold them and cut them in fourths. Using the pizza pieces as models, they can readily see that $1/2$ and $2/4$ of a pizza represent the same amount, but that $1/4$ of a pizza is less than $3/4$ of a pizza.

Cardinal and Ordinal Numbers

As children use numbers to tell "how many," they use numbers in their *cardinal* sense: 108 children on the playground at 11:00, for example. As they use numbers to tell an order or position, children use numbers in their *ordinal* sense: Jody is first in line; our class came in third place in the recycling contest. Uses of numbers in their cardinal and ordinal senses are best introduced in realistic, natural ways and practiced often over a period of time.

Ordinal numbers can be reinforced as children learn and work with cardinal numbers. When three- and four-year-olds help to prepare a soap solution for blowing bubbles, the teacher might model language such as, "First we will get bowls of water. The second step is to add one squirt of soap to each bowl. Then we can blow bubbles." As they read and discuss the numbers on the calendar, kindergarten and primary children learn that 18 follows 16 and 17. They can use the notion that the numeral 18 represents the 18th day of the month.

Numbers, Numerals, and Number Names

It is natural to add number symbols—numerals and written words for number values—as children gain understanding of numbers. Adults can help children build number-numeral-number name associations through their natural, constant use. For example, a teacher of three-year-olds can occasionally count the number who are present and absent and record the results on a chart. As the children compose a group story, the teacher can include numerals or number words as they occur in the narration and read back over the chart or story, so the children see symbols for their ideas. Educators can also make children aware of numerals that occur in the environment—on labels and signs, houses, and in the telephone book. They might keep a running list of "Numbers We See."

As educators plan activities to focus on numbers, they will want to work on the number concepts first and help children talk about, model, and use the number ideas. For example, children need extensive exposure to an idea like "two" before they focus on procedures such as how to write the symbol 2 and the word two. After children have gained some understanding of number concepts, educators can help children use the symbols for the numbers. Premature emphasis on symbolism makes mathematics too abstract for most young children; it may cause confusion and actually delay learning.

When kindergarten and primary children are ready for informal work with symbols, teachers should provide varied opportunities for children to practice writing numerals and number words. Children are motivated to practice when educators offer them a variety of writing materials and a quiet, inviting work area. In this area, children might form numerals from clay, trace numerals in a tray of sand, write on a chalkboard, or use pencils or markers to write lists and notes including numerals. Number books, newspaper ads, catalogs, telephone and address books, and neatly written numeral symbols posted near the area provide models as children practice their growing writing skills.

What are other ways to help young children work with numerals and number ideas? "Calculator Capers" offers an idea.

"Do I have enough teddies to put one on each circle?" Using one-to-one correspondence is a way to answer the question.

CALCULATOR CAPERS

This activity combines numeral recognition and number meaning.

Focus: Numeration, numeral writing, communicating, using technology.

What To Do: If kindergarten or primary children are unfamiliar with calculators, let them work individually or in pairs to explore, pressing the keys and talking about the numbers that result. Show them how to clear the display. Have children choose numeral cards, key in the numbers, then arrange counters or base-ten blocks to represent the numbers. Encourage children to check each other and count aloud.

Adjustments: Provide calculator-style and manuscript numeral cards. Have the children match the cards, then key in numbers and arrange counters to match.

Ongoing Assessment: Talk to the children about what they are learning and how they are checking. Note whether they relate numbers and numerals with ease, count successfully, and represent numbers accurately. Write notes for the children's anecdotal records.

Place Value

Our decimal number system uses just 10 digits—0 through 9—and yet because of place value, we can express any number, no matter how large or small. Our place value system involves three qualities: number symbols are used for values; each symbol has a place; and the value of the numbers in each place are added to give a total value for the number. For example, in 147 the symbols 1, 4, and 7 have meanings that most

Figure 7.1 *Example of grouping in various sizes.*

Working with 25		
Groups of	How many groups?	How many left over?
2	12	1
3	8	1
4	6	1
5	5	0
6	4	1

people understand: the 1 is in the hundreds place and so it means 100; the 4 is in the tens place and means 4 tens or 40; the 7 is in the ones place and means 7 ones. The total value of the number is 100 + 40 + 7 or 147.

Because grouping is so essential in our number system, helping kindergarten and primary children make equal-size groups is very beneficial. For example, the teacher might ask 25 children to form groups of several sizes and record the results. The children could group themselves as 12 pairs, with one child left over; they could make 8 groups of 3 children each with 1 left, and so on. The results of making groups of other sizes are shown in Figure 7.1.

Primary children can use other materials such as counters, mittens, and pencils to make groups of equal size with some left over. Using language such as "5 groups of 6 and 2 extras" helps set the stage for place value language where the children use sets of tens and ones: 26 means 2 groups of 10 and 6 more.

As children work with numbers, 10, the base for our number system, is important. As shown below, work with ten-frames (2-by-5-space grids with room to arrange counters, developed by Wirtz, 1974) helps children picture 10 at a glance. Using ten-frames, they get used to the idea that numbers less than 10 do not fill the frame. Ten fills it exactly; numbers greater than 10 fill the frame with some extra counters. After children fill several ten-frames, they can count the total number by tens and ones— 10, 20, 30, 31, 32, 33, 34, for example (Figure 7.2).

As children continue their work with larger numbers, educators can help them organize their thinking by forming sets of 10 and discussing the results. From a pile of 36 blocks for example, first grade children can form

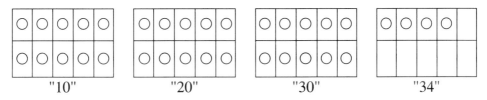

     "10"   "20"   "30"   "34"

Figure 7.2 *Using ten-frames, students can count a number by tens and ones.*

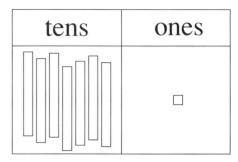

tens	ones

"17 means 10 and 7"

tens	ones

"71 means 7 tens and 1"

Figure 7.3 *Base-ten manipulatives.*

3 sets of 10 and have 6 left. A group of 14 paper clips can be arranged as 10 clips—perhaps linked together in a chain—and 4 more clips.

Teachers should realize that many children will be confused as they encounter symbols for numbers in the teens. For example, 17 means 10 and 7, yet we say the seven part first; some children may write 71 for 17, indicating the order in which they hear the 7 and 10 parts of the number. They may be helped by lots of work recording tens and ones in a chart as they work with base-ten manipulatives (Figure 7.3).

Children arrange base-ten blocks on a mat labeled with place values.

As children continue their work with base-ten materials, educators can guide them to discover and verify that they can trade 10 single unit blocks for a 10 rod or strip, or trade a 10 rod for 10 unit blocks. After much exploration and use of numbers less than 100, older children work with trading 10 tens for 1 hundred and 10 hundreds for 1 thousand. "Target 50" and "Hundreds Day," presented below, provide opportunities for picturing numbers.

TARGET 50 (OR ANOTHER NUMBER)

Composing a number such as 50 gives primary children concrete experience with trading and representing numbers.

Focus: Numeration, number sense, counting, place value.

What To Do: Prepare a number cube marking its faces with dots or numerals for 0, 1, 2, and 3, or use an ordinary die, replacing 6 with a 0. Show children how to play a game taking turns rolling the cube and choosing the appropriate number of counters. They then place the counters on ten-frames until they fill five frames. When they have 50, children can count them one by one, or by fives or tens. Have children work together, taking turns to reach 50, or work individually until everyone has reached the target of 50.

Adjustments: Show the children how to drop clothespins in a coffee can, taking turns until they think they have 20 in the can, then counting and grouping the clothespins by tens. Children might also work with larger numbers and a greater target number.

Ongoing Assessment: Have the children self-evaluate their work. What did they learn? What was hard about it? What was easy? How well did they work together? How could they vary the games?

HUNDREDS DAY

This activity, intended for kindergarten and primary children, requires long-term planning, but the benefits are many.

Focus: Counting, place value, estimating, number sense, connecting to measuring time.

What To Do: On the first day of school, have a special helper put a counter aside and write the number that shows how many days you have been in school. Have the children speculate on when the 100th school day will be. Each day take a short time to talk about the ordinal number of the day. Let a helper record the appropriate data and add to the pile of counters. With children six years and older, group the counters by tens and practice counting them. On the 23rd day of school for example, you will have two groups of 10 and three more counters: 10, 20, 21, 22, 23.

Before the 100th day, plan with the children some special activities for the day—bringing old T-shirts to decorate with 100 designs, making collections of 100 objects, or serving special "100th day foods" (100 carrot sticks to share, 100 pieces of popcorn for each child). Develop feasible activities; appoint committees of children and family members to carry them out. On the 100th school day, recount the counters with fanfare. Carry out your special activities. Write a group composition.

Adjustments: Help children videotape their sets of 100 objects.

Assessing Progress: Observe the children for signs of understanding and skill. Can they make groups of 10? Do they count confidently and use ordinal numbers?

Primary children can use the calculator when working with place value. They might arrange base-ten materials, key in their values, and read the number in standard form from the calculator display. Teachers can introduce a game where one child says a number while the others key in the number on their calculators. The children can then compare answers, tell the place values, and arrange base-ten materials to represent the numbers. Another calculator activity, "Wipe Out," follows.

WIPE OUT

This versatile calculator game builds place value ideas.

Focus: Place value, representing numerals, number sense, using technology, communicating.

What To Do: Show primary children how to key in a two- or three-digit numeral, then use the + or – key and one number to make a designated digit become 0. For example, if 78 is keyed in, they can change it to 70 by pressing the – and 8 keys. To make 325 become 305, children can key in – 20 (not 2).

Adjustments: Let children draw numeral cards and key in the numbers. Have children represent their numbers with base-ten blocks, both before and after they have "wiped out" digits.

Assessing Progress: Evaluate the children's understanding by asking them to explain what they are doing and why it works. Have children write about the activity for their portfolios.

Working with a hundreds chart helps primary children see relationships of numbers and solve problems involving values of numbers. Children might start with a familiar number—perhaps 28, the number of students in their classroom. They could count to 28 and represent 28 with base-ten blocks. The teacher might pose questions such as the following and have the children both study the chart and represent the numbers with their blocks. What if 10 more children joined us? How many would

Figure 7.4   *The hundreds chart.*

0	1	2	3	4	5	6	7	8	9
10	11	12	13	14	15	16	17	18	19
20	21	22	23	24	25	26	27	28	29
30	31	32	33	34	35	36	37	(38)	39
40	41	42	43	44	45	46	47	(48)	49
50	51	52	53	54	55	56	57	58	59
60	61	62	(63)	64	65	66	67	68	69
70	71	72	(73)	74	75	76	77	78	79
80	81	82	83	84	85	86	87	88	89
90	91	92	93	94	95	96	97	98	99

It's easy to find 10 more or 10 less than a number when we use the hundreds chart.

there be? Can you tell without counting? How are 28 and 38 related? Where are they on the chart? Are their tens the same? Their ones? What is 10 more than 38? Ten more than that? How are the numerals the same and different? If we keep on adding tens, what numbers will we have? Find them on the chart in Figure 7.4.

Over a period of days the teacher and children might pursue other patterns in the chart, seeing how its rows, columns, and diagonals are organized and how the numbers are related. After some understanding of numbers less than 100 has been established, children need opportunities to practice counting sets of objects, learning to say the numbers by rote. They will typically need to give attention to transition points such as these: after reaching 79, we start on numbers in the eighties; after reaching 99, we start on numbers in the one hundreds—100, 101, 102, 103 . . . .

Fractions and Decimals

Work with whole numbers is complemented by study of fractions and decimals. Numbers like 3.1, $3\frac{1}{2}$, 3.68, and $3\frac{7}{8}$ let people deal with quantities between whole number values—those greater than 3 and yet less than 4. Fractions and decimals are important in measuring. Eight-year-olds may find, for example, that a classmate's height is between 130 and 131 centimeters. Calling the height "*about* $130\frac{1}{2}$ centimeters" or "*close to* 130.5 centimeters" lets children use fractions or decimals meaningfully.

"Two of my six blocks are red." "I made hexagons with different fractions."

Figure 7.5 *Children's statements about pattern block designs.*

From experiences with sharing, children are familiar with the idea of breaking wholes into parts. Often they know the names of parts such as halves or thirds. Children can also be exposed to the "part of a group" interpretation of fractions and decimals as they work with classifying and graphing. For instance the children might find that 4 of a group of 10 are wearing knee socks, while 5 out of the 10 are wearing short socks, and 1 out of 10 has tights. They might see that as 23 children marked a picture graph of interesting animals, 14 of them picked gorillas, 5 out of 23 picked giraffes, 3 out of 23 chose anteaters, and 1 out of 23 picked hippos.

Whatever experiences they plan for children, educators should remember that children construct fraction ideas slowly, so it is crucial that teachers use physical materials, diagrams, and real-world situations to represent them. Geometric designs and art projects as well as social situations are stimuli for picturing and discussing fractions and decimals. For example, Figure 7.5 shows pattern block designs and some of the statements children made about them.

Activities such as "Work with Halves" increase children's understanding of fractions.

 WORK WITH HALVES

Children should work with many different models for fractions such as $1/2$.

Focus: Fractions, number sense, communicating, reasoning, connecting to everyday life.

What To Do: Ask each kindergarten or primary child to bring a healthy, nonperishable snack to school. Let the children describe their snacks. Tell the children that they will divide their snacks in half, eating half in the morning and half in the afternoon. Let the children work in groups and show how they will split their snacks. Once the group agrees that the halves will be equal pieces, they can break the snacks in two. Have the children compare their snack pieces and see if the pieces are approximately the same. As children enjoy their snacks, discuss foods that are divided in halves before eating.

Provide paper and crayons for the children to draw pictures of foods divided into halves. Extend the children's understanding of halves by making a group composition about halves people use.

Adjustments: Provide modeling dough, plastic knives, and plates. Let the children make models of foods, cut them in half, then check their pieces to be sure they are halves.

Ongoing Assessment: Observe the children for understanding. Do they realize that halves involve two equal parts? Do they use the word "half" as they work? Can they make halves several ways?

Only after much work with fraction and decimal *concepts* should educators focus on their symbols (Rowan & Bourne, 1994). Premature emphasis on symbolism may confuse or mislead children. Although adults may want to use fraction and decimal symbols informally as they help children record data, children's mastery of written symbols can be delayed until the middle grades. For example, second- or third-grade children might use egg cartons with 2 sections cut off, leaving a carton with 10 sections. After arranging interlocking cubes or other small objects of at least two colors in the sections of the egg cartons, they can make statements about the numbers and colors of blocks they used. After students have considerable experience with talking about parts of the whole set of 10, a few may be ready to label their arrangements with symbols that show the fraction or decimal for each color (0.7 for 7 out of 10 for example).

Young children can work informally with equivalent fractions. In work with pattern blocks, children can see that a hexagon ($\bigcirc$) can be covered with two trapezoids ($\triangle$), three diamonds ($\diamondsuit$), or six equilateral triangles ($\triangle$). Thus they gain exposure to the idea that $1 = {}^2/_2 = {}^3/_3 = {}^6/_6$. They may also begin to understand that if a hexagon represents a whole, then a trapezoid and three triangles cover the same area ($^1/_2 = {}^3/_6$).

Objects such as quilts provide good models for fractions. After looking at a quilt displayed by a resource person, children might try to duplicate its pattern. They could start with single paper blocks, which they can color half red and half white. Adding another similar block makes four parts. While the mini-quilt is still half red and half white, it can also be described as $^2/_4$ red and $^2/_4$ white. As more blocks are added to the quilt, it can still be described as half red and half white, but many other equivalent fractions can be used (Figure 7.6).

Estimating with Numbers

As children learn number concepts, educators can provide ongoing work with a variety of estimating experiences. An estimate is a quick but "informed" guess (rather than a wild guess) about a quantity. Estimating is a fast mental process; estimating is not a time to count objects or figure on paper. For practical estimating purposes, a range of answers for estimates is acceptable. An estimate of 85 people is as good as an estimate of 78 people when there are 81 people at a school meeting. Saying that "75 to 85 people are present" is also a good answer.

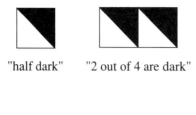
"half dark"   "2 out of 4 are dark"

"4 out of 8,
but still half"

"9 out of 18 are dark"

Figure 7.6 *Quilts work as models for fractions.*

Children should estimate with familiar numbers. If many children of a kindergarten class have good understanding of the numbers 1–10, their teacher might ask them to guess how many teddy bear counters are in a jar that she briefly shows them, then hides behind her back. When second graders are comfortable with numbers to 100, their teacher might show plastic bags containing different numbers of pennies, letting the children estimate the number of pennies in each bag. After children make their estimates, many will be curious about the actual number, so a child might lead the class in counting the objects together.

Good estimators use a variety of strategies as they judge numbers and quantities. One strategy involves using a *benchmark* or mental image of a known quantity to make decisions about an unknown quantity. Teachers can help kindergarten and primary children practice using benchmarks by asking them to guess the number of objects in a box. Having the children write down their estimates or whisper them to a partner builds suspense about the number of objects and helps children remember their estimates. Next the teacher can show the children a benchmark number of objects—perhaps 10—and allow them to compare the benchmark and the number of objects in the box. A final step in the estimating process is determining an actual number. Children can count the objects, perhaps grouping them by tens.

Another estimating strategy is *unitizing.* Here children break a larger quantity into smaller equal parts—thinking of a jar of pennies as having layers of about 10 pennies each. *Chunking* is an estimating strategy that also involves breaking a larger quantity into smaller not necessarily equal parts. A child may imagine 50 pennies in one part of the jar and 20 pennies in the rest, thus making an estimate of 70 pennies.

After children make estimates, discussing their strategies aids them in recognizing their mental processes. It emphasizes the idea that there are many good ways to reason and arrive at estimates. Some learners may prefer one method, while a different strategy may work well for another. Children can also tell each other why they think the estimates they have made are reasonable; much adjustment and self-correction can take place during discussion.

As they help children build estimating skills, teachers can encourage children to recognize when estimates are appropriate. They might start a list of situations where estimating is used and add to the list as the children think of more occasions to estimate. Estimating can extend beyond the classroom, as children ask adults about examples of using estimation.

 ## ASSESSMENT SUGGESTION: Performance

To stimulate children's thinking, have them use estimation in problem solving. Pose a problem such as, "Here are a bunch of counters. If we split them into two equal groups, about how many will be in each group? How can we think about this?" Children's responses will reveal much about their number sense.

SUMMARY

Children's work with numeration and number sense is an important part of their foundation of mathematics. It includes work with counting, making sets, comparing numbers, using cardinal and ordinal numbers, working with numbers greater than 10 and their place values, estimating, and informal work with fractions and decimals. Educators must focus on helping children build understanding of numbers. Use of many experiences and varied materials helps children build ideas of numeration and number sense. Children must use varied communication forms to share ideas they are learning and what numbers mean. As they work, children can use numbers in reasoning and problem solving. When numbers are connected to the real world and children's interests, learning about them is motivating, relevant, and memorable.

◆ *APPLICATIONS: THINKING AND COLLABORATING*

You have read suggestions for helping young children develop and use number ideas. To broaden your understanding of the chapter's topics, choose one or more of the following options.

1. Read the entire "Numeration and Number Sense," "Estimation," or "Fractions and Decimals" standard for grades K–4 (NCTM, 1989). Try to capture the flavor as well as the content of the material. Write about or discuss what the section said and its implications.

2. Choose a topic from this chapter with which you are not particularly comfortable or familiar. Read more about it. Talk to an experienced teacher or colleague who is more confident about the topic.

Based on what you learned, make a presentation to share with classmates or colleagues.

3. The *Curriculum Standards* (NCTM, 1989) present problem solving, reasoning, and communicating as three important areas for learners of all ages. Choose a number topic (such as numbers 0–9, place value, comparing sets, or fractions) and plan ways to incorporate at least two of these three areas as you work with young children. Try some of your ideas with children, then share your ideas and results with classmates or colleagues.

4. Choose a type of commercially made math manipulative material. If possible, read about the manipulative or observe an experienced teacher using the material with children. Get your own material and carry out some activities, trying to explore as children might. Choose one or two of your best ideas to demonstrate to colleagues.

5. Create some manipulatives for counting, telling number stories, representing fractions, or teaching place value. You could gather counting materials, make felt board cutouts, create reusable estimating forms, or collect items to bundle together to represent tens and hundreds. Try your materials with children, then show them to colleagues.

6. Select a counting book to present to children, perhaps reading it aloud and leading a discussion. Plan a follow-up activity where the children practice or extend ideas from the book. If possible, gather samples of the children's work and show it to your colleagues. Evaluate your work: What was valuable? What did the children's responses tell you about their thinking? How could you make the experience more valuable?

7. If you began a mathematics autobiography in Chapter 1, add to it or write a few paragraphs describing your early work with numbers. Comment on ways number sense helps you with other areas of mathematics and in everyday life.

◆ REFERENCES

Bredekamp, S. (1993). *Developmentally appropriate practice in early childhood programs*. Washington, DC: National Association for the Education of Young Children.

National Council of Teachers of Mathematics. (1989). *Curriculum and evaluation standards for school mathematics, K–12*. Reston, VA: Author.

Palmer, H. (1981). *Hap Palmer favorites: songs for learning music and movement*. Sherman Oaks, CA: Alfred Publishing.

Raffi. (1980). *The Raffi singable songbook*. New York: Homeland.

Reys, R. E., Suydam, M. M., & Lindquist, M. M. (1995). *Helping children learn mathematics*. Boston: Allyn and Bacon.

Rowan, T., and Bourne, B. (1994). *Thinking like mathematicians: putting the NCTM standards into practice.* Portsmouth, NH: Heinemann.

Taylor, B. (1995). *A child goes forth.* Upper Saddle River, NJ: Prentice Hall.

Wirtz, R. (1974). *Drill and practice at the problem solving level.* Washington, DC: Curriculum Development Associates.

Van de Walle, J. A. (1994). *Elementary school mathematics: teaching developmentally.* New York: Longman.

◆ SELECTED CHILDREN'S BOOKS

Hall, Zoe. (1994). *It's Pumpkin Time.* New York: Blue Sky Press. Connecting to seasons and growth of plants, the book offers opportunities for counting and sequencing. Its bold collages develop the story of maintaining a pumpkin patch.

Heinst, Marie. (1992). *My First Number Book.* New York: Dorling Kindersley. This oversized book features photographs that show 1 through 20 as well as 50, 100, 500, and 1000. Pages also address sorting, measurement, adding and subtracting, and shape. The book's pictures are ideal for small group use.

McMillan, Bruce. (1991). *Eating Fractions.* New York: Scholastic. Anyone who likes to eat will love this book "written, drafted, cooked, and photo-illustrated" by McMillan. The book's vivid photos show halves, thirds, and fourths of healthful foods such as bananas, pizza, and jello. For classroom use, recipes are provided.

Onyefulu, Ifeoma. (1995). *Emeka's Gift: An African Counting Story.* New York: Dutton. Emeka visits his grandmother in the next village and along the way he sees many things he might take her as presents—4 brooms, 5 big hats, 9 mortars and pestles. With colored photos, the book presents realistic views of African life.

Pomeroy, Diana. (1996). *One Potato: A Counting Book of Potato Prints.* San Diego: Harcourt Brace. This book features an amazing variety of potato prints, embellished with ink. It illustrates the numbers 1 through 10, 20, 30, 40, 50, and 100 with images of fruits and vegetables.

Watson, Amy. (1992). *The Folk Art Counting Book.* New York: Harry N. Abrams. This book includes folk art from Williamsburg and asks readers to perform tasks such as, "Count 3 horses, then tell how many men are included." Colonial artifacts and people of many races appear in works of art—textiles, painting, statuary, and carvings.

Wong, Herbert Lee. (1996). *Mrs. Brown Went to Town.* Boston: Houghton Mifflin. A cow, two pigs, three ducks, and a yak have a series of misadventures while Mrs. Brown is in the hospital. This amusing book invites counting and problem solving.

Operation Concepts and Skills

8

◆◆

Arturo teaches first grade. He has been attending a series of workshops relating to the NCTM standards and how to apply them in his classroom. His main concern regarding the standards stems from how he was taught mathematics. He feels that basic operations are vital to instruction. How will paper-and-pencil computation and mastery of basic facts relate to these new mathematics standards? What role do basic facts play in the new reform?

Hardly a decade passes without concern being expressed over the general level of children's attainment in mathematics, the quality of their learning, or the nature of the mathematics curriculum (Gray & Tall, 1994). Recent reform efforts distinguish between the skills or procedures that individuals need to acquire in order to do things and the ideas behind the skills or procedures, which they are expected to know, on which they operate with their skills. Procedure refers to specific algorithms for implementing a process. The term *mathematics operations* falls under the category of procedures.

In mathematics, basic operations are addition, subtraction, multiplication, and division. These basic operations are central to knowing mathematics (Van de Walle, 1994). People use mathematics operations in their jobs and in everyday activities throughout their lives. Historically, computational skills, or working through these basic mathematical operations, were considered the most important part of mathematics for most people, and these skills drove the mathematics curriculum (Battista, 1994). The idea of prescribed rules for every procedure is still in the forefront of many teachers' minds as we enter the twenty-first century. Traditional approaches to teaching mathematics operations are generally accepted but provide a limited approach to mathematics (Post, 1992). While reform efforts have called for different approaches and topics for mathematics teaching, these four important operations are not to be excluded or ignored when working with young children.

 WHAT DO *YOU* THINK?

The methods you use to solve mathematics problems as adults often differ considerably from the methods you learned in school. Consider how you would work the following problems:

1. 333×3
2. A buffet at a local restaurant costs $7.50. How much would three buffets cost?
3. $100.00 \div 10$

Compare the methods and steps you use in solving each of these problems with traditional methods and steps taught in school. Record the methods and steps you used to solve the above problems and discuss with your peers to see how many different approaches were used.

Traditionally mathematics operations are done with paper and pencil or on the chalkboard. The 1990s have brought technological advances that have all but eliminated the need for paper-and-pencil, complex or lengthy computational skills (Battista, 1994). Consideration of technology and the

Using calculators can be a natural part of learning operations.

needs of children in the learning process changed the nature of mathematics teaching. This does not mean that operations are no longer important or vital to mathematics teaching, but that new methods of using these skills are called for. In the last quarter of a century, the widespread use of calculating devices and aids has reduced the premium placed on calculation skills and placed it on applications and interpretive ability, and an appreciation of the nature of mathematics operations (Post, 1992).

While numerous national and international studies have shown that the widely practiced method of the teacher explaining what to do and the children practicing with paper and pencil have failed to foster mathematics achievement, these studies do not indicate that basic operations are no longer needed for mathematics achievement (Lo, Wheatley, & Smith, 1994). Adults are used to performing mathematical operations in their heads, with calculators, or on paper, and often no longer take the time to consider the meaning of mathematical operations. If children are to understand mathematics operations and recognize situations in which it is appropriate to use them, educators must help them through relevant activities, experiences, and discussions to attach meaning to each of the operations. As we explore what research and practice reveals about each of these mathematics operations, think of ways you can relate their use to everyday living.

OPERATIONS AND OPERATION SENSE

The mathematics curriculum for young children should include addition, subtraction, multiplication, and division of whole numbers so they can relate the mathematical language and symbolism of operations to problem situations. In the process children should develop operation sense. The *Curriculum and Evaluation Standards for School Mathematics* (National Council for Teachers of Mathematics [NCTM], 1989) emphasizes the meanings of the operations and the development of operation sense.

Standard 7: Concepts of Whole Number Operations

In grades K–4, the mathematics curriculum should include concepts of addition, subtraction, multiplication, and division of whole numbers so that students can

◆ develop meaning for the operations by modeling and discussing a rich variety of problem situations;

◆ relate the mathematical language and symbolism of operations to problem situations and informal language;

◆ develop operation sense. (NCTM, 1989, p. 41)

It is important to realize that the goal of operation meaning is separate from mastery of basic facts and computation. Many children can solve problems like 2 + 3 and still have little understanding of when to add or subtract or how to use this information in different settings. Often students fail to solve simple one-step word problems because of inappropriate selection of a working strategy. Understanding operations like addition, subtraction, multiplication, and division are central to knowing mathematics. Many researchers in a variety of contexts and grade levels have found that identical mathematics problems posed within the context of manipulatives versus abstract can produce correct answers in the non-abstract form but not in the abstract form (Carraher, Carraher, & Schliemann, 1987). Children could demonstrate 3 + 4 = 7 when using counting cubes, but could not work the same problem when written on paper.

In order to understand an operation it is necessary to recognize real-world situations that indicate that the operation would be useful in that situation. Educators often forget to communicate to children the mathematical nature of the world around them. Every day opportunities to solve computation problems occur. Estimating time amounts of class activities, graphing children's choices, collecting data from other classes, the entire school, and the local community, and many other opportunities occur during each day. A plastic tableware drawer insert that has the shapes of different pieces indented in it can encourage young children to sort. Place tableware in unsorted piles and encourage the children to first feel the shapes of the plastic indentations and then have the children sort, count, or work simple add-on problems.

By the time young children enter school they can use objects and counting to solve different kinds of problems. Children often are of the opinion that formal, symbolic school mathematics has nothing to do with the mathematics they have learned on their own at home or in the community. Much of children's mathematics knowledge depends on social transmission, often from parents, siblings, or friends. Educators should encourage this social interaction in the classroom by allowing children to have conversations daily about mathematics. Class discussion of a wide variety of problems helps children prepare for understanding operations.

Another element of understanding operations includes building an awareness of models and the properties of an operation. Development of the basic facts and later work with multidigit examples are based on a clear understanding of mathematics operations. Models help children to understand addition, subtraction, multiplication, and division by representing a situation.

Other elements involved in understanding operations are seeing relationships among operations and acquiring insight into the effects of an operation on a pair of numbers (NCTM, 1989). Although all four basic operations are clearly different, there are relationships among them that children need to understand. Young children may at first have a difficult time understanding these relationships. With teacher guidance children can see that both combining two sets to make one larger one and breaking up a set into smaller parts are part-whole processes. Understanding that subtraction is related to addition is appropriate for young children, particularly if based on real-life experiences, such as the actual taking away or disappearance of objects (Krogh, 1995). Teachers should remove objects, but keep them in sight to help very young children understand how the parts and whole are related.

Multiplication begins to come naturally to children as they count in twos, threes, and so on. Teachers can encourage this thinking by having children count things in the classroom like wheels on cars, eyes, gloves, and so on. Division is traditionally thought of as the most difficult of the processes to understand (Krogh, 1995). However, young children can use two types of division from a very early age: sharing with friends and trying to find how many objects can be purchased with money. Multiplication and division, like addition and subtraction, are inverse operations. Children need to understand this relationship through physical manipulation. Furthermore, multiplication can be viewed as repeated addition and division can be viewed as repeated subtraction.

 **ADDING FISH**

Computation can be introduced through problem-solving situations. The educator can easily find useful real-world examples to develop computation skills. The following problem is suggested for five- or six-year-olds.

Focus: Meaning of addition.

What To Do: Buy four new fish for the class aquarium. Tell the children that there were already two fish and that you have added some more fish. Ask the children to count the number of fish in the aquarium. The fish will be hard to count because they will be moving about among the plants and rocks. Suggest that the children use paper plates and blocks to represent the fish. Tell the children to use two blocks to show the original fish on one plate. Then have them count four more blocks to represent the new fish on another plate. Have the children take numeral cards and place them under each plate—a 2 and a 4. Tell the children to put both groups together just like the fish were added to the aquarium. Have the children count how many blocks they have when they combine 2 and 4. Direct the children to find numeral cards that represent the correct number of blocks and fish.

Adjustments: Have the children draw the correct number of fish (2 + 4). Do the problem again using crayons or markers available in the classroom. Use more numbers to increase the complexity of counting.

Ongoing Assessment: Make short notes on self-sticking mailing labels regarding the ability of the children to combine blocks and match correct numeral cards. Place notes in each child's file for narrative report documentation.

The NCTM standards recommend that instruction on the meaning of operations focuses on concepts and relationships rather than computation. Young children need informal experience with problem situations and language prior to symbolic work with operations. Informal experiences with all four operations should begin when children are young and should continue at least through grade 4. Instruction should include the mathematical language and symbols of each operation. In addition to problems with joining and separating structures, teachers should provide problems comparing and equalizing (NCTM, 1989).

Often young children may not be exposed to the language of mathematics. Terms like addition, sum, subtraction, addend, minus, number line, and regrouping are mathematics specific and rarely used during casual conversation. The vocabulary for students defines the core of what children will learn about addition and subtraction as they mature (Schultz, Colarusso, & Strawderman, 1989). Young children need to talk about mathematics; experiences to develop meanings need to be put into words. The language of basic operations—"difference," "factor," "multiple," "product," and "quotient"—can be introduced and informally worked into conversations.

Ms. Lucero provides 1-inch colored tiles and 1-inch graph paper for her children to explore. She has them select multiplication problems to work using the colored tiles and graph paper. Saberly has chosen 3 × 4 to illustrate. She places three rows of four tiles on her graph paper. Ms. Lucero asks Saberly to illustrate other ways to make 12 using the colored tiles. Saberly makes 1 row of 12 tiles and 6 rows of 2 tiles. Ms Lucero tells Saberly that those are the factors of the number 12. She encourages Saberly to choose other numbers and explore factors. Ms. Lucero also provides hundred charts for her students and encourages them to shade in multiples of numbers. She has her children find numbers that are multiples of two, multiples of three, and so on. On one chart Saberly shades in the multiples of two with an orange pencil. She soon realizes that there is a pattern as she works. Ms. Lucero also encourages Saberly to look for common multiples.

As the children work it is important for the educator, like Ms. Lucero, to use mathematics words to describe what the children are doing. As children find numbers that are multiples of two and multiples of three they are introduced to the concept of common multiples. This provides a good opportunity to introduce calculators to explore multiples of a number through repeated addition.

 CALCULATOR FUN

Children need to be comfortable with calculators. Young children often find calculators interesting and fun, and educators should encourage children to explore and use calculators from an early age. This activity can be used with five-year-old children or older.

Focus: Operations and computation.

What To Do: Direct children to key in a number like 2 and then continue to press the + function 10 times. What number did they get? Talk about how 10 twos equals 20. Children can also work with mystery numbers to experiment with addends or factors. One child of a pair can key in a number and show it to a partner. The partner can "secretly" add a number to it and return the calculator to the first child. The first child must guess what number was used.

Direct children to enter a number like 6 and press + 1. Now have the children close their eyes and press the = key repeatedly. Tell the children to stop when they think they have reached 12. How many times did they press the equal key?

Adjustments: Use more complex operations. Allow children to make up their own problems.

Ongoing Assessment: Have the children dictate or write about their calculator experiences.

Properties of an operation are a key component of operation sense. After children notice that reversing the order of two addends does not change the sum, they may use this idea to solve 2 + 5 by starting with 5 and counting 2 more. As children explore manipulatives and mathematics activities, the properties of operations should become evident. It is up to educators to plan and prepare activities that will enhance the children's capabilities.

Mr. Carnera often joins his four- and five-year-old class during learning center time. He sits at the table with one or two children and initiates games with manipulative materials. This week they are studying their community. One day he placed three red houses and four green houses on one side of a street of a community map the children had made. He asked Raul to count the houses. Next Mr. Carnera placed four red houses and three green houses across the street from the other houses and asked Raul if the number of houses were equal. At first Raul said, "No, because there were three red houses at first and now there are four." Mr. Carnera encourages Raul to count and copy the number of houses using different colors. After a few minutes, Raul says, "Mr. Carnera, it doesn't matter which color is three and which color is four. It still makes seven."

Mr. Carnera has helped Raul discover a simple property of addition. Raul was allowed to explore the different colored cubes and given time to think about the problem. Mr. Carnera never forces his children to write problems, but lets them decide for themselves when they are comfortable enough to go from manipulative to symbolic work. Often his children switch back and forth between manipulative and symbolic activities. Sometimes Raul will want to count out seven houses and sometimes he will want to practice using a numeral written on paper to represent the number of houses on the map.

 ## THE MISSING PARTS GAME

The following game uses manipulatives such as interlocking cubes, beans, or any appropriate materials. After the children take away a certain number of manipulatives, discuss what happens when they put the missing pieces back with the whole group. Four-, five-, and six-year-olds should be able to participate.

Focus: Simple operations and communication.

What To Do: This game can be played in pairs or small groups. The children are given a fixed number of counters (interlocking cubes, large dry beans, plastic animal counters, and so on). One child places all of the counters under one hand and then removes some. Interview the other children and have them orally describe what has happened. "There were six counters all together. You showed us four." The children use their counters to copy the problem and then count how many are left under the hand of the first child. "There are two counters left under your hand." The children take turns hiding the counters.

Adjustments: The children can use more complex problems. Older children can write the number of counters as the game progresses.

Ongoing Assessment: Monitor the children as they work to determine their levels of operation sophistication.

Time devoted to conceptual development provides meaning and context to subsequent work on computational skills. Young children must spend much time exploring and working through operations with manipulatives before being introduced to symbolic representation. The NCTM is not suggesting that computation is not needed, but rather that computation should not be the entire focus of mathematics instruction.

Whole Number Computation

In grades K–4, the mathematics curriculum should develop whole number computation so that students can

◆ model, explain, and develop reasonable proficiency with basic facts and algorithms;

◆ use a variety of mental computations and estimation techniques;

◆ use calculators in appropriate computational situations;

◆ select and use computation techniques appropriate to specific problems and determine whether the results are reasonable. (NCTM, 1989, p. 44.)

Almost all computation today is done with calculators and computers; however, people still use mental computation to determine daily problems. Children need to learn a variety of ways to compute as well as the usefulness of technology.

The NCTM states that "strong evidence suggests that conceptual approaches to computation instruction result in good achievement, good retention, and a reduction in the amount of time children need to master computational skills" (NCTM, 1989, p. 44). Children need to explore materials and experiment with relationships in order to accomplish this level of understanding.

Mr. Lujan provides his multilevel primary class many types of manipulative materials. He works with small groups of children during center time. Today he has placed square blocks on the table along with a data recording sheet. The sheet has "How many ways can you make a rectangle with these blocks?" written across the top. Down the left side of the paper are numerals and picture representatives of the number of blocks to use. The right side of the paper is blank to allow the children to record their findings.

As the children work Mr. Lujan asks the children things like, "How did you know to rearrange those blocks to create more rectangles?" and "How many squares would it take to cover this entire sheet of paper?" The children are encouraged to use the squares to create other shapes. Mr. Lujan asks things like, "Could you make a circle with these squares?" "How could you make other shapes with your blocks?" As the children work he points out to younger children that they have added a certain number of blocks to create different shapes. The older children are asked to explain the number added or subtracted to make the new shapes.

BEANS IN THE HANDS

Informal activities enhance the comfortable development of number skills. Inexpensive materials like beans can be used in many operations games. Even children as young as three or four can play this game in small groups or in pairs.

Focus: Subtraction.

Playing "Beans in the hands" helps children explore subtraction concepts.

What To Do: Place a given number of beans in each child's hand. The player places both hands behind his or her back and shifts some of the beans to the other hand. Both hands are clenched and presented to another player. One hand is chosen and then opened, revealing some of the beans. The player must then guess how many beans are in the other hand. The child opens the other hand and both children count to validate the guess. The child guessing should say that the number of beans minus the beans in the closed hand equals what is left.

Adjustments: Have primary children write equations for each other then have classmates work the problems with beans.

Ongoing Assessment: The teacher observes for mastery. Who is guessing and who has grasped the idea?

Models for mathematics operations include countable objects, arrays of objects arranged in rows or columns, and number lines, rods, or segmented strips. Children can illustrate relationships with these models by moving or arranging the materials and drawing additional lines to indicate various relationships. As children are working with models they should verbalize the relationships they make. By emphasizing underlying concepts, using physical materials to model procedures, linking the manipulation of materials to the steps of the procedures, and developing thinking patterns, teachers can help children master basic facts (NCTM, 1989).

Mental computation and estimation are cognitive algorithms. Most people have not been taught how to use mental computation and computational estimation. It is important to remember that there are many mental algorithms to learn and it is not always clear as to which method to use. Different people will use different methods in different situations. But there are specific methods or procedures that can be taught and practiced. Van de Walle (1994, p. 157) presents the following example:

> 48 widgets at 13 cents each equals how much?
> Some possibilities:
> "Let's see, 48 is about 50. 50×10 cents is $5.00. 50×3 cents is $1.50 more. About $6.50."
> "13 cents is close to 10 cents. 50 at 10 cents is $5.00. Probably more—say $6.00."
> "Think of 50×13. 5×13 is 65. Must be $6.50 because $65 or 65 cents doesn't seem right."
> "Instead of 48 and 13, use 50 and 15. Now 5×15 is 75. But I made both numbers bigger—$7.50 is too big. Probably less than $7.00"

These approaches illustrate estimation activities. Look at the following problems and try both estimation, mental computation, or a combination of both to solve them.

 WHAT DO *YOU* THINK?

Have everyone in your group use mental computation and/or estimation to solve the following problems. As you work through them write down your thinking. Compare your thinking processes with three colleagues. Were they exactly the same? Was there any two in your group who used the exact same approach? More? How many?

1. How much would 10 pairs of shoes cost at $15.65 a pair?
2. If one ticket to Puerto Rico is $456.00 round-trip and the second ticket is half-price, what is the total for two people traveling together?
3. Mr. Alvarez lives 17 miles from his place of employment. If he comes home for lunch every day, how many miles will he travel in five days?

Did any two people in your group approach the mental computation the same way? Try other problems and see what happens.

Computation should be approached with a developmental prospective in mind. Premature expectations can cause poor initial learning, poor retention, and waste a large portion of instructional time. Inappropriate instruction focuses on memorizing facts and rules for carrying out procedures rather than on the real-world use of operations. Children need to master the basic facts of mathematics that are essential to fluency with computation, however, mastery should not be expected too soon. Children need to learn the sequence of steps and the reasons for them. Success is possible for almost all children when given careful developmental instruction.

 NUMBER TABLES

In this activity children explore the numbers from 1 to 10 in a variety of ways. Three- and four-year-olds may participate, as well as five- and six-year-olds. Level the task according to the developmental level of the children involved.

Focus: Number concepts and beginning operations.

What To Do: Provide a variety of materials such as beans, interlocking cubes, color tiles, toothpicks, pattern blocks, stones, and wooden blocks. Place like materials on different tables. Encourage the children to move freely among the tables and explore each material. Increase the number of assigned exploration items as children become comfortable with the procedure. Encourage the children to make as many number arrangements as they can with each group of materials. Have the children describe their work. "I have made a group of four toothpicks." "I have two groups of three color tiles." As the children work help them see the groups they have created and how the groups combine to make larger groups.

Adjustments: More mature children can be assigned addition and subtraction problems with the manipulatives. Some children may be ready to group fives and tens to illustrate multiplication operations. One child might make 5 groups of 10 color tiles and write an equation to illustrate.

Ongoing Assessment: Take photographs of children grouping materials to be placed in portfolios. Monitoring of number tables will provide insight into the developmental level of children. Make decisions on what you have observed.

Algorithms are specific procedures used to compute exact answers to arithmetic problems. Each algorithm is based on the meaning of an operation and the meaning should be familiar to the children before formal equations. It should also be clear that the algorithm result applies to all meanings of the operation. Algorithms depend conceptually on the place value system of numeration to make them work. Sequential grouping or trading activities with base-ten materials should be totally familiar both conceptually and orally to any class being taught computational algorithms (Van de Walle, 1994). Young children may not have this knowledge and cannot talk about trading in a meaningful manner.

The end goal of algorithms development is a reasonably efficient use of procedures without models. However, it is vital for children to have use of models in the early development of these procedures. Base-10 models or base-10 bean sticks are usually used for these activities.

The process of selecting and using the right techniques and operations is done intuitively by children in the prenumber years. When children enter school, this intuitive understanding is often taken away as teachers begin to focus on drill and textbook learning (Krogh, 1995). When real-life experiences and applications are used with children, it makes it easier for them to make logical choices of computational techniques. Children need many opportunities to decide whether they need an exact answer and how they will complete a computation.

PRESENTING AND DEVELOPING MEANINGS OF OPERATIONS

What do the operations of adding, subtracting, multiplying, and dividing mean? Each has two or more interpretations or aspects to its meaning. In order to fully understand the operations, children must be systematically exposed to each of the aspects in familiar problem-solving situations. When children know all the aspects of an operation, they can use it more effectively and recognize it more readily when the operation occurs in everyday life.

As children work with the meanings of mathematics operations, they use reasoning and problem-solving skills and models, words, and actions to communicate. Let's look at some of the meanings or interpretations in the context of making and eating sandwiches in the school cafeteria.

Addition

One meaning of addition is *combining sets.* In the cafeteria a "super sandwich" may require two pieces of bread and six fillings. When they are combined, how many ingredients do you have? Children can use real sandwich fillings, paper, or clay ingredients to find out as they create model sandwiches. Combining materials helps children grasp the idea of "putting things together" and determining a total.

Another meaning of addition is called *static.* Here learners think of the total without actually combining sets. The cafeteria may have two signs on its back door and three signs on its front door. Learners can determine how many signs there are in all without actually moving the signs together. For instance, they might count the signs in front, then count the signs in back.

Thinking of *continuous increases* is a third interpretation of addition. The temperature near the cafeteria oven may rise as the oven is used to bake bread. The temperature in the oven itself rises dramatically when the oven is turned on. In these cases, whole numbers of degrees of temperature are not actually added or tacked on; instead we see a gradual increase. Children can actually see evidence that the temperature rises on a thermometer or you can demonstrate the process on a model thermometer.

Subtraction

Subtraction has at least four interpretations: take away, comparing, missing addend or missing part, and decrease. The *take away* interpretation is perhaps the easiest to model. For example, the cafeteria cook has prepared four sandwiches and one is sold. How many are left? Children can easily act out the situation and see the answer.

Ms. Cervantes uses snack time as a subtraction exercise, relating snacks to thematic topics. The class is studying pond life and today the four- and five-year-old children have prepared "Frogs on a Log." (Peanut butter on celery sticks with raisins on top. The recipe is in Chapter 7.) As the children eat their snack Ms. Cervantes directs them to eat one frog and then tell her how many are left on each child's "log." Ms. Cervantes always uses daily activities to help her children practice mathematics skills.

The *comparison* model or interpretation of subtraction involves making a comparison between two sets and seeing how many more one set has than the other. If Bobby eats four sandwiches and Omar eats two, how many more does Bobby eat than Omar? If the children model this situation, they can easily see the answer.

COMPARISON SUBTRACTION

This game is played with a partner as a way to connect the comparison relationship in subtraction. Children should be mature enough to understand subtraction concepts when they are about six or seven.

Focus: Subtraction.

What To Do: A bar of interlocking blocks is lined up on one side of a table or the partner's work area. One child places another interlocking cube bar across from the first bar. The other child must tell how much longer one bar is than the other (or in the case of equal bars, the difference is zero). Help the children relate the differences they see to subtraction. Help them identify the relationship. For example, "The difference between nine and three is six." If children are having trouble, place the bars side by side so children can clearly see the difference. Change the number of cubes for each turn. Allow the children to make equations with number cards or cards that have numbers on them and equal, subtraction, and addition signs.

Adjustments: Allow the children to make up their own problems. After the players have looked at the first bar and know the number of cubes, hide the bar so the children will have to practice mental computation. Use more complex operations.

Ongoing Assessment: Check the children's equation cards or listen to the children to determine the accuracy of their thinking.

The *missing addend* or *missing part* meaning for subtraction involves knowing part of the whole and trying to find the other part. Perhaps the cafeteria cook needs five packages of cheese to make sandwiches for the day. She has only three packages. How many more does she need? Children can actually arrange objects and count to find the answer.

OVERHEAD SUBTRACTION

Visual aids that are used as kindergarten and first-grade children work through problems with manipulatives at their desks help children retain important concepts.

Focus: Subtraction.

What To Do: Place a number of transparent colored tiles on the overhead projector and ask the children to replicate the number at their work stations. Hold a piece of posterboard to shield what is being done on the overhead while separating the counters. Place the posterboard over one section of separated tiles and ask the children to adjust their tiles and say what number is missing and the subtraction sentence: "Seven minus four is three." The subtraction equation may be written as the children work.

Adjustments: Allow the children to pose the problems on the overhead for the class to solve. Switch back and forth between addition and subtraction to allow children to determine the operation being used.

Ongoing Assessment: The teacher observes the children for participation and understanding.

Finally, subtraction may involve a *decrease.* After the oven is turned off, the temperature falls. "If the temperature was 350 degrees, and it falls to 85 degrees inside the oven, how many degrees did the temperature go down?" is a decrease situation.

Young children can explore multiplication and division in concrete ways, see how the operations are related, and model the operations when developmentally appropriate. Memorization of multiplication and division facts as well as multidigit problems are best presented in later grades.

Multiplication

Multiplication can be interpreted three ways. The *repeated addition* model involves thinking of the same number being added to itself a number of times. If the children at a table eat three trays with four sandwiches each, the number of sandwiches could be thought of as $4 + 4 + 4$ or as 3×4. Children, already familiar with addition, usually relate well to the repeated addition model.

Multiplication on a number line concerns movement to the right so that each displacement has equal steps. Movement always starts at zero and a pattern emerges by recording the "landings." Manipulatives such as

Figure 8.1   *Problems like 4 × 3 can be modeled using real-life examples. Here children determine the amount of bread needed to make sandwiches.*

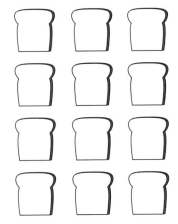

Cuisenaire rods and a number line made to match the unit size of the material can be used to illustrate the hops. It is important for children to remember that the unit distances are the focus and not the number points.

The *area* or *row-by-column* interpretation of multiplication involves thinking of a multiplication situation as a rectangular arrangement. When the cook lays out pieces of bread to be spread with toppings, he lays out five rows with two pieces of bread in each. If the arrangement involved four rows of three pieces of bread each, the problem 4 × 3 can be modeled as shown in Figure 8.1.

The *combinations* interpretation of multiplication involves thinking of the number of combinations that can be made using given numbers of factors, usually two sets. Multiplication can be used to express the number of possible pairings. The need to count possible combinations or outcomes is important in simple probability problems. For example, suppose the cook uses two kinds of bread—wheat and white—and four kinds of sandwich toppings—cheese, vegetable, ham, and turkey. How many different open-face sandwiches with one piece of bread and one kind of topping can she make? The children might draw or use paper or modeling-dough sandwich parts to make the eight possible different combinations.

 ## COMBINATIONS OF CLOTHES

Children are usually interested in their clothing and color combinations. Looking at sets can help second- and third-grade children explore the combination model of multiplication.

Focus: Grouping, addition, and multiplication.

What To Do: Either provide real clothing, paper cutouts, or have the children choose the following articles of clothing from a magazine: two pairs of different color jeans and three different color shirts. Ask the children to determine how many different outfits they could wear by combining different color jeans and shirts. Children may want to draw combinations or illustrate as below.

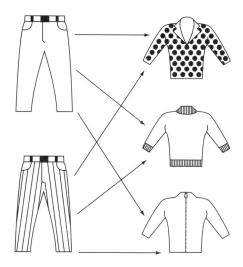

Help the children develop an organized approach to identify all possible outfits. Have the children check to be certain they have all possible combinations and whether they have repeated combinations.

Adjustments: Add more jeans and shirts to increase the possible combinations. Add two different pairs of shoes and see how many possible combinations the children can come up with.

Ongoing Assessment: Allow the children to illustrate their thinking on combinations and place their work in their portfolios.

Division

Division situations can be thought of in two ways: *repeated subtraction* and *distribution* or *"fair sharing."* Repeated subtraction builds on children's understanding of subtraction. The cafeteria cook has 12 pieces of bread. She makes sandwiches that use two pieces of bread each. How many sandwiches can she make? Repeated subtraction can be used to get the answer. Children can model the situation and the teacher can record the work. When one sandwich is made, 10 pieces of bread remain. When a second sandwich is made, eight pieces of bread remain, and so on. In all, the chef can make six sandwiches. Learning division makes the process shorter and easier.

The distribution interpretation of division involves a situation with which children are familiar: objects are passed out or shared to make equal sets. They can model the operation by passing out 12 sandwiches to each of five children, being sure that each gets the same number of sandwiches. In this case, each gets two sandwiches with two left over. The leftovers can be split further or they can be kept whole "for the cook." If a quantity is to be measured into sets of a specified size, then division expresses the number of such sets that can be made. Sometimes there is a remainder and sometimes there is not.

Adults should note that in the repeated subtraction interpretation we know the number of objects in each set, but not the number of sets. In the partitioning interpretation we know the number of sets, but not the number included in each set. Division as repeated subtraction can be illustrated by hops on a number line. All movement is to the left, toward zero, and starts at the number to be divided.

Multiplication and division share a close relationship. Educators can capitalize on the relationship between these two operations by using the same situation to illustrate multiplication and division problems and by discussing the relationship as it becomes evident in the children's work.

Jesse brought a package of rolls to school for a special class lunch. The class noticed that there were four rows with six rolls in each row in the carton. Mr. Fenton asked the class to help find out how many rolls were in the package. He asked his class to draw a picture to verify their responses. He allows the children to use counting tiles to make a model of the package. After the children have determined the number of rolls in the carton, Mr. Fenton asks the children how they can find out if there are enough for the entire class of 12. Jesse suggests using the counting tiles to illustrate how many groups of six are in 24 to find out how many rolls each child might have. Then he regrouped his tiles to show two groups of 12.

BASIC FACTS

Basic facts for addition and multiplication are considered those combinations where both addends or both factors are less than 10. Subtraction and division facts correspond to addition and multiplication. Mastery of basic facts means that a child can give a quick response without resorting to such things as counting.

Eventually children will have to memorize basic facts. Quick, effortless recall of basic facts makes them readily "available" for use in problem solving. For example, as children learn to work mentally with multiples of 10, basic facts are vital. For example, adding 40 + 80 builds on knowledge of 4 + 8. Estimating answers to computations also builds on knowledge of basic facts.

Memorization of facts is most effectively built on understanding. People can memorize and retain better when they understand the material. After children have worked with the modeling operations, are familiar with their many interpretations, and have worked with the patterns and relationships of the facts, they are ready to memorize. Memorization is best done in short, regularly spaced periods. For example, 10 minutes a day, four days a week devoted to memorizing is generally more effective than a single 40-minute period each week.

 WHAT DO *YOU* THINK?

The following game helps children gain experience with factors. It may be helpful to compile a reference book of factors for all numbers through 66.

Prepare a 100 square like the one below. Be sure to include the numbers 1 to 9 and the number 11 in each row.

5	11	4	7	2	6	9	1	3	8
4	8	3	1	6	5	11	7	2	9
11	2	7	6	3	1	8	9	4	5
7	8	2	6	9	11	3	5	1	4
3	4	9	7	5	8	11	1	2	6
9	3	5	1	6	2	4	7	11	8
1	5	3	7	6	2	11	9	8	4
6	2	5	9	8	11	7	3	4	1
2	7	8	11	1	9	4	6	3	5
7	9	1	5	4	3	2	8	6	11

Play this game in groups of two to four. Provide different color counters, two dice numbered 1 to 6, and a calculator. Have the children take turns throwing two dice and deciding which two-digit number they want (15 or 51). Use a counter to cover any factor of that number. The first player to get five in a row wins.

After you have played this game, write a short narrative about your approach to deciding which combination of numbers to cover.

Educators should help children set goals for themselves in memorizing facts. One child may be able to commit two or three times as many facts to memory as another child. Individual goals help children feel successful. Children might make their own flash cards, then file them in a box as they are memorized. If the box has sections for "Facts I'm Working On" and "Facts I Know," each child can review known facts as well as see progress toward knowing all the facts.

As children begin to memorize facts, they must understand that their purpose is to memorize; it is not to discuss or model facts or "work them out" by drawing pictures. Children need feedback as they memorize facts. A variety of self-checking devices can help them see immediately whether they are right or wrong in their answers. If children see both the problem and the answer in the feedback, it often helps them to build associations and remember the fact.

When children "miss" facts, it may help them to redo them using a different communication form than the one they initially used to practice the facts. That is, if a child is practicing facts by saying them aloud, he might write a missed fact, then also say it. If a child is practicing facts by writing them, she might trace a missed fact in a sand tray, then say it.

 BASIC FACT ACTIVITIES

Many activities enhance the mastery of basic facts. This group of games is focused on addition and subtraction appropriate for first- and second-grade children.

◆ Ask "What is one more than nine?" As soon as the child answers, ask "What is one plus nine?" or hold up a 9 + 1 flash card. Be sure to make the connection that 10 is one more than 9.
◆ Make number cards. Have the children play a match game where they are given a number and they have to find the card that matches one, two, or three more.
◆ Make and match flash cards for doubles, with pictures of the doubles images or double domino dot patterns. Say the doubles fact with each match.
◆ Roll a single die with numerals and have the children double the number rolled. Change the game to require the children to add one, two, or three to the number rolled.
◆ Make a mat with two ten-frames on which students can place counters. On one of the ten-frames draw in nine counters. Give students flash cards for the minus nine facts. Have them use counters to build the sum starting with the nine drawn counters. Repeat with all the "minus" facts.
◆ Prepare addition and subtraction fact flash cards. Have the children match the subtraction fact with a helping addition fact.
◆ Use the calculator to practice "minus" numbers. Make flash cards for all numbers in the families of subtraction and addition facts.

Children enjoy practicing facts in familiar game formats. Fact searches, tic-tac-toe (where players must say a fact before making a mark), or fact bingo are old favorites. Children can also toss number cubes or use number spinners to produce numbers on which to practice operations. Children can make their own game boards and establish rules for basic fact games.

MULTIDIGIT OPERATIONS

Learning to do multidigit operations such as 18 + 75 + 125 or 85 - 27 should be attempted after children understand the process of operations,

WHAT DO *YOU* THINK?

Look at this list of numbers. Try to spend about one minute memorizing it so that you can either write or repeat it verbally.

2581114172023

How did you approach the task? Some of you may have separated the list into smaller chunks, 258-111-417-2023. The chunks are easier to remember than the entire string of separate numbers. How long do you think you will remember this list? Try two different approaches to memorizing this list. Say the list aloud, invent a rhythm, or write it down a few times. There is a pattern involved in this list. Can you find it?

have modeled and worked with basic facts, and have memorized most of the basic facts. It is also vital that children have place value understanding.

Working with multidigit operations is a long process. If it is to be meaningful to children they should first work with manipulatives to model the operations in meaningful problem situations; they must discuss what they are doing and use symbols to represent what is happening. Next, the children can explain what they are doing using symbols alone. Finally, children practice working with symbols as performing the operations becomes automatic. It is important that educators avoid presenting work with operations as a series of rules or mysterious procedures.

To introduce multidigit addition, a teacher might generate interest in finding out how many children are present in the school or part of the school each day. The children can count the numbers present in several classrooms or work areas, then report the numbers. They might estimate a number for the total before they begin. The teacher can show the children how to represent two or more of the numbers with place value materials, then combine the pieces to find the sum. As they combine the materials, children will see some tens and ones represented. Some may choose to combine tens first, then ones, or some may combine ones first then tens. If 10 or more ones are found, the children can regroup (trade or exchange) them for tens, then name the number for their final answer.

The children might gain more practice in multidigit addition by continuing to add on the numbers of children they have found in other classrooms. If they continue the project for several days, the final sums will probably be about the same, and the children can try to predict the next day's attendance based on the data they already have. Using real-life situations lets children work with some numbers where regrouping is necessary and some numbers where it is not. They do not overgeneralize that every problem requires or does not require regrouping.

As soon as children recognize positional notation and master some of the basic subtraction facts, the teacher should present situations that require the subtraction of two-digit numbers. Such exploration usually occurs when children are about six years of age. It is vitally important for children to use manipulative materials. Multidigit subtraction might be introduced in the context of making change in the school store or seeing how many supplies are left after purchases are made. The children can start with designated amounts of money and plan for their purchases. They can then use subtraction to see how much money they will have left.

SUMMARY

The NCTM recommends that children develop operations after many experiences with real problem situations. Children develop meaning for mathematics operations by modeling and discussing a rich variety of problem situations. The language of mathematics should be modeled and encouraged as children explore material. Children should be able to relate mathematical language and symbolism of operations to problem situations and informal language. The scope of a single mathematics operation can apply to a wide variety of problem structures. Educators need to help children develop operation sense.

The NCTM establishes several goals for computation. One goal is for children to model, explain, and develop reasonable proficiency with basic facts and algorithms. Children need to learn a variety of mental computation and estimation strategies to help them master mathematics. Calculators and technology have altered the traditional view of teaching computation and should be used regularly with young children prior to and while they learn paper-and-pencil computation. Children also need to be able to determine if their results are reasonable.

The four basic operations associated with mathematics are addition, subtraction, multiplication, and division. Each operation has different interpretations. Addition has three interpretations: combining sets, static, and increases. Subtraction has at least four interpretations: take away, comparing, missing addend or missing part, and decrease. Multiplication can be interpreted three ways: repeated addition, area or row-by-column, and combinations. Division has a distribution and repeated subtraction interpretation.

◆ *APPLICATIONS: THINKING AND COLLABORATING*

1. Set your calculator to count by ones and count to a number such as 20, 50, or 100 several times. Watch the numbers and try to imagine what young children would think about as they did the same counting. Describe a lesson that can relate such counting to learning operations.

2. Design a counting activity by threes for a six-year-old child. Indicate how counting by threes relates to addition or multiplication. Describe the mathematics to be learned.

3. Researchers debate whether young children store basic fact information in long-term memory or use an efficient production system to generate the answer to a basic fact question. What do you think? Interview other adults in your group, then organize and analyze your data.

4. Using all the digits from one to six each only once, make two numbers and multiply them such that you get the greatest possible product. For example, $12,345 \times 6 = 74,070$. Can you do better? Explore this problem and then explain how you solved it to a member of your group.

5. Use a calculator to solve the following problems:

$0 \div 1$ $0 \div 2$ $0 \div 3$ $0 \div 100$ $0 \div 9999$

What can you say about dividing zero by any number? Interview some children about zero and what they know. How can they explain about zero and division to a friend who does not understand?

◆ REFERENCES

Battista, M. (1994). Teacher beliefs and the reform movement in mathematics education. *Phi Delta Kappan, 75*(6), 462–470.

Carraher, T. P., Carraher, D. W., & Schliemann, A. D. (1987). Written and oral mathematics. *Journal for Research in Mathematics Education, 18,* 83–97.

Gray, E. M. & Tall, D. O. (1994). Duality, ambiguity, and flexibility: a 'perceptual' view of simple arithmetic. *Journal for Research in Mathematics Education, 25*(2), 116–140.

Krogh, S. L. (1995). *The integrated early childhood curriculum.* New York: McGraw-Hill.

Lo, J.-J., Wheatley, G. H., & Smith, A. C. (1994). The participation, beliefs, and development of arithmetic meaning of a third-grade student in mathematics class discussions. *Journal for Research in Mathematics Education, 25*(1), 30–49.

National Council for Teachers of Mathematics. (1989). *Curriculum and evaluation standards for school mathematics.* Reston, VA: Author.

Post, T. R. (1992). *Teaching mathematics in grades K–8.* Needham Heights, MA: Allyn and Bacon.

Schultz, K. A., Colarusso, M., & Strawderman, V. W. (1989). *Mathematics for every young child.* Columbus, OH: Merrill.

Van de Walle, J. A. (1994). *Elementary school mathematics, teaching developmentally.* White Plains, NY: Longman.

◆ *SELECTED CHILDREN'S BOOKS*

Brett, Molly. (1993). *The Untidy Little HedgeHog.* London: Medici Society, Ltd. This delightful story revolves around a hedgehog who encounters many animal friends. The illustrations lend themselves to simple addition and subtraction problems when comparing the different animals.

Caduto, Michael, & Bruchac, J. (1989). *Keepers of the Earth.* Golden, CO: Fulcrum. This is a collection of Native American legends and folk tales. Each story has suggestions for integrating activities that relate to the story. There are several addition and subtraction opportunities in this authentic book of the first Americans.

Hawkins, C. & Hawkins, J. (1993). *I Know an Old Lady Who Swallowed a Fly.* Glenview, IL: Scott Foresman & Co. This traditional rhyme is about an old lady who adds on many interesting things as she continues to swallow a sequence of materials. Counting and adding or subtraction can easily be pulled from this beautifully illustrated book.

Heller, Ruth. (1989). *Many Luscious Lollipops.* New York: Grossett and Dunlap. This attractive book offers children a delightful counting experience. The brightly colored lollipops will lead children through wonderful counting exercises that can easily be adjusted into operation activities.

Hoberman, Mary Ann. (1991). *Fathers, Mothers, Sisters, Brothers.* New York: Penguin Books. This book is a collection of family poems that will delight and charm any reader. The opportunities to assign operation problems abound as children compare and contrast families in the poems.

McGrath, Barbara. (1994). *The M & M Counting Book.* Watertown, MA: Bridge Charles. This colorful book is full of counting, addition and subtraction activities. The illustrations are as colorful as actual M&Ms. The ideas can be implemented with real M&Ms.

McMillan, Bruce. (1991). *Eating Fractions.* New York: Scholastic. The photographs in this book illustrate whole and part relationships and lend themselves to addition and subtraction.

Pinkney, Andrea Davis. (1993). *Seven Candles for Kwanzaa.* New York: Dial. This Newberry Award–winning book focuses on the seven-day holiday in Africa. During the holiday an array of gifts are given to participants. The vivid colors and clear illustrations lend themselves to addition and subtraction activities.

Sharmat, Majorie. (1979). *The 329th Friend.* New York: Four Winds. This wonderful story can be the source of many sequencing and counting activities as 329 guests arrive for lunch. Children can easily practice adding as more and more guests arrive.

Ukrainian fairy tale. (1994). *The Mitten.* Moscow: Maylsh. This classic adventure about a mouse who takes winter shelter in a mitten is known throughout the world. Different animals keep adding to the group living in the mitten until the whole thing blows up. The children can also subtract the animals.

Zimmerman, Andrea, & Clemesha, David. (1993). *The Cow Buzzed.* New York: Harper Collins. This charming book can be used to enhance children's data skills. Using the wonderful illustrations and story, children can record data about each of the animals and add the total of facts about each animal.

Working with Data and Probability

9

◆◆◆

Mrs. Haviland asks her principal, Ms. Washington, to come and see something her kindergartners have worked on. The children, as part of their study of families, discussed pets and made clay models and drawings of pets. The children displayed their drawings and models

185

on squares of paper and arranged them on the floor to make a large graph. When Ms. Washington enters the room, several kindergartners greet her with, "Come see our graph. See, we have lots of pets ... some clay and some on paper ... more drawings than clay models." How might Ms. Washington react? Is making a graph a typical or unusual activity for five- and six-year-olds? Will Ms. Washington see it as a valid learning experience? Why?

At the beginning of a new school year, Mr. Black wants his second graders to get to know each other and learn to work together. Since he has also set a goal for using more realistic problem solving, he decides to pose a problem for groups of children: What can you find out about your classmates and groupmates? As the children absorb the problem, Mr. Black helps them develop subquestions: What would we like to know? How can we find out? How can we share what we have found?

As the children solve the problem, they use many different approaches. Marty's group makes short questionnaires including, Do you have a pet? How many brothers and sisters do you have? and What do you like to do after school? They give their questionnaires to classmates, then discuss and count the responses and report to the class.

Ingrid's group takes a different approach, asking classmates to draw pictures of their favorite school lunches. They then sort the pictures into categories and arrange them on a graphing mat made from a vinyl tablecloth. The children show the graph to their classmates and ask questions about the graph: "How many children picked pizza?" "What was our favorite lunch?"

Other groups use still different approaches for gathering, displaying, and interpreting their data. Mr. Black helps the children summarize and begin to apply some of the ideas they have been working on when he asks, "What are some important things we learned? How did we gather and share our data? How can we use what we learned about each other as we work together this year?"

Overall Mr. Black is pleased with his students' work. The children were interested in learning about each other; they worked together and built communication skills and cohesiveness. Mr. Black is proud of the fact that he has informally introduced the children to solving realistic problems and working with data.

DEVELOPING STATISTICAL THINKING

The authors of *Curriculum and Evaluation Standards for School Mathematics* (National Council of Teachers of Mathematics [NCTM], 1989) offer guidance for planning experiences in working with data and probability with young children. Describing the need for children to learn to work with data in an information society, they describe a spirit of investigation that permeates activities in which children pose and investigate questions that are important to them. They point out that problem solving, reasoning, and communicating are involved as children conduct interdisciplinary data investigations.

The *Curriculum Standards* (NCTM, 1989, p. 54) include the following:

> In grades K–4, the mathematics curriculum should include experiences with data analysis and probability so that students can

♦ collect, organize, and describe data;

♦ construct, read, and interpret displays of data;

♦ formulate and solve problems that involve collecting and analyzing data;

♦ explore concepts of chance.

The NCTM standards further describe graphs that children can make as they find answers to questions such as, "What's the favorite ice cream flavor in our class?" "How do the temperatures in our town compare to those in New York or Sydney, Australia?" or "Which spinner is more likely to give us a red?" (NCTM, 1989, p. 56; see Figure 9.1).

In our information-filled world, people constantly use quantitative terms and statistics to describe phenomena. They encounter statistical claims and must make sense of data presented in graphs and charts. Probability situations abound in a world characterized by chance occurrences and uncertainty. Therefore it is important that young children have concrete experiences in collecting, organizing, and interpreting data and in exploring ideas of chance. Publications such as the *Curriculum Standards* (NCTM, 1989), the *Quantitative Literacy Series* (American Statistical Association [ASH], 1989), and *Used Numbers* (Russell, Cirwin, Freil, Mokros, & Stone, 1992) have brought to educators' attention appropriate ways for young children to explore statistics and probability.

Use of many representational forms reinforces the assertion of the National Association for the Education of Young Children (NAEYC) (Bredekamp, 1993) that literacy and understanding are enhanced by activities such as drawing, dictating, and writing about experiences and by making

Figure 9.1 *Spinners help children explore probability in a concrete manner.*

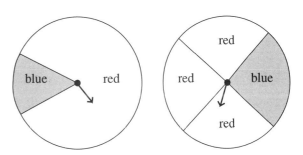

After collecting a variety of natural materials, children arrange them on sorting mats.

books. Early experiences in working with data lay a firm foundation for later, more formal work that elementary students will encounter in a balanced mathematics curriculum.

MATERIALS FOR INVOLVING CHILDREN IN WORKING WITH DATA AND PROBABILITY

Many simple materials can be used to enhance children's work with data and probability. When children sort materials, using paper plates, boxes, or baskets for placing items that are alike helps children organize their thinking. Paper sorting mats help children make groups of small objects. For larger objects—or people—educators can prepare sorting mats on plastic tablecloths, shower curtains, or pieces of shelf paper.

When children work with simple graphs, large graphing mats can be made in the same ways as sorting mats. For bar graph formats, columns or squares can be drawn with permanent marker or outlined with tape. Children can also use poster board graph forms ruled into columns by adults, or they can work with duplicated polling forms attached to cardboard with paper clips (Figure 9.2).

For picture graphs, children can draw on equal-sized squares, making possible clear comparison of results. Self-adhesive notes are easy to arrange in sets to make graphs on a bulletin board or poster board. Children can make simple circle graphs from paper plates or circles folded into four or eight equal portions.

For work with probability, number cubes are available in many designs including dice with 4, 6, 8, 10, and 20 faces. Number cubes can be made from classroom blocks or foam pieces with numerals or symbols written

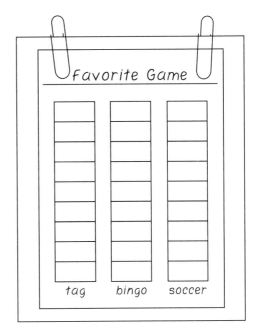

Figure 9.2 *Graphing mats help children see the results of their data collection.*

on. A wide variety of spinners are commercially available. Teachers and children can also make spinners on pieces of poster board with paper clips or paper arrows attached with brads. For sampling activities, opaque containers such as paper or cloth bags work well.

GATHERING, ORGANIZING, AND DISPLAYING DATA

How might a teacher help children get started in working with data in meaningful ways? Consider the ways a teacher of four-year-olds informally lays the groundwork for working with data. Miss Giametti's children love playing in the block center, and she has worked to help them clean up responsibly. Miss Giametti posted pictures of the different shapes and sizes of blocks on the shelves so the children could replace the blocks.

As the children work, Miss Giametti let them describe how they know they are placing the blocks in their correct places. At a "class meeting," children offered examples of organizing things at home and at school—laundry, doll clothes, dishes, silverware, and shoes. Miss Giametti decided that most of the children grasped the idea of sorting things that are alike, so she planned activities where children could sort a variety of objects—wooden beads, pictures, buttons, and discarded keys. Thus the children gain considerable experience with the idea of categorizing and organizing sets of material. "Sorting Kids" describes more ideas for extending sorting skills.

 **SORTING KIDS**

For children of any age; an ever-present and interesting resource for sorting is the children themselves.

Focus: Gathering and organizing data, reasoning, communicating, connecting to real life and to fractions.

What To Do: Have four or five children stand. Others suggest ways to sort these classmates into two or more groups. After one child suggests a basis for sorting, let another move the standing children into groups, then ask for more sorting suggestions for other volunteers.

Adjustments: Encourage kindergarten and primary children to use fraction language when describing ways to sort classmates; perhaps two out of six are wearing blue, one out of six red, and three out of six other colors. Sort children's name tags by numbers of letters or in other ways. Suggest sorting experiences children can do at home.

Ongoing Assessment: Have the children describe the groups they make. Note children who might help less-confident classmates with sorting. Set up pair or small-group activities and let these children work together.

Let's imagine an extension of sorting for older children. During her second grade's unit on the grocery store, Miss Kenyon and parents collected many lids from jars, bottles, and other containers. She displayed the lids in a basket and invited groups of children to arrange them. As Kelli worked with the lids, she arranged them all with the hollow side up, then with the hollow side down. When Miss Kenyon asked, "Can you put them in groups?", Kelli made sets of large ones and small ones. Miss Kenyon invited Kelli to show Wanda what she was doing. Wanda had been stacking her lids and counting them. After listening to Kelli, she proceeded to arrange her lids in groups by size—large, medium, and small-sized lids.

As with any topic, children's sorting abilities vary. Miss Kenyon noticed that Donald often "wandered" from a sorting scheme he started. For example, he began arranging lids by size, but then started to focus on color. At times Miss Kenyon prompted him, saying, "Show me what you're doing . . . how can you stay with that way of sorting? . . . does this one belong in the large or small group?" At other times, she stood back and realized that Donald was not able to sustain his focus on one sorting attribute; this is not atypical for a child his age.

Miss Kenyon realized Horace and Denise needed a challenge, so she invited them to use centimeter rulers and set definitions for "small," "medium," and "large" categories that they were making. After some experimentation and discussion, Horace and Denise decided that their "small" group of lids would be those less than 5 centimeters across, "medium" would be lids about 5 to 10 centimeters, and "large" would be lids greater than 10 centimeters across. Horace and Denise enjoyed showing their groups of lids to others, "playing teacher" and helping others measure.

As children worked, the question, "What different ways can we sort the lids?" prompted more sorting: by color, shape, and material. Miss Kenyon made a list of the ways the children sorted, displayed it near the sorting center, and asked the children to show several ways of sorting in their math journals.

Finally, Miss Kenyon placed a large graphing mat on the floor for the children to place the lids in rows. As the children worked, they counted and compared the numbers of lids in their groups: more lids with writing than without, for example. They enjoyed Miss Kenyon's request, "After you're done, ask someone else questions about the way you sorted."

More ideas for sorting follow in "Secret Sorting Rules."

 ## SECRET SORTING RULES

This activity emphasizes reasoning and extends kindergarten and primary children's thinking about sorting.

Focus: Organizing data, reasoning, communicating.

What To Do: Use a collection of 8 to 10 toys, books, or objects from your desk drawer. Tell children to watch closely as you begin to sort the objects into two groups. Ask children to decide what the "secret" rule for sorting the objects is and raise their hands when they think they know what the rule is. As children raise their hands, let them tell in which group to place the next object, but ask them not to announce the rule. After many children seem to know the rule, let several explain their versions of the rule while others check.

Adjustments: Let children play the game in smaller groups, deciding on "secret rules" and leading the game.

Ongoing Assessment: Let children tell how they decided on sorting rules and whether they did a good job playing the game.

SOURCES OF DATA

Much data can be gathered about concrete materials; people's characteristics, personal experiences, and opinions provide other rich sources of data. Interesting information can also be found in a variety of print sources—books, catalogs, picture sets, magazines, reference books, newspapers, and other print media. Classroom experiences are rich in opportunities to predict, gather, and analyze data (Isaacs & Kelso, 1996; Jorgensen, 1996).

After reading *Each Orange Had 8 Slices* (Giganti, 1990), Miss Walton helped her four-year-olds wash and slice several oranges with plastic knives. She led the children in counting each orange's slices and recording the numbers. On subsequent days the children focused on other aspects of their snack foods—numbers of seeds in apples, grapes in small bunches, and sections in tangerines. Thus the children were exposed to much data about fruits through reading and hands-on experience.

 WHAT DO *YOU* THINK?

Children's past experiences, home settings, and cultures might provide rich sources of data. What could you do to facilitate children's organizing, displaying, and analyzing this data in the classroom?

Children might examine informational books such as almanacs, record books, or encyclopedias to find factual data. Books with pictures and words fit the varying levels and needs of children. For example, Usborne Books' series of factual books are appealing publications that contain a variety of unusual and intriguing facts for young children.

Mrs. Ross's first graders were studying animals. The children read and looked at pictures in a variety of books, then each drew a picture of an interesting idea. They wrote words on their pictures, dictated narration for Mrs. Ross to record, or used oral language to convey information. After the children had shared, Mrs. Ross suggested grouping the pictures by whether the interesting information concerned animals' appearance, habits, diet, or other areas. The children sorted their pictures, then bound them in a class book.

GRAPHS FOR YOUNG CHILDREN

Once data is collected and organized, it can be shared in many ways. Devices such as written narratives and illustrations present data; charts or organized lists display facts, figures, and pictures. Still another way to organize data is to display it on graphs. Used frequently today, graphs let people display much data in small spaces, offering vivid pictures of information.

Graphing votes is a realistic activity that engages children in communication and reasoning. To help children make independent choices, educators might let each child use one piece of paper or place one object on a graph; otherwise some may want to vote for every category. Teachers should stress each child making up his/her own mind about topics, rather than watching the graph-making process and voting for the "winner."

To this end, children might select graph markers or jot down their choices before seeing their classmates' votes. Voting could be introduced by sharing the book *The Day Gogo Went to Vote* (Sisulu, 1996).

Young children can be involved in making and interpreting several different kinds of graphs. A natural progression of introduction to types of graphs is starting with the real graph, then exploring picture and bar graphs. Children should start with graphs of just two categories, then use three or more categories for data. Second- and third-graders can make circle graphs showing small numbers of equal parts.

ASSESSMENT SUGGESTION: Checklist

As children engage in sorting activities, use a checklist with items such as the following to document their progress.

◆ Follows sorting scheme
◆ Suggests sorting schemes
◆ Describes basis for sorting and making decisions
◆ Is able to sort on a number of bases

"We're lining up the tie shoes and the buckle shoes."

Real Graphs

In a real graph, the most concrete type of graph, children arrange themselves or real objects in categories. For example, as they get acquainted, children might line up according to the numbers of children in their families—those with just one child, two children, three children, and four or more children. During cold weather four-year-olds could lay their "hand warmers" in piles—gloves and mittens—and compare the numbers. At any season, each might remove a shoe, place the shoes in piles, and compare the numbers of shoes with ridged, patterned, smooth, or other kinds of soles. "How Does Your Jacket Fasten?" describes another real graph.

 HOW DOES YOUR JACKET FASTEN?

Graphing clothing is interesting to children of any age.

Focus: Graphing, communicating, reasoning, connecting to the real world.

What To Do: On a chilly school day, have the children model their jackets and other cool weather garments. Discuss features of the garments and let the children demonstrate their fasteners—zippers, buttons, velcro, snaps, and drawstrings.

Ask the children how they might sort their garments—perhaps those with zippers and without. Arrange the garments in a clean place, or let the children hang them in your coat rack area, using the categories they have devised. Have the children help you make signs for the categories and count the numbers of garments.

Adjustments: Guide younger children to make just two graph categories. Invite the children to examine other aspects of their clothing and make more real graphs based on clothing features.

Ongoing Assessment: Have the children draw and write in their math journals about the experience.

Data should be displayed in both horizontal or vertical form. As children place objects (or themselves) on a real graph, they should start at a base line rather than placing objects in categories in random arrangements. Graph interpretation skills are fostered if groups of data are arranged starting at the left or bottom, the form used in most one-quadrant graphs (Figure 9.3).

Picture Graphs

Teachers must help children make the transition from real graphs to a less concrete graph form, the picture graph or pictograph. Instead of using real objects, picture graphs use representations of data. Miss Michaels, after noting her class's interest in the topic, How many people are in your family?, had her first-graders line up to form a real graph of

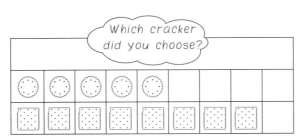

Horizontal graph format   Vertical graph format

Figure 9.3 *One-quadrant graphs.*

this data. After they counted the number in each category, she questioned, "If we sit down, can we remember all this? How can we show it to someone else?" The children suggested drawing pictures of themselves and their siblings.

Miss Michaels provided squares of paper for the children's pictures and they stood in categories holding their pictures. Miss Michaels helped the children compare their arrangement to the real graph they previously made. Next she had the children lay their pictures on the floor and verify the idea that the pictures showed the same information as their real graph.

Miss Michaels was pleased with the children's apparent understanding of the picture graph and planned several picture graph topics for the upcoming week: each child's favorite character in a story, the beverage chosen by each child for lunch, and each child's favorite lunch. Another day she let the children decide on the topic for their graph. The children made their picture graphs in several formats: another floor graph, pictures pinned to a bulletin board, and self-adhesive notes attached to a blank poster board. The children also made a "Photo-graph" as follows.

 PHOTO-GRAPHS

Use children's photographs for easy markers for picture graphs.

Focus: Graphing, communicating, connecting to everyday life.

What To Do: Take photos of children or photocopy their class pictures. Have each child mount his/her picture on a square of paper, adding a name to it. Use the photos as markers for a variety of picture graphs. Children might arrange their photo markers by month to represent their birthdays, or use the photo markers for a graph on preferences, perhaps favorite fruits or sandwiches.

Adjustments: Let the children suggest topics for picture graphs using their photo markers.

Ongoing Assessment: Observe children's reactions to graphing activities. Do they enjoy the experience and seem proud of the personalized markers? Does each show interest in graphing? Make notes for children's anecdotal records.

As a transition from pictures to more abstract forms, teachers can ask children to write names or symbols on squares of paper to be placed on a graph form. For example, they might count the number of pockets in their clothes and categorize the numbers as less than six, six, or more than six. Children might make a graph of favorite ball games by placing name tags on a form to show whether each prefers soccer, softball, or kickball.

Bar Graphs

Bar graphs show data in rows or column-like categories. They are not as concrete as real or picture graphs because the objects or people they represent are not shown specifically; rather they are represented with parts of a continuous bar. Teachers might use interlocking cubes to help children make a transition from real and picture graphs to bar graphs. Each child in a small group might pull five cubes out of a box containing red and green cubes. The children can then count their cubes of each color, join them together, and tell whether the numbers of red and green cubes are the same or whether one color appears more often than the other. Next the group might trace around their cubes, coloring in rectangles to represent the cubes and comparing their resulting "bar graphs." They can also make "Paper Bar Graphs" as described below.

 PAPER BAR GRAPHS

Using real-size bars is a concrete way of introducing children to bar graphs.

Focus: Graphing, measuring, problem solving, reasoning, communicating.

What To Do: Set up a learning center where children can cut strips of paper or paper adding machine tape to the sizes of real objects. Each might cut paper to the length of the writing instrument he/she is using, then tape it to a form to make a bar graph. For other bar graphs, children might help each other cut bars to represent the lengths of their arms, pointer fingers, or feet. Each can label the strip, then arrange the strips to form a bar graph. Work with children to establish titles for the graphs and to describe the results.

Adjustments: For beginners, limit the number of bars to five or six. Let the children decide on other topics for paper strip graphs.

Ongoing Assessment: Let the children help each other evaluate their paper strip graphs. Did you measure carefully? How? Did you check your measurements? How can you describe your graph?

Children can also color squares on predrawn graph forms to make bars of various lengths. For example, a teacher may help a pair of confident children develop a topic for a graph—What is your favorite kind of milk: Chocolate or white? The children can help to fill out a "poll" form such as the one shown in the photo, then using a clipboard, circulate among their classmates, letting each color in a choice. The poll takers can then present their findings to the class. Children can take turns conducting polls.

ASSESSMENT SUGGESTION: Portfolio

As children take polls, ask each to write and draw about the experience. Include their descriptions, as well as their poll forms, in their portfolios.

Circle Graphs

Circle graphs show parts of a whole. A circle is divided into sectors of sizes to show the proportions of its parts, which can be colored for easy size comparison. Young children should work with circles showing "easy" parts such as fourths, eighths and tenths. Because they show wholes and parts, working with circle graphs complements learning about fractions.

It's fun to act as a pollster and record opinions on a graph.

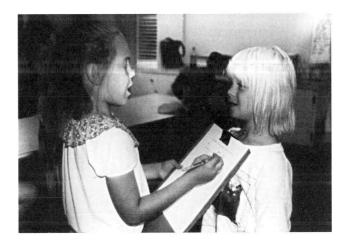

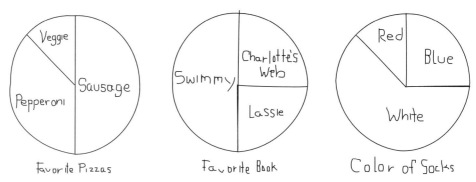

Figure 9.4   *Circle graphs.*

Kindergarten children can fold paper circles or paper plates into two, then four equal parts. The teacher can have the children count the sectors and establish that each sector is a fourth of the circle. Then the children might toss four coins and lay a coin on each fourth of the circle graph. As the children report their findings, teachers can encourage them to use fraction language—two out of four of my pennies were heads, for example. Children can then devise a color code, perhaps red for heads and blue for tails, and color in the sectors of their graphs. Other topics for circle graphs abound. Primary children might form groups of eight and make circle graphs to show some of their favorite things on circle graphs. They might make designs of eight blocks, then use circle graphs to show what kinds or what colors of blocks they used. For homework, children might question four or eight people, then use circle graphs to report their results. Several circle graphs are shown in Figure 9.4.

Children might work with partners to poll 10 classmates on a topic of their choice, then show the results on a teacher-drawn form. As Mrs. Ramirez's third graders did this, some of the topics they developed were toothpaste used, favorite baked potato topping, numbers of pets, whether classmates had aunts and uncles, and number of buttons on clothing. Another topic for a circle graph is described in "Chip Circle Graphs."

 CHIP CIRCLE GRAPHS

Do all chocolate chip cookies have the same number of chips? Kindergarten and primary children can graph their findings.

Focus: Graphing, counting, communicating, connecting to everyday life and to fractions.

What To Do: Provide a chocolate chip cookie, a paper towel, and a toothpick for each child. Ask the children to delay eating their cookies while you discuss predictions for the questions, How many chips might be in your cookie? or Will the cookies have the same number of chips? Record some predictions. Let the children work carefully to remove the chips. Have them count the chips and discuss the findings. Were all the numbers the same? Close? How can we explain the results?

Help the children work in groups of 8 or 10 and fill in circle graph forms of their data. Have them discuss the data, using fractions, then share their results and add written narratives.

Adjustments: Let the children compare different brands of cookies. Instead of circle graphs, show the results on bar or picture graphs.

Ongoing Assessment: Note which children understand the problem clearly, follow instructions, play leadership roles, and those who need support. Consider pairing these more and less confident children for future graphing activities.

Line Graphs

Line graphs show change over time or trend data. Sometimes they are called broken line graphs because they show line segments linking dots that represent numbers. Unless the numbers are the result of a constant trend, the line is made up of several segments. The broken lines show fluctuations in data, and often line-graph readers comment about "ups and downs" in the data.

Primary children might keep track of the number of students present each day. After showing this data on a bar graph, the teacher might introduce the idea of a line graph, making points on a graph form to show the numbers, then connecting these points with line segments rather than using bars. Bar graph and line graph formats for the same data are shown in Figure 9.5.

Other topics for line graphs might include temperatures over several days, amounts of money raised in a fund drive, or numbers of pieces of trash collected each day for a cleanup campaign.

"Graphing Software" offers a choice of formats for graphs.

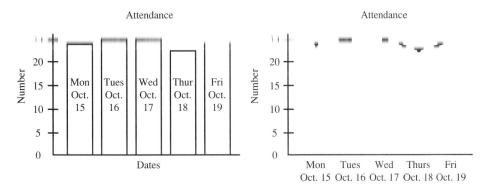

Figure 9.5 *Bar and line graphs.*

▲②③ GRAPHING SOFTWARE

Many simple-to-operate computer programs are available, adding a technological touch to children's work with graphs.

Focus: Graphing, using technology, problem solving, communicating, reasoning.

What To Do: Help children learn to use a graphing program. Typically they need to gather data; perhaps primary children could investigate different numbers of coins for a sum of money such as 45 cents. Children then enter their data as the program asks for it. In this case, numbers of each coin, a title, and names for the graph's categories. Demonstrate these steps, then let partners or small groups try to make graphs independently.

Adjustments: For preschool and kindergarten children, use a program that lets children "stamp" counters on a grid, making a graph-like arrangement on the screen.

Ongoing Assessment: Observe children's abilities to operate the computer. Note their attitudes—helpfulness, ability to explain to others, and willingness to share time and materials.

INTERPRETING DATA

Gathering and displaying data is interesting and valuable, but making sense of the data is also essential. Adults must stimulate children to interpret data they have collected, organized, and displayed.

Discussing Data

Talking about displays of data is a natural process. Questions such as, "What does this graph show?" and "Tell me some things about this data," invite children to answer in many ways. Open-ended questions such as these invite more answers than questions with single, simple answers: "How many pictures show animals? How many words in our list start with W?" After several answers to an open-ended question, the teacher may want to add focused questions such as: "How many more people marked _____ than _____?" or "How many people in all are shown on this graph?"

The teacher may also pose questions that require children to speculate beyond the data shown on a particular display. If children have graphed shoes in three categories—shoes with ties, shoes with velcro fasteners, and "others"—the teacher may pose a question such as, "How might the shoe store manager use our data?" or "If a child from another room walked in to visit us, what kind of shoe would you guess he/she might be wearing?" Such application or inferential questions are challenging, and they also let children glimpse reasons for data collection.

Writing About Data

After displaying data, children might write about it. Three- to five-year-olds might contribute ideas for a group composition. After reading the children's composition back to them, the teacher can post the story near the data display. To start their own writing, older children might work in groups, discuss several things to write about, then write individually or dictate their comments. Some children may enjoy writing on strips of paper or self-adhesive notes to post near a graph.

Another writing technique involves children writing questions for others to answer about a data display. In a primary classroom, several groups could poll their classmates on different topics. Each group could make a graph of results, then write questions for others to answer as they share their results. The questions can start oral discussions and might also be used for children to use to study and answer in writing.

Mathematics journal writing is a powerful technique to use for interpreting graphs as well as other math topics. Students might be asked to describe in their journals how they gathered and organized data and what they found out. Evaluative comments might address questions such as, "What was interesting about the process?" or "What parts were your best work?" For young children, drawings are a valuable part of journal writing, and sketches of graphs should be included in their journals.

Simple Statistics

When graphs and other data displays involve numerical data, kindergarten and primary children can learn to use simple statistical concepts to describe the data. Range, mode, and median are ideas that young children can easily grasp if they are presented informally and in concrete terms.

The *range* of a set of numerical data is the difference in the highest and lowest values. If second graders were studying families and found out their grandparent's ages, each child might write the ages on a piece of paper. The children could gather around a table and lay out their papers. The teacher might ask, "How can we organize all this information?", then illustrate the range concept by guiding the children to order their numbers from youngest to oldest ages. In describing what they see, the phrase "The ages range or go from 39 to 65" might emerge. Second- and third-grade children could also calculate the difference using subtraction and say, "There's a range or difference of 26 years." To compare ranges, children might write and arrange their own ages and see that the difference between their oldest and youngest ages is less than their grandparents' ages (Figure 9.6).

Another simple statistical concept, *mode*, is easy for children to see and understand. The mode is the most-frequently occurring value or values in

Figure 9.6 *Graphic representations help children identify the
mode.*

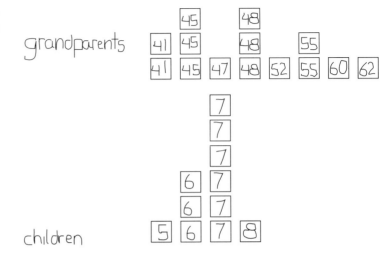

a set of data. The mode—7—of second graders' ages is obvious above; children often say it "sticks out the most." Sets of data may have more than one mode—for the grandparents' ages, both 45 and 48 are modes.

The *median* is the middle value in a set of numerical data; it gives an idea of a typical value. Like the range and mode, the median can be picked out visually. For the set of numbers that are shown below—the number of buttons on children's garments—the children might be able to see that the median is "somewhere close to 4 or 5." Children might start at both ends of the numbers, eliminating values two at a time: the median is not 0 or 12; it's not 0 or 11; it's not 1 or 9, and so on. If they move papers with the numerals on them slightly as they seek the middle number, the median—4—becomes even more visually clear.

$$0\ 0\ 1\ 1\ 1\ 2\ 3\ 4\ \underset{\uparrow}{4}\ 5\ 6\ 6\ 7\ 8\ 9\ 11\ 12$$
median

Children can work with these statistical ideas as part of interpreting any set of numerical data, even if the terms are not used formally. The *mean,* or arithmetic average of a set of numbers, is best reserved for older children who work routinely with division.

PROBABILITY

"We can probably rent a movie this weekend." "It sure looks like rain." "Chances are, we'll be at grandma's by six o'clock." Statements like these are made and heard by almost every young child. They deal with probability or chance, ideas that occur often in our world. Because of its usefulness, relevance, and intrinsic interest, the authors of the *Curriculum*

Standards include the idea that K–4 children should "explore concepts of chance" (NCTM, 1989, p. 54). The *Curriculum Standards* authors point out that ideas of chance occur often in social studies and science, so including them in the mathematics curriculum not only links math and other areas, it also presents a broad view of mathematics. Work with probability offers opportunities for children to explore and discover mathematical ideas, recommended by NAEYC (1993), in investigating occurrences.

But isn't probability too "deep" a subject for youngsters? Perhaps it is for preschool children, but if approached with a spirit of "let's find out" and activities that let children explore and experiment, kindergarten and primary children can learn many things about probability. For example, to start his kindergarten children working with chance, Mr. Bonner talked to the children and helped them make a chart of things that will happen "for sure," things that might happen, and things that couldn't happen in our real world. Among the things the children named that were sure to happen were: it will get dark tonight and a book will fall when dropped. The children named many things that might happen: we will have pizza for lunch this week, we might play in the block center, and Mr. Bonner will read us a story today. After Mr. Bonner asked for things that could never really happen, they added these ideas: dogs never talk with words, cats never fly with wings, and neither do people.

To "explore ideas of chance" as recommended in the NCTM standards (1989), children might work with materials such as number cubes, mystery bags, spinners, and coins. After experimentation with the materials, educators can ask the children to work in a cycle that includes *predicting* outcomes, *testing* predictions, and *keeping track* of results. Children might also make graphs of the data they have gathered. In discussion of the results, they should explain why they think their results happened and make more refined predictions for subsequent activities. As the children work, educators should remember to keep the focus on *exploration of ideas* rather than on theoretical explanations about occurrences.

Let's look at this cycle in Miss Carter's second grade. As children were using coins while setting up a class store, each child worked with a handful of coins. They examined both sides of the coins. Miss Carter encouraged the children to make statements about their coins and notice their heads and tails. Miss Carter asked the children to shake their coins in their hands, drop them on the table top, then see if the heads and tails had changed. A lively discussion ensued.

After the children had established that their numbers of coins did not change, but that their coins might land on heads or tails, Miss Carter focused their attention on predicting. She asked that each child in the group choose one coin to work with and plan to toss it 10 times. She drew a chart to record predictions and results.

The children worked in pairs; each child made 10 tosses. They took turns telling their numbers of heads as Miss Carter recorded their responses.

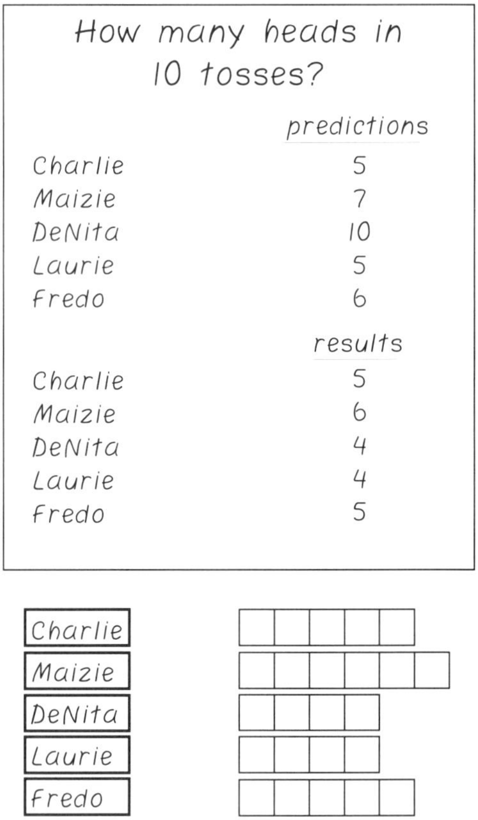

Figure 9.7 Converting data to
a concrete graph shows children
the connection between numbers and graphic representations.

How many heads in 10 tosses?

	predictions
Charlie	5
Maizie	7
DeNita	10
Laurie	5
Fredo	6

	results
Charlie	5
Maizie	6
DeNita	4
Laurie	4
Fredo	5

Charlie
Maizie
DeNita
Laurie
Fredo

Miss Carter next had each child use unifix cubes to show the number of heads. They arranged their cubes to make a bar-like graph (Figure 9.7).

Miss Carter said, "We got lots of 4s and 5s and 6s, but never all 10 heads. Why do you think this happened?" As children offered various explanations, Billy's was insightful: "Well, it might be heads and it might be tails—one happens about the same as the other. Each has the same chance, so all of them being heads won't happen very often."

Since several of the children seemed interested in pursuing the activity, Miss Carter invited any who wished to continue to record predictions and results on the chart. Debby and Seth stayed with the coin tossing activity a long time. They tallied their total numbers of heads and tails; their final chart showed impressive numbers—185 heads and 191 tails.

Primary children can use other materials to investigate many different aspects of chance. Partners might use pairs of spinners labeled with numbers 1–10 and see if they get more even numbers or odd numbers. They might use the same spinners for a "Target 60" game, where they take the numbers of interlocking cubes shown on the spinners and link them together until each reaches a total of 60.

Common materials such as string and tape can be used to explore chance. Jones, Langrall, and Thornton (1996) describe attaching tape of two or more colors to the ends of pieces of yarn. The yarn is then draped over a board so that the tape does not show. Children pull two strings and reveal the colors at the end. If they match, it's a "win." After trying the game and determining how often they win, children might discuss whether the game is "fair" or not.

Using number cubes can lead to many investigations, such as using two cubes and seeing whether the numbers match or not after the cubes are tossed. Will the numbers match on each toss of the cubes? Will they ever match? What matches are possible? Children could use one number cube for ones and another cube to represent tens. After rolling both cubes, they can talk about the resulting two-digit numbers they get and represent the numbers with base-10 blocks as well as numerals.

Dice with 10 faces are available; if their faces are labeled with 0–9, then any two-digit number can be represented. Children can use these dice, predict whether they will roll more numbers under 10, 10–19, 20–29, and so on, then conduct 30 or 40 trials. They can use hundreds charts and mark the numbers they roll, then check their predictions when they analyze the results. "Mystery Bags" suggests another kind of probability activity: sampling.

 ## MYSTERY BAGS

Sampling a bag of objects is suspenseful and sets the stage for kindergarten and primary children to learn more about chance.

Focus: Probability, communicating, reasoning.

What To Do: Prepare an opaque bag with one red and nine black cubes inside. Tell the children that the bag contains 10 cubes of two colors, but do not tell them what the colors are or how many of each are inside. Let the children take turns pulling one cube at a time from the bag, showing the cube's color to their classmates, then returning the cube to the bag, and shaking it.

You or a child might record the results. At intervals, ask questions such as, "How many reds do you think are in the bag now? What about blacks? Why do you think so? Do you think the bag has any greens? After all the children have had a turn to choose and show a cube, show the bag's contents. Let the children explain why they think they got the results.

Adjustments: Use different proportions of colors and different objects in the bag. Invite the children to prepare "mystery bags" for their peers to sample.

Ongoing Assessment: Observe the children to gauge their interest and understanding. Do they propose reasonable guesses? Do they adjust their guesses according to the samples they see? Can they keep track of the results?

ASSESSMENT SUGGESTION: Self-Assessment

As children work with ideas of chance, have them discuss their work and feelings about it. Are the topics interesting? How do they relate to real life? Do the children understand the ideas? What other ideas would they like to explore? What aspects are harder and easier?

 WHAT DO *YOU* THINK?

If teachers model appropriate behaviors and attitudes, they set good examples and high expectations for children. Using this chapter's material, brainstorm how you, as a teacher, could model dispositions such as persistence, curiosity, enthusiasm, and cooperation as you help children work with data or chance.

SUMMARY

Working with data and chance are interesting, appropriate topics in mathematics for young children. These topics are part of a broad curriculum as advocated by the NCTM. Work with data, a necessary part of math literacy in our modern world, can begin with sorting and keeping track of ongoing occurrences.

Starting in preschool and through the primary grades, work with data involves gathering, organizing, and displaying information and interpreting it. Young children should begin exploring ideas of chance in kindergarten and extend their notions of probability in the primary grades. As children become involved in activities to promote their understanding of data and chance, they use problem solving, reasoning, and communication abilities constantly. The skills and understanding gained can be applied to almost any curricular area and to the real world.

◆ *APPLICATIONS: THINKING AND PROBLEM SOLVING*

Apply and extend things you have learned in this chapter by completing one or more of the following options and sharing it with others—children or adults.

1. Choose a topic related to your everyday life and gather data on the topic for a period of three or more days. You might keep track of the

fat grams you consume or the numbers of vegetables you eat. If you are feeling tired, getting a handle on how many hours you sleep would be useful. Make a form for gathering your data. Plan time each day to recall and record your data. Display and share your data with an appropriate audience.

2. Adult-made sorting and graphing mats help children organize their thinking, but making different mats for every activity is time consuming. Make two or more reusable sorting or graphing mats to use for several different activities with young children. Use them with children, then display your mats for colleagues.

3. Carry out an activity with young children in which you involve the children in sorting, organizing data, and graphing. Try to use an interesting topic or one to fit in with what children are studying. Plan some questions to stimulate discussion and interpretation of the graph. Write up your results or take a photo of the children and their results.

4. Like other math topics for young children, working with data and probability have the potential for enhancing children's problem-solving, communicating, and reasoning abilities, and for connecting to everyday life. Consider an activity from this chapter or devise one. List at least 10 ways that children's skills and understandings in these four areas can be strengthened. Share your list with a colleague, improve and revise it, then present it to a larger group for their comments.

5. Find library books and other print materials for children to use as data sources. Plan ways for children to find information from the books, translate it into another form such as pictures, then organize the data on a chart, graph, or other display. Carry out some of your ideas with young children. Write up or photograph your results and share them with colleagues.

6. Writers from the Wisconsin Center for Education Research (1994) report that little research has been done on teaching and learning statistics in elementary school. Take this idea as a challenge and plan how to investigate some aspect of working with statistics with young children. Carry out a short term study. Share your findings with colleagues, or extend your study and write for publication an article about your findings.

◆ REFERENCES

American Statistical Association. (1989). *Quantitative literacy series.* Palo Alto, CA: Dale Seymour Publications.

Bredekamp, S. (1993). *Developmentally appropriate practice in early childhood programs serving children from birth through age 8.* Washington, DC: NAEYC.

Giganti, P. (1990). *Each orange had 8 slices*. White Plains, NY: Cuisenaire Company of America.

Isaacs, A. C., Kelso, C. R. (1996). Pictures, tables, graphs, and questions: statistical processes. *Teaching Children Mathematics, 2*(6), 340–345.

Jones, G. R., Langrall, C. W., & Thornton, C. (1996). Using data to make decisions about chance. *Teaching Children Mathematics, 2*(6), 346–350.

Jorgensen, B. (1996). Hamster math: authentic experiences in data collection. *Teaching Children Mathematics, 2*(6), 336–339.

National Council of Teachers of Mathematics. (1989). *Curriculum and evaluation standards for school mathematics.* Reston, VA: Author.

Russell, S. J., Cirwin, R. B., Freil, S. N., Mokros, J. R., & Stone, A. (1992). *Used numbers.* Boston: Lesley College Technical Educational Research Centers.

Sisulu, E. B. (1996). *The day Gogo went to vote.* Boston: Little Brown.

Wisconsin Center for Education Research. (1994). *NCRMSE research review: integrating statistics into the school curriculum.* Madison, WI: Author.

◆ SELECTED CHILDREN'S BOOKS

Bresler, Lynn. (1987). *The Usborne Book of Facts and Lists: Records, Lists, Facts, Comparisons.* London: Usborne Publishing. This book presents a variety of interesting factual data using realistic pictures and words.

Giganti, Paul. (1990). *Each Orange Had 8 Slices.* White Plains, NY: Cuisenaire Company of America. The beautifully designed pictures of this book invite discussion and exploration of shapes, sizes, and fractions.

Miller, Margaret. (1992). *Where Does It Go?* New York: Greenwillow. This book, suitable for even the youngest learners, shows photos of familiar objects and invites readers to tell what set each belongs to.

My First Look at Sorting. (1991). New York: Random House. With clear, colorful photographs of common objects, this book challenges young readers to figure out objects that don't belong, match identical objects, and find pairs.

Mysteries and Marvels of Nature. (1989). London: Usborne Publishing. This book is packed with facts about animals, plants, and places. Vivid pictures and brief descriptions convey information.

Reid, Margarette. (1990). *The Button Box.* New York: Dutton Children's Books. Pastel drawings show a boy exploring his grandmother's button collection and sorting buttons in many ways. The sorting schemes could be applied to other materials.

Sisulu, Elinor Batzat. (1996). *The Day Gogo Went to Vote.* Boston: Little Brown. In this realistic, lavishly-illustrated book, a young South African girl accompanies her grandmother in the first multi-racial election ever held in that country.

Geometry

◆◆

A teacher of four-year-olds observes that Kenisha, Gracie, and Lawrence play regularly together in the block center whenever they have a choice of activities. They build large structures and are remarkably cooperative as they work. Is this "just play" or should their teacher use their interest as an opportunity to teach the children some things about geometry? If she tries to do so, what concepts and skills should she start with?

Astrong, balanced mathematics program for young children includes much work with geometry. The authors of the *Curriculum and Evaluation for School Mathematics Standards* (National Council of Teachers of Mathematics [NCTM], 1989) state, "Children are naturally interested in geometry and find it intriguing and motivating; their spatial capacities often exceed their numerical skills, and tapping these strengths can foster an interest in mathematics and improve number understandings and skills" (p. 48). Geometry builds children's problem-solving and reasoning abilities, developing spatial sense, an essential ability for writing, following directions, and visualizing objects (Bruni & Seidenstein, 1990).

Geometry helps with communication too. Knowledge of geometry concepts enables people to interpret pictures and graphics (Hoffer & Hoffer, 1992). Children's work with geometry sets the foundation for later, more formal experiences and for the geometry they will encounter in the world and in their future occupations (Van de Walle, 1994).

To make sense of the world, humans rely on perceptions of space, shapes, and patterns. Nature, as well as designs and artifacts made by people, embodies geometric forms. Geometry for young children can help them interpret, understand, and appreciate their world. As children work with positions in space and three- and two-dimensional objects, they gain implicit knowledge of forms and relationships.

Work with geometry can be active, involving, and multisensory; it is very suitable for young children. Some children excel in work with numbers, others "shine" in work with geometry and spatial sense. Many learners find enjoyment and beauty in their work with geometry. Despite preferences, without ideas of both quantity and space, mathematics is incomplete.

Geometry plays a more prominent role in the mathematics curriculum in other countries than in our own. Geometry should not be considered an "add-on" or enrichment topic, rather it is an important and integral part of the mathematics curriculum.

WHAT DO *YOU* THINK?

"Geometry . . . should be a central topic throughout school mathematics curricula. Unfortunately this is not always the case. In many schools the geometry chapter is delayed until the end of the school year. . . . It is no wonder that [international comparisons] found geometry achievement in the U.S. ranks in the bottom 25 percent of all countries . . . because many students have never had the opportunity to learn these important ideas" (Hoffer & Hoffer, 1992, p. 249). Was your study of geometry minimal, as described? Share some recollections of geometry when you were a child.

How might the classroom look as young children are engaged in the developmentally appropriate study of geometry? Let's look in on a first-grade classroom as children focus on triangles in a unit on "shapes." In a large group, the children show examples and sketches of triangular objects found at home. Bethany comments that she and her mother found triangles in their drapes' designs. Harry describes triangles in a quilt pattern. The children share other examples such as crackers, door stops, wedges of cheese and cabbage, shelf braces, tops of buildings, and rafters. Mrs. Washington, their teacher, shows magazine pictures of windows; the children locate some triangular windows.

Mrs. Washington next leads a short activity where the children work with partners. One arranges geobands to form a triangle on her geoboard, then hides it. The partner tries to copy the shape and the children compare the results. They talk about the sizes and positions of their designs. The partners then switch roles and make more triangles to be copied.

Mrs. Washington asks the children how they could sort their geoboard triangles. Kerry says that all the geoboards belong in just one pile because they're triangles, but Jose suggests sorting them as large and small triangles. Jose leads his classmates in making these two sets, and the children count and compare the numbers in each set. Jamie suggests that they make sets of designs that go "straight across" and those that don't. The children rearrange their geoboard triangles in this new scheme.

Mrs. Washington moves the children into small-group activities, showing the children several learning center activities: continuation of work with geoboards, making triangles with three, four, five, six, seven, and eight toothpicks, looking for more examples of triangles in magazines and newspapers, and pressing small blocks into modeling dough and examining the imprints.

After the children have worked for about 30 minutes, Mrs. Washington asks them to describe some of the things they noticed and learned. The children offer several ideas. Since some seem interested in the discoveries made by others, Mrs. Washington announces that they may use the materials again later in the day. After the children straighten and clean up the materials, they write and draw for several minutes in the books they have been making—"All About Shapes." As they work, Mrs. Washington circulates, asks several children to clarify or expand on their writing, and comments on their drawings. She is pleased with the children's interest in shapes and the ways they express themselves with oral language, pictures, and written words.

This vignette illustrates some of the in-depth, active, investigative work young children use to explore geometry. Such classroom work lets children use reasoning and problem solving as they make models, discuss and compare results, and find examples of geometric ideas in the real world. The teacher moves among the groups facilitating involvement with materials and asking questions as recommended by the National Association for the Education of Young Children (NAEYC) (Bredekamp, 1993).

What principles and theory should guide educators' as they plan experiences with geometry? The following sections will provide guidance, direction, and examples of learning activities.

GEOMETRY FOR YOUNG CHILDREN

The NCTM *Curriculum Standards* (1989) include the following about teaching geometry to young children:

> In grades K–4, the mathematics curriculum should include two- and three-dimensional geometry so that students can

♦ describe, model, draw, and classify shapes;

♦ investigate and predict the results of combining, subdividing, and changing shapes;

♦ develop spatial sense;

♦ relate geometric ideas to number and measurement ideas;

♦ recognize and appreciate geometry in their world (NCTM, 1989, p. 48).

Describing the role geometry plays in helping children develop mathematical thinking skills, the authors stress the value of investigative, hands-on experiences.

Meaningful work with geometry can also help to alleviate children's misconceptions about geometric ideas. For example, children may believe that only equilateral triangles, with horizontal baselines, are triangles. They may think that every four-sided figure is a square (Clements & Battista, 1992). Children need exposure to a variety of shapes and orientations of these shapes, as well as time to discuss and make figures to help them advance their thinking about geometry.

As they facilitate children's work with geometry, teachers can expose children to many vocabulary words. They can introduce and model the use of precise terms such as "prism," "cylinder," "sphere," and "octagon," while also accepting children's use of more common terms such as "box," "can," "ball," and "stop sign."

MATERIALS FOR INVOLVING YOUNG CHILDREN IN GEOMETRY

Meaningful work with geometry involves use of a variety of concrete materials to embody concepts and to allow creativity in modeling ideas. The idea of materials for exploring geometric ideas is not new. Frederick Froebel, inventor of the term "kindergarten," created "geometrical gifts" or shapes for children's use. Such materials, relevant to real life, are more meaningful to children than are workbooks, flashcards, and ditto sheets

(Bredekamp, 1993). For example, to pursue the idea that four-sided figures can assume different shapes, children might use magnet strips, arranging them on a magnet board to represent shapes around them, then compare and share their figures.

Geoboards, wooden and plastic models, pattern blocks, mirrors, and tangrams are examples of multiuse materials to stimulate children's thinking. Geoboards feature 25 pegs around which children can arrange rubber geobands to make designs. Flat and three-dimensional models of figures such as rectangles, squares, prisms, and cylinders can be touched, rearranged, and compared to real-world objects. Pattern blocks, manufactured in plastic, wood, or rubbery "manipulite," are designed to fit together to make a variety of designs. They typically feature yellow hexagons, red trapezoids, blue diamonds, orange squares, green triangles, and tan diamonds. Children can use small mirrors to reflect designs and check for symmetry. Tangrams, seven pieces that fit together to form other shapes, are based on an ancient Chinese puzzle.

Classroom supplies such as clay, modeling dough, blocks, poster board, hole punchers, toothpicks, and yarn let children make models and other representations of geometric concepts. Children can arrange, manipulate, describe, sort, and explore real-world objects such as cans, boxes, and balls.

THEORY FOR TEACHING GEOMETRY TO YOUNG CHILDREN

What theoretical background can help as educators plan and implement geometry lessons? The work of van Hieles and Del Grande, described in the following sections, offers guidance.

The van Hieles Model

The late Dina van Hiele-Geldof and her husband Pierre van Hiele were Dutch educators who studied people's development of geometric ideas and described sequential stages of understanding. Rather than being a function of age, the van Hieles pictured the stages as a function of experience and education. They posited that although students may memorize material and discuss it in a rote fashion, true understanding does not result until students have experienced certain phases of instruction (Clements & Battista, 1992; Fuys, Geddes, & Tischler, 1988). Descriptions of the van Hiele levels of geometric thought are included in the following section. More detail is provided for levels 0 and 1, the levels of most young children.

Level 0—Visualization
In this basic level, learners recognize and are able to name figures according to general, holistic impressions of the figures. They perceive figures as wholes; they may identify a triangle "because it looks like one." They

may think a shape is no longer a triangle when it is moved to an "upside down" position.

In level 0 children can learn to name geometric figures. They can match figures that are alike and can copy figures—from geoboards to geopaper, for example. They can sort or classify figures on the basis of their overall appearance. Four- and five-year-olds may make a set of rectangles and say that the rectangles all go together because they "look alike" or because they are "shaped like doors." Learners at level 0 do not exhibit explicit knowledge of attributes of shapes. That is, level 0 learners would not describe a door as having four square corners, and two longer and two shorter sides.

In level 0, learners should have many experiences using physical models of figures and making models with many materials. They might compare balls of various sizes to objects such as oranges or grapefruits. Level 0 learners should add to and subdivide figures, manipulating materials such as tiles, blocks, and paper polygons, using them to form designs and patterns.

Clements and Battista (1992) describe a level of understanding even more basic than the van Hiele level 0. Children at this level lack the perceptual ability to form appropriate visual images to let them reconstruct figures after seeing the figures. Clements and Battista call this level *pre-recognition.* At this level, children may be unable to identify common shapes. They may distinguish between figures that are curved and linear, but they do not make distinctions among figures in each class. That is, they may recognize that an oval is different from a triangle, but may not differentiate a triangle from a square. Many three-year-olds are at this stage. Adults should not press them to make recognizable drawings or paintings and to name everything they create (Bredekamp, 1993).

Level 1—Analysis
At this stage learners are able to move beyond holistic impressions of shapes and focus on attributes of figures. They should continue to work with and construct models and classify figures on the basis of their attributes. For example, first-grade children, after exploring the idea that many things have square corners, could make sets of figures with square corners and those without. They could group three-dimensional figures by their number of faces (flat surfaces) or corners. The same first graders might be able to see that "boxes" have six faces, while cylinders have just two circular faces and another curved surface.

As children on level 1 describe figures, they are likely to name many properties of the figures rather than the minimum number of properties needed to define each figure. For example, a child may describe a rectangle as having "4 sides and 4 right angles and 2 longer sides and 2 shorter sides" rather than defining it in the briefest way: as a "parallelogram with 1 right angle." Educators should accept this extended kind of definition. They might actually help children focus on figures' many attributes by displaying models and asking children to list as many properties as possible for each model.

Level 1 learners are not able to work very successfully with classes of figures and their relationships. For example, although a learner at level 1 recognizes and discusses characteristics of squares and rectangles, he/she does not ordinarily understand that squares are special rectangles—they are rectangles with the additional requirement that all sides are equal. In a similar way, a level 1 learner may not realize that sets of right triangles and isosceles triangles have many members in common: right isosceles triangles.

Level 1 learners must continue to work with models, but educators should help them focus on and solve problems with properties of the figures. Students can sort figures according to their characteristics and compare the properties of two or more shapes. Six-year-olds might use attribute blocks and make sets and subsets of blocks that are alike—large triangles and small triangles, large circles and small circles, and so on. They might use three or four blocks to play a "one of these doesn't belong" game, supporting their judgments of shapes with common properties and those without the properties.

Children at level 1 should describe the features of figures and match shapes with written or oral descriptions of the shapes. They can recognize and describe the attributes of classes of figures. With a small group of first graders who seemed to be functioning in van Hiele's level 1, Mrs. Turner played "Show Me." They used sets of precut paper shapes; each child's shapes were different. As Mrs. Turner asked the children to "show me a shape with a square corner" or "show me a shape with two equal sides," she found that children not only examined their own shapes to find examples, they glanced around, checking the shapes that groupmates offered. The children soon began to ask each other for shapes; the game became child-directed.

Level 2—Informal Deduction
At this level learners construct relationships between classes of figures. They make logical conclusions and can follow simple, logical proofs. Level 2 learners develop and use definitions that are not redundant. Most young children do not reach this level, although concrete exploratory experiences and communication about properties and relationships lay the groundwork for work on level 2.

Level 3—Formal Deduction
This is the level of traditional high school geometry in which learners use formal logic, develop proofs based on axioms and theorems, use abstract definitions, and make formal arguments about relationships.

Level 4—Rigor
Mathematicians work on this level; it includes elaborating on and comparing axiomatic systems.

Clements and Battista (1992) state that people may be on different van Hiele levels for different topics. For example, a person may operate on level 1 when working with two-dimensional figures, but on level 0 with three-dimensional figures. When exploring new concepts, learners may lapse back to lower-level thinking. In any group of children, individuals are likely to be on different levels in their geometric thinking. Therefore it is important for educators to offer a variety of engaging activities that might be completed successfully whether learners are on one level or another.

Del Grande's Aspects of Spatial Perception

Canadian educator John Del Grande offers useful ideas on spatial perception. He defines spatial perception as "the ability to recognize and discriminate stimuli from space and interpret those stimuli by associating them with previous experiences" (Del Grande, 1987, p. 126). Recognizing that even young children have had years of experience in the three-dimensional world, Del Grande (1990) underscores the importance of spatial perception in geometry. He describes seven spatial abilities that seem to have strong relationships to academic development and to the development of geometry ideas.

Eye-motor coordination is the ability to synchronize vision and body movements. It is important in drawing, arranging figures, and manipulating materials. Working with a variety of materials will enhance eye-motor coordination. Without this ability, children's movements are clumsy, their attention is absorbed by the physical aspects of a task and they cannot focus on geometric aspects of a situation.

Figure-ground perception, recognizing figures embedded in a background, is used in work with overlapping figures and pictures with "hidden" parts. Having children complete and color around figures is a valuable experience.

Perceptual constancy is the ability to recognize that "a figure has invariant properties such as size and shape in spite of the variability of its impression as seen from a different viewpoint" (Del Grande, 1987, p. 128). This ability lets people recognize shapes regardless of their positions. To develop this ability, children can arrange objects and view them from different positions.

Position-in-space perception concerns the relationship of one object to another and to the observer. It includes "rotations and reversals of whole figures, change of position in detail, and mirror patterns" (Del Grande, 1987, p. 131). Children use position in space when they differentiate among letters such as *b, d, p,* and *q.*

Perception of spatial relationships is closely related to position in space. It involves people seeing two or more objects in relation to other objects, and requires them to perceive effects that motions or transformations such as slides and flips have on shapes. As children make patterns by flipping or turning over paper shapes, they are working with perceptual relationships.

Visual discrimination involves noting similarities and differences between objects and figures. As children sort objects, visual discrimination is important. Children may find like figures or pick out unlike ones—circles from a group of squares, for example.

Visual memory or recalling objects or designs that are no longer in view is the final spatial ability. To promote this ability, children might work in pairs with geoboards. One can make a simple design, show it to his partner for several seconds, then hide the shape. The partner then tries to copy the design from memory. As the partners compare shapes, they can check for perceptual constancy and positions in space of their figures.

Del Grande recommends that educators recognize the need to develop children's spatial abilities as they plan learning activities. Processing visual information is important and should be "integrated into a well-rounded program that takes into account the child's total development" (Del Grande, 1987, p. 135).

GEOMETRY TOPICS FOR YOUNG CHILDREN

The following sections present geometry topics appropriate for young children. Included are activities that allow children to work with important ideas and ways to assess children's learning.

Geometry in the World

Drawing children's attention to geometric shapes and examples of geometric concepts in the environment is important. Through repeated experiences

"These match." Many aspects of spatial sense can be developed as children work with geoboards.

that increase their awareness of the geometry around them, children see the beauty and usefulness of geometry.

Opportunities to focus on geometric concepts abound in the early childhood classroom. As preschoolers work at the sand table, they can create and describe flat, curved, and bumpy surfaces. They can press objects into dry and slightly damp sand and see what imprints remain. The children can make straight and curvy paths or roads in their creative play and games. "Shapes on the Playground" offers more sources of geometry.

 ## SHAPES ON THE PLAYGROUND

What better place to look for a variety of shapes than on the school playground?

Focus: Geometry, three- and two-dimensional shapes, positions and paths, connecting to the real world.

What To Do: On the playground children of any age can locate various shapes. Perhaps supports for the swing, climbers, and other equipment have circular, triangular, and rectangular parts. The children might be able to find geometric shapes on the paved surfaces. They can describe the edges of the playground and the paved surfaces as they walk, hop, and run along the edges.

Adjustments: Show children how to play "Run and Find It." A leader gives an instruction such as, run and find something straight, then the group scatters and each holds onto something straight. The leader checks them, then chooses a new leader.

Ongoing Assessment: Let children self-evaluate their work, discussing questions such as, Did you cooperate? Did you look hard for shapes? Can you suggest other things to look for?

An important part of the children's world is books. Many books have potential for geometric concepts. An educator might start by reading a book like *Butterflies* (Bailey & Butterworth, 1991) and have the children discuss what they noticed in the pictures. The book shows many symmetrical views of butterflies. This might lead to noticing and making a list of symmetrical things in the classroom, or things with straight and curvy parts. The children could draw pictures and write about them, then bind their work together to make a book like *Butterflies*. Assessment suggestions for a book-making project follow.

 ## ASSESSMENT SUGGESTION:
Product Analysis, Self-Evaluation

Check a product such as a child-made book by looking through it for pertinent examples. Are ideas creative? Have children found unusual examples or decorated the book in unique ways? Talk to the children about your observations, or for children who can read, write narrative comments. Let children show parts of the book they like best and share ideas for subsequent books.

Shape walks at school and in the neighborhood let children find examples of many geometric ideas—traffic and street signs, buildings, and natural objects. Children can take clipboards and draw pictures of the things they find. Shape walks can have a theme such as looking for rectangles, for shapes with square corners, for tesselated surfaces, or for round things—circles, spheres, and others. Shape hunts can also extend to children's homes.

WHAT DO *YOU* THINK?

Where in your community can you find common and unusual examples of geometric shapes? What workers or hobbyists can act as resource persons to share their work with shapes? List 5 to 10 ideas.

Positions and Paths

Children's school work with geometry is based on prior experience of moving about in a three-dimensional world. Children are expected to follow directions that use positional words such as over and under, up and down, and right, left, and middle. Educators can help children refine

Children can find many examples of geometry on a shape walk.

their understanding and usage of positional words by leading games using positional words—perhaps a version of "Simon Says" with children placing a toy or marker in various positions.

A book such as *Abuela* (Dorras, 1991), with its fanciful flying characters, can be used to introduce the children to the idea of looking down at objects and talking about what they see. Such a bird's-eye view is the basis for mapping. To develop the idea of mapping, children might use a large, flat box to create a three-dimensional map or model of the classroom. They might talk about and try to represent the basic shape of the classroom, then add details such as rugs and tables. Such a project involves much adjustment to properly place objects.

Even the youngest children can enhance their spatial sense. "Here To There" offers several possibilities.

 HERE TO THERE

Exploring ways of getting around lets children of any age illustrate positional words, and develop the concept of paths.

Focus: Geometry, paths, positional words, connecting to language arts and to everyday life.

What To Do: Introduce the topic by talking to the children about the "paths" they take in the classroom—from the coat area to their seats, or from the bookshelf to the reading table. For an indoor game, let the children show how to move from one place in the classroom to another in several different ways. As they do so, have their classmates use descriptive words to describe the paths: Are they straight? Curved? Were corners turned? How did the child move—fast, slow, up high, down low? Have children discuss and demonstrate paths for getting to places in the school. With choices of many paths from one place to another, which path is better to take? Why?

Adjustments: Help the children create paths outdoors, filling milk cartons with water and placing them to outline a long path. Let the children traverse the path many ways—running, skipping, or walking backwards.

Ongoing Assessment: Note whether the children can follow instructions that involve movements along paths. Can they describe the paths using words such as straight, curved, zigzag?

Three-Dimensional Figures

Children's work with geometric figures might begin with three-dimensional shapes, the kind found most in life. Children can gather objects from the classroom and sort them many ways—large, small, and medium ones; shapes that roll and don't roll; objects that stack easily and those that don't; things with flat surfaces, curved surfaces, and a combination of surfaces. Children four years and older might describe a collection of three-dimensional shapes and sort them by shape names—ones round like a ball or "spheres" and those not spheres; those that are like boxes or "prisms" and those that are not.

Getting a feel for three-dimensional shapes as well as looking at them is important. To introduce three-dimensional shapes to his four-year-old class, Mr. Arento prepared a mystery bag with several blocks and balls inside. He displayed similar shapes outside the bag and invited the children to take turns feeling inside the bag and finding shapes like the ones he designated. Children described the shapes they found in the bag; later several played the game independently.

To extend their work with three-dimensional shapes, children can use the shapes to make and extend patterns, a problem-solving experience. Classroom blocks as well as other objects can be used for patterning. Examples of simple patterns to start with are cube, cylinder, cube, cylinder, . . . , or long block, pyramid block, pyramid block, long block, pyramid, pyramid, and so on.

Children can make models of three-dimensional shapes using clay or modeling dough. They might predict what the impressions will look like if they press plastic and wooden shapes into clay or dough, then check the results of doing so (Figure 10.1).

Other materials facilitate making three-dimensional shapes. Children can construct three-dimensional shapes of straws or toothpicks held together with small balls of clay, small gum drops, or mini-marshmallows. Pipe cleaners can also be twisted together to make three-dimensional figures. Flexible drinking straws (Prentice, 1989) can be used to make sturdy

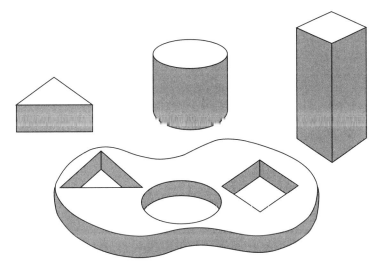

Figure 10.1   *Three-dimensional shapes made from clay or modeling dough.*

Figure 10.2 *Three-dimensional shapes made from clay and toothpicks and clay balls.*

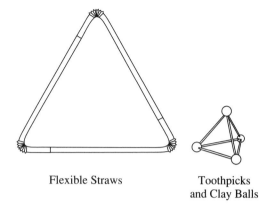

Flexible Straws   Toothpicks
                         and Clay Balls

three-dimensional structures. Children put the straws together by slightly compressing the short end of the straw, then inserting it into the longer end of another straw to make a firm, flexible joint (Figure 10.2). After the children use straws to make several polygons, they can fasten them together with twist-ties.

Two-Dimensional Figures

Work with two-dimensional or plane figures follows naturally from work with three-dimensional figures and discussion of their surfaces or faces. Children can feel, describe, and name the faces of solids. Primary children can make paper "jackets" for figures and see that many solid figures can

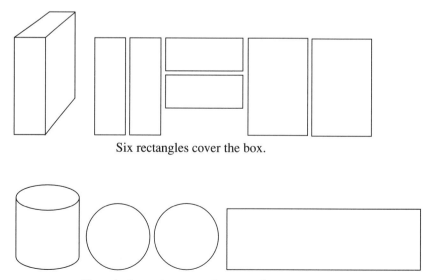

Six rectangles cover the box.

Two circles and a rectangle cover the can.

Figure 10.3 *Comparing surfaces of solids.*

be covered by a number of flat shapes. Some of the surfaces of a three-dimensional figure are likely to be the same size and shape. The children can verify this idea by tracing around the surfaces, then cutting them out and comparing them (Figure 10.3).

Young children often think that when positions of shapes change, the figures themselves change. Activities such as "Shape Dances" may help to dispel such ideas.

 SHAPE DANCES

Paper shapes stay the same no matter how they are turned in space. "Dancing" shapes help children internalize this idea.

Focus: Geometry, perceptual constancy, reasoning, communicating, connecting to music.

What To Do: Have the children cut out shapes such as circles, triangles, or rectangles. Play lively music for the children to "dance" with their shapes. Say "Shapes dancing, shapes dancing, turn them around. Shapes dancing, shapes dancing, up and down." Ask the children to "freeze" in their dancing positions, look at their shapes, and see if the shapes have changed or not.

Adjustments: Let the children decorate their shapes, making various creatures to dance with, name, and display.

Ongoing Assessment: Note the children's enjoyment of the activity. Can they tell what happens to shapes as their positions change?

Computers also help children work with two-dimensional shapes. In programs such as *Logo*, children specify a series of steps to make the computer draw and vary shapes. Other programs allow children to draw and "stamp" predetermined shapes in a variety of positions or select shapes and layouts from "print shop" menus. Children can make designs and patterns, then print out their work to color, describe, and compare.

To further their work with two-dimensional figures, children can locate "flat" shapes or plane figures in the environment—rugs, table tops, walls, and pieces of paper. They can reach into a mystery bag and tell whether the shapes they feel are flat or three-dimensional. Children might choose a shape, describe it, let classmates sketch it, then reveal the shape for classmates to compare.

Children can use paper and plastic shapes for a variety of games. Partners can play "Guess My Shape," sitting back to back and giving each other clues about shapes they hold. They can make patterns and designs using the same shape in different positions or using different shapes. Children can play "Walk Across," naming shapes as they walk on large cutouts arranged on the floor or walking only on shapes of a given kind. They can walk in an "attribute path," stepping on shapes

Careful work with pattern blocks produces neat geometric designs.

with a given attribute only. For instance, children might walk only on shapes with straight edges, only on shapes with square corners, or only on circles or ovals.

Children can make pattern block designs, then have a "walk around," where classmates circulate, admire, and comment on each others' designs. Children who are especially proud of their designs can copy the designs freehand, with pattern block stamps, or paper shapes. Photos of the children's pattern block designs might be displayed or filed in portfolios.

The idea of tessellations, or tilings, builds naturally from experiences with pattern or parquet blocks. The word *tessellation* is derived from "tessera" or tile. It applies to covering a surface with flat shapes that do not overlap or leave "holes." Tessellations can be made with a single shape or with a variety of shapes. Many pattern blocks tessellate. Children will enjoy using the word "tessellate" to describe their designs.

Children as young as three or four can create plane figures using materials such as yarn arranged on a flannel board or glued to paper. Each child in a small group might use the same number of strips of paper or toothpicks and see what different figures they can create. "Geometric Designs" and "Quilt Patterns" offer other suggestions.

 GEOMETRIC DESIGNS

Making designs increases children's hand-eye coordination while they explore an aesthetic side of mathematics.

Focus: Geometry, two-dimensional figures, communicating, problem solving, hand-eye coordination, connecting to art.

What To Do: Provide a variety of materials for the children to use in making geometric designs. Cut shapes from manila folders for children to place under thin paper to make rubbings. They can trace around templates made of cardboard or cut from sections of milk cartons. Children can carefully glue scraps of thick yarn to cardboard to make geometric figures. They can then dip the figures, yarn side down, into thin paint, and make prints on large sheets of paper.

Kindergarten and primary children can also work on squares of smooth carpet, and punch around templates with large nails, making a series of closely spaced holes. They can then punch out the resulting shapes and display the punched shapes and their "negatives."

Adjustments: Cut sponges or potatoes to make geometric prints.

Ongoing Assessment: Watch the children as they work on their geometric designs. Mark on a checklist items such as interest, neatness, originality, and ability to describe designs.

Shape puzzles such as tangrams and alphagrams (Perl, 1989) offer many opportunities for solving spatial problems. The alphagram uses eight pieces instead of the tangram's traditional seven pieces. These pieces and an alphagram puzzle are shown in Figure 10.4. Children use the pieces to make a variety of shapes.

Before working with traditional tangrams or alphagrams, children might combine shapes, making designs and creations of their own, then let peers duplicate the shapes and name and describe their creations. Puzzles with actual-size outlines are easier than are puzzles where children copy shapes shown in a smaller version.

Geoboards, another versatile manipulative, allow children to easily create a variety of shapes. Kindergarten and primary children can make designs for their classmates to copy and pose problems for others to solve. They might work according to directions such as "make a triangle," then compare results and see the rich variety of triangular shapes. They can make a shape, change it in one way, and then show others the results.

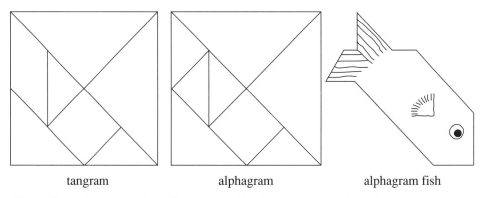

| tangram | alphagram | alphagram fish |

Figure 10.4 *Shape puzzles offer opportunities for solving spatial problems.*

As they work with geoboards, children should transfer their designs to paper. The process of transferring figures from geoboards to paper takes careful work and self-checking, and most children will need to begin with simple shapes. They might work with partners, checking and supporting each other. More suggestions follow in "Geoboard Challenges."

 GEOBOARD CHALLENGES

A variety of questions can prompt spatial problem solving.

Focus: Geometry, spatial sense, problem solving, communicating, reasoning.

What To Do: Pose geoboard problems for kindergarten and primary children to solve.

◆ Make some shapes where the bands touch 6 pegs and enclose 2 pegs. (Vary the numbers for this problem—touching 8 pegs and enclosing 3 for example.)

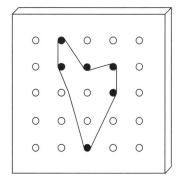 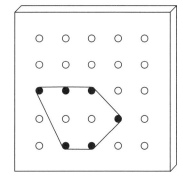

◆ Classify the shapes you have made at least two different ways.
◆ Compare the number of squares and parts of squares that are enclosed.

Let the children work in small groups and compare their answers. Children may wish to draw their solutions on geopaper.

Adjustments: Begin by letting children make designs that enclose some pegs and touch others. Have them count the pegs and show their designs. Are any of the children's numbers the same? Are their designs the same? Let the children make problems for each other, sharing their problems and solutions with others from a "mathematician's chair" (Buschman, 1995).

Ongoing Assessment: Have the children draw and write about their experiences with geoboard problems in their math journals.

 ## ASSESSMENT SUGGESTION: Problem Solving

Present problems for children and assess their problem-solving abilities as well as their strategies, and their abilities to get many solutions, persevere, and describe their reasoning. Examples of problems for seven- or eight-year-olds are

◆ How many different triangles can you make from 10 toothpicks and bits of clay?
◆ Mr. Giordano has 10 small square restaurant tables that can seat one person at each side. What are some ways to arrange the tables to seat different numbers of people?

Have the children solve the problems by manipulating materials, drawing, and using other means. Invite the children to tell how they solved the problems and how they know they are correct. Do they have all the possible solutions or might there be more solutions?

 ## ASSESSMENT SUGGESTION: Checklist

To help you document the children's work with three- and two-dimensional geometry, use a checklist such as this one.

◆ Sorts geometric shapes into two or more piles.
◆ Matches three-dimensional shapes.
◆ Matches two-dimensional shapes.
◆ Constructs simple three-dimensional shapes.
◆ Constructs simple two-dimensional shapes.
◆ Describes shapes.
◆ Extends patterns with three- and two-dimensional shapes.
◆ Describes patterns with shapes.
◆ Names shapes in spontaneous conversation.
◆ Recognizes shapes in the classroom and environment.
◆ Makes geoboard designs.
◆ Duplicates geoboard designs made by others.
◆ Transfers geoboard designs to paper.
◆ Seems to enjoy work with geometry.

◆ Chooses geometry when offered a choice of activities.
◆ Works creatively.

Congruence and Symmetry

As children work with plane figures, ideas of congruence and symmetry emerge naturally. If figures are the same size and shape, they are congruent. Kindergarten and primary children can check figures for congruence by placing one atop the other and seeing if the shapes match "exactly." Their exploration of symmetry can start with line symmetry—figures with two congruent, mirrored halves. Children can use plastic mirrors or fold paper figures to check for line symmetry.

To further explore congruence, children can make paper figures, cutting or tearing through two layers of paper. A group of children can mix up their figures, then sort them, finding those of the same size and shape. They can verify whether the shapes are congruent by placing one shape atop another. For more work with congruence, one child can make a simple geoboard figure for a partner to copy; the children can then compare their figures and see if they are congruent.

Using hole punchers can enhance primary children's understanding of symmetry. Children can fold paper, then punch holes through both layers. They can predict how many holes they will see when they unfold the paper and where the holes will be. Partners can check each other by unfolding their papers.

To produce symmetrical figures, children can fold paper and cut through both layers, keeping the fold line at least partially intact. When they unfold their shapes they will see congruent halves—mirrored images of each other. Each child can fold a paper, draw half a design, then have a classmate complete the drawing by making another symmetrical half. Children can also examine seasonal designs and natural objects and show each other whether these are symmetrical. Children can also fold paper twice and cut through all the layers to make designs that have two lines of symmetry (Figure 10.5).

Another activity is described in "Symmetrical Masks".

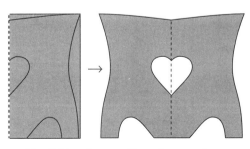

One fold makes one line of symmetry.   Two folds make two lines of symmetry.

Figure 10.5 *Learning about symmetry.*

SYMMETRICAL MASKS

In this activity, children make designs with line symmetry.

Focus: Geometry, symmetry, problem solving, communicating, reasoning, connecting to art and to everyday life.

What To Do: Show kindergarten or primary children a teacher-made or purchased mask with line symmetry. Let the children point out features that are the same on both sides of a line that extends from the middle of the forehead, between the eyes, and through the nose and mouth. Children will also enjoy discussing how their faces are symmetrical. Provide materials—paper bags, markers, yarn, and other things for children to make masks with symmetrical designs and features. Have a parade with the masks.

Adjustments: Help the children cut eye and nose holes.

Ongoing Assessment: Have the children describe their masks' designs and point out symmetrical features.

SUMMARY

Geometry is an active subject in which children can explore and communicate about shapes, positions, and their relationships. Geometry, an important part of the world and of school mathematics, also provides many opportunities for children to reason and problem solve, and to compare and share their discoveries. Geometry connects well to real life and to other subject matter areas. As they work in geometry, children and teachers can use a variety of simple materials as well as technology to promote understanding and to stimulate conversation and vocabulary development. Assessment of learning is easy and natural as educators and children use a range of techniques to gather data.

◆ *APPLICATIONS: THINKING AND COLLABORATING*

To extend your thinking about geometry for young children, complete one or more of the following exercises.

1. Study the K–4 geometry section of the NCTM *Curriculum Standards*, generating more examples to use with children. Plan to share the information with other teachers, students, or parents. Make and evaluate your presentation.

2. Read more about the van Hiele model of geometric thought. Based on your reading, think about a geometry activity you would enjoy doing with young children. What would its van Hiele level be? Are there ways to adapt the activity so that children on both level 0 and

1 could learn from it? Develop one or more activities to challenge children on both levels 0 and 1.

3. First-grade students of Sherry Swain (1993) worked with geoboards to make and compare sets of three triangles. The children drew some of their triangles and wrote about why the figures were triangles. Some of the children's work is reproduced in Figure 10.6. On which van Hiele levels might each be? Try a similar task with a small group of young children. Interpret your results for a group of colleagues.

4. Choose a geometry activity to enhance children's reasoning and problem-solving skills. Present the activity and analyze the children's work. What geometry skills or concepts were involved? What kinds of thinking and problem-solving occurred? What would you change if you used the activity again?

5. Explore uses of technology to enhance young children's understanding of geometry. Do some reading, watch children using a computer program such as *Logo* to create shapes on the screen, or view some videotapes on geometry. Write up your findings; reflect on ways to use technology to promote geometry learning.

6. There are many commercially and teacher-made manipulative materials such as geoboards, tangrams, pattern blocks, flannel board pieces, and building tiles. Choose one kind of manipulative. Use it yourself to explore geometry ideas. Read about the material or ask an experienced teacher about it. Plan a time to demonstrate your findings to colleagues.

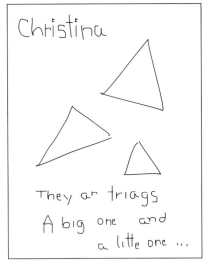

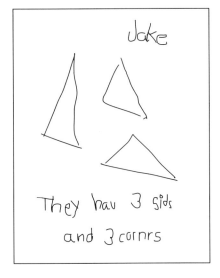

Figure 10.6 First-graders' geoboards.

7. Think about what you have learned about teaching geometry to young children and add your reflections to the math biography you started in Chapter 1 of this book.

◆ **REFERENCES**

Bailey, D. & Butterworth, C. (1991). *Butterflies.* New York: Steck-Vaughn.

Bredekamp, S. (Ed.). (1993). *Developmentally appropriate practice in early childhood programs serving children from birth to age 8.* Washington, DC: National Association for the Education of Young Children.

Bruni, J. & Seidenstein, R. (1990). Geometric concepts and spatial sense. In J. Payne (Ed.), *Mathematics for the young child.* Reston, VA: National Council of Teachers of Mathematics.

Buschman, L. (1995). Communicating in the language of mathematics. *Teaching Children Mathematics, 1,* 324–329.

Clements, D. H. & Battista, M. T. (1992). Geometry and spatial reasoning. In D. A. Grouws (Ed.), *Handbook of research on mathematics teaching and learning.* Reston, VA: National Council of Teachers of Mathematics.

Del Grande, J. A. (1987). Spatial perception and primary geometry. In *Learning and teaching geometry.* (pp. 126–135). Reston, VA: National Council of Teachers of Mathematics.

Del Grande, J. A. (1990). Spatial sense. *Arithmetic Teacher, 37,* 14–20.

Dorras, A. (1991). *Abuela.* New York: Dutton.

Fuys, D., Geddes, D., & Tischler, R. (1988). *The van Hiele model of thinking in geometry among adolescents.* Reston, VA: National Council of Teachers of Mathematics.

Hoffer, A. R. & Hoffer, S. A. (1992). Geometry and visual thinking. In T. R. Post (Ed.), *Teaching mathematics in grades K–8: research-based methods.* Boston: Allyn and Bacon.

National Council of Teachers of Mathematics. (1989). *Curriculum and evaluation standards for school mathematics.* Reston, VA: Author.

Perl, T. (1989). *Alphagrams.* New Rochelle, NY: Cuisenaire Company of America.

Prentice, G. (1989). Flexible straws. *Arithmetic Teacher, 37,* 4–5.

Swain, S. (1993). Personal communication.

Van de Walle, J. A. (1994). Elementary school mathematics: teaching developmentally. New York: Longman.

◆ **SELECTED CHILDREN'S BOOKS**

Bailey, Donna and Butterworth, Christine. (1991). *Butterflies.* New York: Steck-Vaughn. This factual book provides detailed pictures of butterflies, showing symmetry and details of their bodies.

Dorras, A. (1991). *Abuela.* New York: Dutton. A Latino girl's imagined flying ability lets her view objects from unusual angles! This book's idea of looking down on objects introduces the basis for map making.

Grifalconi, Ann. (1986). *The village of round and square houses.* Boston: Little, Brown. In the African village featured in the book, men and women live in houses of different shapes. With realistic drawings, the book presents ideas about shapes and culture.

McMillan, Bruce. (1992). *Beach Ball—Left, Right.* New York: Holiday. McMillan captures the path of a colorful beach ball as it crosses a part of a beach. The pages, labeled right and left, invite readers to tell which position the ball is in.

McMillan, Bruce. (1993). *Mouse Views: What the Class Pet Saw.* New York: Holiday. Oops! A mouse is loose in a classroom, and it looks at objects from different perspectives. With amusing text, the book invites children to guess the objects and view them from different angles.

Tompert, Ann. (1990). *Grandfather Tang's Story.* New York: Crown. How did the tangram come into being? What can we do with its versatile seven pieces? This book answers these questions with vivid pictures and an entertaining story.

Measurement

✓ **Measurement for Young Children**

✓ **More Principles for Teaching Measurement**

✓ **Materials for Involving Children in Measurement**

✓ **Exploring Measurement Attributes**
    Length
    Area
    Capacity
    Volume
    Weight
    Time
    Temperature
    Angles

✓ **Summary**

✓ **Applications: Thinking and Collaborating**

◆◆

Anna Kelly is anxiously awaiting the day when the preschool class in which she is student teaching takes a trip to the grocery store. The class will walk three blocks to the store, then spend about an hour taking a tour of the store and making purchases. Ms. Kelly's supervising teacher has asked her to plan some measurement experiences for the children preceding, during, and after the trip. What are some things she might have the four-year-olds do as they prepare for their trip? What measurement concepts might the children explore on the trip? What follow-up activities might enhance the children's understanding?

Measurement is a topic with much potential for engaging young children in active learning. As they work with measurement concepts young children explore many attributes such as length, weight, and time. Children start building measurement ideas by comparing sizes. They later progress to using ordinary objects as units of measurement, and finally use standard units of measurement such as inches, kilograms, and hours. Work with measurement strengthens children's number concepts and estimation skills; it lets children use geometric ideas. Measurement is a topic that lends itself well to integration with other subject areas and real-life applications. Therefore, a broad mathematics curriculum emphasizes measurement.

What might children do as they engage in measurement activities? In Jerry O'Malley's first-grade room, the children studied healthy habits and compared their heights, weights, and lengths of various body parts such as feet, arms, and smiles. The children compared body parts directly—standing in lines of three or four, holding arms side by side, and so on. They cut paper strips and pieces of yarn to represent their measurements.

Mr. O'Malley next introduced the idea of using small classroom objects—paper clips and blocks—as units of measurement. As they laid paper clips on paper footprints and counted the clips to determine the lengths of the prints, Jody and Kenneth commented that it was hard to arrange the individual clips. They suggested linking paper clips together for easier handling. After they shared their idea with classmates, it caught on quickly. Children found objects that could be linked in manageable sizes—interlocking cubes and plastic links.

Some children had been using dry lima bean counters and adapted these for measuring by gluing beans, end to end, to strips of paper. The children had practiced counting by tens, so several made strips with 10 beans, enabling them to quickly count the numbers of beans. They found that their bean strips had the advantage of being flexible—they bent the strips around wrists or ankles. Thus the children "invented" tools comparable to tape measures for determining length. Mr. O'Malley suggested that the children post signs on the objects that they measured, and the children wrote in their math journals.

As Mr. O'Malley reflected on his students' progress, he was pleased about several things: The children used numbers and comparative words naturally as they worked. They used measuring tools to verify statements such as "the table is shorter than the door." The children worked well together, helping each other, settling differences, and suggesting ways to streamline their work. Mr. O'Malley also considered individualization of the measurement activities he was planning. He decided to let children help devise some learning center activities for more work on length. He planned to have the children compose a story about their activities to share in his monthly family newsletter.

WHAT DO *YOU* THINK?

What were some ways Mr. O'Malley let his first graders initiate activities and construct their own knowledge of measurement? How did Mr. O'Malley connect their activities to a unit topic and to everyday life? What activities could you plan to extend the children's learning at school? At home and in the community?

MEASUREMENT FOR YOUNG CHILDREN

As with other topics, the *Curriculum and Evaluation Standards for School Mathematics* (National Council of Teachers of Mathematics [NCTM], 1989, p. 51) offers guidance for helping children learn measurement:

> In grades K–4, the mathematics curriculum should include measurement so students can

- ◆ understand the attributes of length, capacity, weight, area, volume, time, temperature, and angle;
- ◆ develop the process of measuring and concepts related to units of measurement;
- ◆ make and use estimates of measurement;
- ◆ make and use measurements in everyday situations.

The authors of the NCTM standards emphasize the importance of the process of measurement—choosing attributes to be measured, selecting suitable units, covering or balancing objects with units, and counting the units. For weight, children must handle objects, lifting and comparing them. They might use a balance scale as a tool for measuring and verifying ideas. They might place the box of crayons in one pan of the balance and use pennies in the other pan until the pans balance. The number of pennies expresses the weight of the crayons.

All measurement is approximate. Errors are inherent as people use and read measuring tools. Therefore, educators should encourage children to use words such as "about" or "almost" as they report measurements.

The Curriculum Standards authors indicate that as children use non-standard units for their initial explorations, they "develop some understandings of units and come to recognize the necessity of standard units to communicate" (NCTM, 1989, p. 52). Finally, the authors stress the importance of measurement in natural, problem situations, measuring attributes of real objects and making objects of chosen sizes. "Textbook experiences cannot substitute for activities that use measurement to answer questions about real problems" (NCTM, 1989, p. 53).

MORE PRINCIPLES FOR TEACHING MEASUREMENT

Besides the guidelines offered by the NCTM standards, we suggest three more principles for helping children learn measurement.

Use stages for exploring measurement attributes. As they explore any measurement attribute, children should first directly compare pairs of items. Children can use real objects, physically manipulating objects or placing them side by side (Souviney, 1994). Comparison activities must involve each child working with the materials to build measurement concepts.

A second stage for measurement activities is *ordering* or *seriating.* Here children work with three or more objects and arrange them along a continuum—perhaps from shortest to longest or longest to shortest time durations. Children must work with ordering in direct ways—lining up classmates to see who is tallest, or placing their hands in cold, very warm, and cool water to order the samples of water by temperature.

Children can next work with *nonstandard units* of measurement as small, equal-sized units. For example, they can use small scoops and measure the capacities of larger bowls in "scoop units." Children might find that it takes about 8 scoops to fill one bowl and 15 to 16 scoops to fill another bowl. Work with nonstandard units helps children grasp the idea that measurement involves telling how many of an appropriate unit are needed to match the object being measured.

After many experiences with comparing, ordering, and using nonstandard measurement units, children are ready for work with *standard units* of measurement. In this stage they work with units familiar to many people: centimeters, feet, hours, and liters. Such units are considered to be unchanging; they represent ideas agreed upon and used by many people.

Preschool children's work with measurement should focus almost exclusively on comparing. Most kindergarteners will work with comparing and ordering; they often progress to working with nonstandard units. Primary children can be engaged in all four stages as they work with measurement.

Help children develop measurement benchmarks. To understand measurement well, children must be able to estimate and problem solve using measurements. Developing benchmarks or mental images of measurement units helps them with these processes. Benchmarks are developed through experience. As second graders work with centimeters, for example, they might draw line segments about a centimeter long. They might also find body parts—perhaps the distance across a finger—that are about one centimeter, and collect many objects to represent a centimeter. Thus through many examples the centimeter unit becomes familiar.

As children develop ideas of measurement units, they can estimate based on those benchmarks. Miss Gaddo worked with second graders all through the school year on weight concepts. At the beginning of the year, they lifted their backpacks and compared the weights. The children explored standard units—pounds—as Miss Gaddo asked each child to bring a one-pound package of food to class and verify the weight on a spring scale. Miss Gaddo next asked the children to find classroom items that might weigh about a pound. The children discussed their items and verified their estimates using a balance scale. As a home follow-up, Miss Gaddo asked the children to list items labeled by weight. Through much hands-on work, the children developed a good sense of the measurement process as well as ideas of a weight benchmark, the pound. They used this benchmark in estimating other weights. After several teacher-directed activities, Miss Gaddo set up a learning center where she placed scales and objects to be weighed. As children used the center, they added objects and devised tasks for others.

Let children make measuring tools. When children make measuring tools they understand more about the measurement process: the use of equal-sized units, and that when these units are linked together, they are often easier to handle than using separate units. Children can also produce measuring tools of which they are proud and use them at home. Child-made measuring tools also enhance the numbers of available classroom measuring devices.

For example, children can make or help to make simple scales. Children place items of different weights into a milk carton suspended by a heavy rubber band and see what happens. They can then mark their results—the relative weights of the items—on a marking board behind the device.

MATERIALS FOR INVOLVING CHILDREN IN MEASUREMENT

Children must use physical objects as they measure, including classroom materials, items from home, and the children themselves. Almost any real

Simple materials make a usable device for measuring weight.

item has a variety of attributes the children can compare and measure. Measurement tools are also important. Some devices can be made from paper. For example, children can use strips of paper, cut to equal lengths, to measure length. For area, children can cut and use paper squares; they can use squared paper, placing flat objects on top, then count squares to determine the approximate areas. To measure angles children can fold paper plates in fourths or eighths, cut apart the sections, and use the pie-piece wedges as units.

Rope or string makes inexpensive measures of length. Four-year-olds might cut lengths of string and use them for comparison, finding objects about as long as their strings, and longer and shorter than their strings. Older children might mark smaller, equal units on strings or ropes, thus making multiunit measuring devices similar to tape measures.

As they study time, children and teachers can make models of both analog (with hands) and digital clocks. Paper plate clocks are favorites; they can be taken home after classroom use. Digital clocks are easily prepared with strips of paper that show numerals through "windows" cut in cardboard backings (Figure 11.1).

For primary grades, purchased measuring equipment is a good investment, useful throughout the school for measuring activities. For measuring length, educators should purchase simple rulers, perhaps calibrated in centimeters or in inches and half inches. Yard and meter sticks are needed for measuring longer lengths. Tape measures wrap easily around curved objects. For longer distances, trundel wheels, devices that children push, have clicking devices to signal each meter that is traveled.

For measuring capacity, sets of plastic cups and cylinders are available. Educators should purchase capacity measures marked with large, clear numerals. Sets of measures including units of 100, 250, 500, and 1000 milliliters (1 liter) and 1/2 cup, 1 cup, 1 pint, and 1 quart are useful. Children's study of volume, measured in cubic units, is enhanced by using small cubes in cubic centimeter or cubic inch sizes.

Figure 11.1   *Digital clock made from cardboard.*

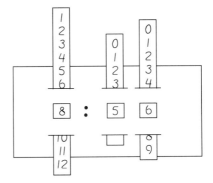

Scales are indispensable as children work with weight. Balance scales feature plastic pans or hoppers in which children can place a variety of objects. Sets of weights, calibrated in grams and ounces, go with the scales. Inexpensive spring scales let children read a gauge to determine weight. Step-on scales allow children to weigh themselves and hold other heavy objects.

Many devices are commercially available for telling time. Large clocks with geared hands let children set times with hour and minute hands in the correct positions. Inexpensive analog and digital clocks are useful, as are small clocks with movable hands. Stamp sets simplify the task of drawing clocks.

For measuring temperature, thermometers are essential tools. Simple, inexpensive thermometers, calibrated from below freezing to about 50° Celsius or 120° Fahrenheit (the temperature of hot water) are available. Room and outdoor thermometers with large scales, simple cooking thermometers, and large demonstration thermometers with movable "mercury" are also available.

EXPLORING MEASUREMENT ATTRIBUTES

For each of the measurement attributes designated by the NCTM standards for young children, we provide discussions and descriptions of learning activities in the subsequent sections.

Length

Length is a linear concept, answering questions such as how long?, how wide?, and how high? Most young children have a sense of length-related words. To enhance and deepen such a sense, a teacher of three-year-olds might play music and ask the children to walk around, stop, and stretch to be very tall, then bend, making themselves shorter, and making themselves shorter still by squatting and crouching. Children might hold their arms at their sides, stretch their arms a little, then stretch to make themselves wide, wider, and wider still.

To complement their naturally occurring comparative language, children can continue exploring length concepts with activities such as "How Far Did It Go?"

 HOW FAR DID IT GO?

This game sets the stage for much informal language about length.

Focus: Measurement—comparing, problem solving, communicating, connecting to everyday life.

What To Do: Set up situations where children of any age move objects and compare the results. Let the children make and fly paper airplanes, use half-sections of straws to blow styrofoam bits on the floor, or race cars from a cardboard ramp. After some practice trials, let the children take turns testing their objects and comparing the results. Younger children can identify the longest and shortest distances; older children can use nonstandard or standard units of measurement to estimate and record distances.

Adjustments: Let the children suggest ways to vary the activity. Second and third graders can record results for three trials each, then identify their longest distances.

Ongoing Assessment: Observe children's work to determine if individuals work cooperatively, initiate conversation about lengths, compare lengths, and use measurement tools.

After comparing and ordering lengths, children measure lengths with nonstandard units, working with units such as strips of paper or hands. In first and second grade, many curriculums include work with standard units such as centimeters and inches. Conversions such as 100 centimeters equals 1 meter are handled in exploratory ways rather than with formulas. Third graders often explore decimeters and yards, other standard measures of length.

In the primary grades curriculum, metric units—based on tens—are often presented along with place value. Customary units—inches and feet—are often handled later in the school year. In work with either measurement system, children must develop mental pictures or benchmarks of the units. "Finding Lengths at Home" and "Make a Meter" help children use benchmarks.

FINDING LENGTHS AT HOME

Locating objects of various lengths at home enhances children's development of measurement benchmarks and consciousness of sizes.

Focus: Measurement—comparing, finding benchmarks, communicating, connecting to the real world.

What To Do: Help primary children make paper strips of specified lengths—nonstandard units such as the lengths or widths of their hands, or strips of standard sizes such as 5, 10, or 20 centimeters. Ask the children to use the strips at home, find several objects close to the lengths of the strips, and bring one object to school. Let children set up a sharing table of their objects, adding signs to tell their lengths.

Adjustments: Suggest that children trace or draw pictures of objects that they cannot bring to school. Let children cut pieces of yarn or string to use as measuring devices.

Ongoing Assessment: As children present their objects, try to judge their interest, asking what they like about the activity and ways to improve it. Observe children's abilities to find objects of designated lengths and communicate findings.

MAKE A METER

This activity helps primary children picture a one-meter length.

Focus: Measurement—standard units, problem solving, communicating, connecting to number concepts.

What To Do: As children explore meters as standard units of length, have them work with partners using a meter stick and base-ten blocks. Have them take turns rolling a number cube and selecting the number of unit blocks that the cube shows, then place the blocks along the meter stick. As the children accumulate blocks for a 10-centimeter section, they trade 10 unit blocks for a 10-centimeter rod.

Adjustments: Use 1-inch cubes and let the children make a yard, trading sets of 12 blocks for 1-foot rulers. Let the children predict the number of die rolls needed to complete the task.

Ongoing Assessment: Observe and guide the children's work, focusing on cooperation, understanding of when to trade, and informal use of measurement vocabulary.

Along with direct attention to length concepts, educators can find many related opportunities to reinforce children's measurement concepts and skills. As children complete art projects, participate in large motor activities, and work with physical properties of objects in science, they compare lengths and use their growing measurement skills.

An extension of length concepts is perimeter, the length around flat objects or plane figures. Primary children usually explore and figure out perimeters of simple figures, they do not use formulas. To start such explorations, children might arrange pieces of yarn to enclose various shapes. They can then choose a favorite shape, glue the yarn to paper in that shape, and make a picture or design inside. Small blocks, used in the following activity, are another good model for perimeter.

BUILDING BLOCK PERIMETERS

"Fences" made from building blocks model perimeter.

Focus: Measurement—nonstandard units, problem solving, communicating, reasoning, connecting to geometry and to everyday life.

What To Do: Provide preschool or primary children with blocks and invite them to make enclosures for "gardens" or "pens." Invite the children to describe and compare the sizes and shapes of the enclosures they are making. Let the children count out the same numbers of blocks—perhaps 24—and make enclosures of different shapes. Extend the children's play by offering plastic animals and paper to draw details.

Adjustments: Introduce the word "perimeter" to older children. Help them locate and measure other perimeters in the classroom, making a list of their suggestions and results.

Ongoing Assessment: Observe the children for signs of understanding of making enclosures and counting their numbers of blocks.

Area

Area is a measure of surface that concerns two dimensions. To understand area, children cover entire surfaces with no overlapping. As they begin exploring area, young children may cover surfaces with nonsquare objects such as pennies or cotton balls, or color surfaces with crayons. As ideas of area become more formalized, learners use square units—square centimeters or square inches, for example.

To introduce children to area concepts, educators might use the words "area" and "surface" informally. As she admires the painting of a three-year-old, a teacher might point out, "Here's an area with lots of red, and this area is covered with blue." As preschool children make collages, caregivers can help them to point out "empty" areas and areas filled with materials.

For informal units of area, a teacher might cut squares of construction paper or newspaper, making them about 15 by 15 centimeters (6 inches square). The teacher then lets the children guess about how many of the squares would be needed to cover a surface such as a small rug or desk top. After recording estimates, children can place the papers, then count the numbers that are used. Some partial squares may be needed to cover

"These squares cover it pretty well." Students use square units as they determine the approximate area of a floor mat.

an area, providing opportunities for children to use language such as "almost 18 squares" or "the area is 16 whole squares and parts of 4 more."

The children's book *Eight Hands Round* (Paul, 1991) features drawings and information about quilt patterns. In making quilts, people design pieces to cover areas in unique ways. Working with quiltlike patterns can extend children's understanding and appreciation of area. They might work with squares of colored paper, arranging the colors in rows, in checkerboard patterns, or in twos to make rectangles of color. They might next use right triangles, arranging these in several ways to cover areas. After experimentation, children can describe favorite patterns and display their work.

Paper ruled with squares, as in "Color and Count" helps children explore area concepts.

 COLOR AND COUNT

This activity lets children six years or older be creative as they explore area concepts.

Focus: Measurement—nonstandard units, problem solving, communicating, connecting to numbers, geometry, and art.

What To Do: Let children cut small rectangles from squared paper—6 by 8 squares, 8 by 8, or 10 by 10. Have them use two or more colors and fill in the squares and make designs. After children mount their designs on rectangles of colored paper, have them count their squares of each color and the total number of squares, sharing this information along with their designs. Model language such as, Joy's design has an area of 48 squares—20 squares red, 14 squares blue, and 14 yellow.

Adjustments: Ask the children to make two or more designs using the same large area, then compare their colors. Specify numbers of squares for each color and let the children make different designs.

Ongoing Assessment: Observe the children, noting things such as understanding directions, counting squares systematically, and sharing results using area-related words.

Capacity

Capacity is a measurement attribute that addresses the question, how much does a container hold? Capacity often pertains to pourable substances—water and other liquids, flour, birdseed, or sand. Units of capacity for young children include liters, milliliters, teaspoons, tablespoons, cups, pints, and quarts. Nonstandard units of capacity may be spoonfuls, scoops, and "cups" using any cuplike container.

Mrs. Thomas, a teacher of three- and four-year-olds, focused children's play in the home living center when she provided large dried beans and

Working with water and other pourable substances helps young children develop a variety of measurement concepts.

rice for them to "serve." As they played, Mrs. Thomas heard the children using capacity-related words such as "lots," "empty," and "full." The preschoolers' understanding of capacity was also enhanced with "Water Table Fun."

 ## WATER TABLE FUN

Playing at the water table is soothing and relaxing, and it also exposes preschool and kindergarten children to ideas of capacity.

Focus: Measurement—comparing and ordering, communication, connecting to everyday life.

What To Do: Provide a variety of transparent and translucent plastic containers at a water table or large tub of water. Invite the children to play with the containers, fill them, and pour from one container to another. As the children talk about what they are doing, introduce or reinforce words such as empty, full, and partly full. Ask the children to compare containers. Which might hold more? How can you find out?

Adjustments: Partially fill a large tub with dry beans or birdseed, inviting pouring and experimentation.

Ongoing Assessment: Take photos of children working. File the photos, along with quotes, in the children's portfolios.

Experiences with foods enhance young children's understanding of capacity. During her four-year-olds' explorations of healthy foods, Miss Lee provided small cups and discussed healthy foods to fill the cups—carrot rounds, apple slices, raisins, and soup. Each day for a week, Miss Lee provided such snacks for the children to eat from the cups, providing opportunities to use capacity-related words such as "full," "partly gone," and "empty." A highlight of the unit came as the children helped to prepare snacks (Partridge, Austin, Wadington, & Bitner, 1996). Starting with a small bowl of unpopped corn, they chose a larger bowl that the popped corn might fill. The children watched with interest as the popcorn emerged from the hot air popper; they found the bowl they had selected was almost full. The children divided the popped corn among their smaller cups for snacking. Finally, the children helped to make whipped fruit gelatin and watched its volume increase as they beat it with an eggbeater.

As in "Will 100 Fill It?", comparing capacities is extended by working with nonstandard units of measurement.

 WILL 100 FILL IT?

Will 100 paper clips fill a small cup? 100 raisins? 100 cubes? Primary children can investigate questions such as these.

Focus: Measurement—nonstandard units, problem solving, communicating, connecting to numbers and to everyday life.

What To Do: Invite the children to work alone or with partners. Each should collect 100 small objects—perhaps classroom materials such as coins, or natural or household objects such as acorns, pebbles, shells, pieces of cereal, pasta, or popcorn. Let the children count and display their collections. Show the children a small container such as a plastic glass or box. Ask them to make and draw predictions of how the collections will appear when placed in the container. Will any collections fill the container? Are any too large or too small for the container? Let the children test their predictions, then illustrate their collections in the container.

Adjustments: Use the activity on the hundredth day of school. Work with smaller numbers—10 to 20 objects.

Ongoing Assessment: Examine the children's pictures for reasonable predictions and showing containers filled to various levels. As the children work, note their use of language about capacity.

As children learn to use standard measures of capacity, they should discuss benchmark amounts. For example, what things come in one-cup sizes? Teachers can ask children to suggest amounts that are much smaller and much greater than a cup. Most children understand that a dose of medicine is smaller than a cup, while a large can of fruit is more than a cup.

Volume

Volume is a three-dimensional concept concerning filling space with *cubic units.* As children see how many cubes can fit in a box or use little cubes to build a structure, they are working with volume. As children develop volume concepts, they must work with cubic units, handling them. Merely looking at pictures or at structures made by others may create misconceptions—that volume concerns flat objects or that volume is the units on the outside or front of a structure.

For preschool and primary children, most work with volume concerns comparing, ordering, and using nonstandard units—the number of cubic units or little cubes that are used to build or fill a structure. Relatively little emphasis is placed on standard units, such as cubic centimeters or cubic inches, or on finding volume by formula.

Miss Ferguson introduced first graders to volume as she had children take handfuls of wooden cubes, build structures from the cubes, then show and describe them. Ronnie told that his structure had four cubes on the bottom layer, three in the middle, and one on top—eight cubes in all. The children next arranged their structures in order from those with the smallest numbers of cubes to those with larger numbers. They displayed their work for others to examine and try to replicate.

Many concrete activities can be used to enhance children's understanding of volume. An example follows.

 SAME VOLUME, DIFFERENT SHAPES

Young children of any age can create many different structures with the same numbers of cubes.

Focus: Measurement—nonstandard units, communicating, reasoning, connecting to geometry and to everyday life.

What To Do: Have the children choose a number of cubes—perhaps 5 or 10. Challenge the children to create as many different structures as they can using the number of cubes they have selected. Let them display all their structures, checking to be sure that various designs are actually different. Discuss real-world shapes that resemble the children's designs.

Adjustments: Increase the numbers of cubes to 16, 24, or 36 and have the children try to make different-looking boxes or rectangular prisms, each with the designated number of cubes.

Ongoing Assessment: Observe the children's work for evidence of creativity. Can each child count the number of cubes used? Does he/she use shape names and positional words in descriptions? Do the children seem to enjoy the activity?

Weight

How heavy? How light? Weight is a concept that addresses these questions. Weight comparisons must be made by lifting objects; children should not be asked to judge weights by merely looking. Three-year-olds might begin exploring ideas of weight as they lift classroom objects—a chair, then a book. Children may comment that the book is smaller and also lighter in weight. Young children might gather several objects to place in paper bags. They can then lift pairs of bags, one in each hand, compare the weights, then compare their judgments.

After her kindergarten children had worked with comparing weights, Ms. Brown helped them set up a scale using a milk carton pan and a rubber band gauge (described on page 237). The children then gathered objects, placed them in the pan, and observed and marked where the pan came to rest. On subsequent days Ms. Brown helped the children add two more pans and rubber bands to the scale setup. They then collected sets of three objects, placed one object in each scale, and were able to observe the pans and order three objects by weight. Vocabulary such as heavy, heavier, and heaviest emerged, as did observations that some objects were very close in weight.

Ms. Brown found that most of her kindergarten children were also interested in using a balance scale. They used pairs of objects and recorded their findings with pictures on a chart. After some guided work, Ms. Brown made the balance available for independent use in the classroom "store" they had set up.

Satisfied that the children were ready for an introduction to using nonstandard units to measure weight, Ms. Brown showed them how to place an object in one pan of the balance and place small similar objects in the other pan until the two pans balanced. She let the children use interlocking cubes for weights one day and pennies and pattern blocks other days. The children counted numbers of nonstandard weights needed to balance classroom objects. Many children were interested in recording the numbers of weights they used, so Ms. Brown provided a chart (Figure 11.2).

How Much Does It Weigh?			
Object	Cubes	Pennies	Blocks
bird's nest	4	5	7
book	26	32	40
marker	2	3	5

Figure 11.2   *Chart used to record student's work with weight.*

In the primary grades, children's work with weight involves hands-on work, lifting objects and using tools to compare and measure weights. Their work, however, can be slightly more sophisticated as they use nonstandard units of weight. Standard weight concepts are developed as children work with ounces or grams. To become acquainted with one ounce, children might lift single-serving size portions of dry cereal. For one gram, children might lift a small paper clip or raisin and observe that although the weight of a gram is quite tiny, it can be felt. A nickel is a handy model for 5 grams. Each child might make a kilogram weight (1000 grams), as described.

 ## MAKING AND USING KILOGRAM WEIGHTS

It's easy for primary children to make one kilogram and develop this important weight benchmark.

Focus: Measurement—standard units, communicating, reasoning, connecting to everyday life.

What To Do: Ask the children to collect one- and two-liter soft drink bottles. Have them lift the bottles, then fill the bottles with water and have them lift them again, seeing that they weigh more filled than empty. Place a bottle on a spring scale and help the children add water until the bottle weighs one kilogram. A one-liter bottle will be almost full; a two-liter bottle will be slightly less than half full.

Let each child make a one-kilogram bottle; seal it tightly. Have the children find classroom objects that weigh about the same as their one-kilogram weights. Children can lift each others' objects and compare them "by hand," then use the balance scale to check.

Adjustments: Let the children add small amounts of glitter to their bottles to make them more intriguing to use. For approximate one-pound weights, use 16-fluid-ounce plastic bottles.

Ongoing Assessment: Observe the children's abilities to follow directions and to find objects that weigh about one kilogram. Let them complete a math journal selection telling about what a kilogram weight is or feels like.

After experiences with balance scales, primary teachers might introduce spring and step-on scales. These scales use a number gauge, and children must be guided in interpreting the scale. Most primary children should not be expected to master spring scales, but educators can help them interpret their own weights and the weights of classroom objects on such scales.

Time

Time, unlike other measurement concepts, is not applied to physical objects; rather it is a concept that people apply to events. Time concerns duration—how long it takes for events to happen—or the placement of

Figure 11.3 *Children keep track of time with a "week line."*

events in longer periods. Although it is hard to imagine life in our modern world without reference to time-keeping devices, teaching children about time is a complex process that takes place over an extended period.

Children are typically first exposed to ideas of time by placing events on a continuum of time. Sequence words are used as preschoolers and primary children follow a routine—before, during, after, first, and last, for example. Times of the day—morning, afternoon, and evening—may be defined by events such as meals. When a four-year-old asks when story time will be, telling him that it follows outdoor time may make more sense than saying that story time will be at 10:30.

People keep track of longer periods of time with terms such as days, weeks, months, seasons, and years. Children are exposed to these names in formal and informal ways. Mr. Nelson introduced the names of the days of the week to his four-year-olds with nursery rhymes and the book *Seven Blind Mice* (Young, 1992). He also made a "week line," using permanent markers to make seven sections and day names on a long piece of plastic shelf paper. He laid it on the floor, and as part of his morning routine let a child stand on the appropriate section of the week line. As the children learned the day names, they walked along on the week line saying the names.

Mr. Nelson used paper clips to attach sheets of paper to the week line. As he summarized some of each day's activities with his children, he renamed the day and added a few words to the papers. When the children started a seed planting project, Mr. Nelson encouraged them to dictate information about their plants. The week line thus became a valuable resource for keeping track of time and exposing the children to keeping written records (Figure 11.3).

Following are more ideas for acquainting children with months and keeping track of longer periods of time.

 MONTH BY MONTH

Posters for each month of the school year help children of any age document and become more aware of the passage of time.

Focus: Measurement—standard units, reasoning, communicating, connecting to science and to everyday life.

What To Do: At the beginning of each month, introduce its name and help the children start a poster of events and weather for the month. Let the children gather specimens or draw pictures of leaves and trees. Add notes about birthdays and other special events. Each week have the children write and add pictures to the poster. Toward the end of the month, review some of the events reflected on the poster. Keep your growing collection of posters in view for the children to refer to as the year progresses.

Adjustments: Encourage primary children to keep individualized miniposters or make notebooks of monthly occurrences. Month and seasonal names might be part of the class spelling list.

Ongoing Assessment: Judge the children's interest as the project progresses. If attention wanders, keep the activities brief and minimal, or involve only children who seem interested.

A MONTH-BY-MONTH BOOK

Adapt this idea to any book that deals with the names of months.

Focus: Measurement—standard units, communicating, connecting to the real world and to language arts.

What To Do: Read *Hermit Crab Finds a Home* (Carle, 1987) to kindergarten or primary children. Discuss the idea that the book's events took place over a long period of time—a year. Review the book's pages and name the months, asking the children to recall special events and to identify their birthday months.

Let individuals or pairs to make pages for a book of months. They might decide to make a book like Carle's. Or perhaps show the children events they might participate in during the various months. Help the children compile their pages in order and bind the pages together. Display it in your library center or offer it to be checked out for home use.

Adjustments: Use a book that features weekday names or seasons. Let the children make a book that features those concepts.

Ongoing Assessment: After you read the child-made book, let the children tell things about their book of which they are most proud. What might they change if they made another similar book?

Young children are familiar with the idea that clocks and watches are time-keeping devices long before they can read them. Ordinarily kindergarten children are exposed to the idea of telling time to the nearest hour. Most first graders master this skill and can tell time to the half hour. In second and third grade many children learn to read clocks to quarter hours, five-minute intervals, and to the minute.

Although she knew she would not focus on telling time on the clock until the spring of the kindergarten year, Mrs. Thompson exposed her children to telling time on the clock all year long. During the first week of school, Mrs. Thompson made a sign that said "clock" and let the children post it near the clock. They discussed the idea that clocks let us know when it is time for events such as story time. Mrs. Thompson also referred to the clock several times a week in casual conversation. Occasionally, a minute or two before the hour, she had the children watch the clock as the minute hand moved to 12, then she helped the children interpret the time. Mrs. Thompson posted the class's schedule on a large chart and talked to the children about the sequence and duration of events during the day. By the time Mrs. Thompson was ready to help the children focus on reading the clock, they already had weeks of rich, casual, but meaningful exposure to time concepts.

As children learn to tell time on the clock, hours and minutes are important; children must gain concepts of these time units relating to real experiences and to everyday life. To help kindergarteners or first graders build time benchmarks, teachers might help them identify examples of events that take about an hour, much longer than an hour, and much shorter than an hour, making a list of their examples.

Engaging children in activities that involve minute intervals is easy. A minute may seem different according to the activity one is doing. Walking to the school office in a minute might be a challenge, but a minute might seem long when holding perfectly still. Children can use a stopwatch to see how many blocks they can stack in a minute or see how many minutes it takes for a dripping faucet to fill a small container. Children can estimate numbers of things they can do in short time intervals such as one or two minutes—how many jumping jacks they think they can do in a minute or how many beans they can drop into a container in a minute.

Children should use real, model, and child-made clocks as they learn to tell time. As they work, they should build associations between the times they show and real events. Kindergartners might establish that they arrive at school about 8:00, have a snack at 10:00, eat lunch before 12:00, and go home at 3:00. As children set and read clocks, the children then have a context for the times the clocks show.

A next step might be having children set their clocks to various times on the hour and tell each other what they might be doing at those times. To add symbols to the process of telling time, the teacher might next add models of digital clocks. She can show a time on the digital clock, help the children read it, then set their analog clock models to the same time.

Children acquire proficiency in reading clocks at different ages. Those with good skills can often help others. Making time materials available for independent use is a practical idea. Clocks, clock face stamps, and pictures of children doing things all stimulate children to think and talk about time and telling time.

Many computer programs are available to help primary children gain skill and understanding in reading clocks. As children use such programs, educators might have children work in pairs and relate the times on the clocks to their own real-life activities. Pairing more- and less-confident children for work on the computer provides support and learning for both children.

ASSESSMENT SUGGESTION: Checklist

You might use a checklist with items such as the following to document children's understanding and skill for time.

◆ Uses "before" and "after" to describe sequences of events.
◆ Compares time intervals using "longer" and "shorter."
◆ Correctly uses time vocabulary—day, week, month, year.
◆ Helps keep track of time with calendars and clocks.
◆ Tells time on the hour.
◆ Reasonably describes events for given times of day.
◆ Tells time on half and quarter hours.

Temperature

How warm? How cool? Temperature is the measurement attribute that addresses these questions, indicating the presence or absence of heat. Children's attention to temperature is often first associated with statements such as "The soup is hot" or "We need coats. It is cold outside."

Children can compare temperatures and use comparative words in a variety of concrete experiences. Three-year-olds enjoy water play with tubs of warm water and water with a few ice cubes added. Four-year-olds can take a walk around the day care center, feeling the cool sides of a metal filing cabinet, touching a sunny window sill, and handling a package of frozen food from the freezer. After such a walk, their teacher might help them write a group story about the experience. Older children might enlarge the scope of such a walk, looking for things that are used for heating and cooling or using thermometers. Children of any age can also make "Temperature Collages" with pictures to suggest temperatures.

TEMPERATURE COLLAGE

Making a temperature collage develops ideas of hot, cold, and "in between" and enhances communication and sorting skills.

Focus: Measurement—comparing, communicating, reasoning, connecting to everyday life.

What To Do: Invite the children to select pictures and add them to a group or individual collage to show "Hot Things," "Cold Things," and "In-Between Things." Let the children describe some of their pictures and relate the experiences to everyday life.

Adjustments: Refocus the collage on a theme like "Hot Foods," "Cold Foods," "Clothes for Hot Weather," or "Clothes for Cold Weather."

Ongoing Assessment: Make notes as the children describe their pictures. Can they categorize pictures and explain their reasoning? Does each speak confidently or need prompting?

Miss Caldwell exposed children in her multiage primary classroom to the thermometer through concrete experiences. When she showed a classroom thermometer and asked about its uses, children described fever thermometers at home, in the nurse's office, and at a health clinic. Many children reported using thermometers to measure room and outdoor temperatures. As the children talked Miss Caldwell wrote down their ideas, displayed the story, and invited interested children to add pictures.

Miss Caldwell next had children work in groups. Helpers filled bowls of water for each table—warm and cool tap water and colder water from the drinking fountain. Miss Caldwell drew the children's attention to the colored liquid in the thermometer and asked each group to predict what the liquid would do when a thermometer was placed in each cup. She had the children attach a self-adhesive note to each thermometer and make a mark each time they tested the thermometer. As they discussed their results, the children established the idea that the thermometer's liquid rises in warmer conditions and lowers in cooler conditions (Figure 11.4).

In small groups, Miss Caldwell let the children handle the thermometer, place it in different conditions—near a radiator, inside a jacket, and with thumbs on the bulb—and try to read the thermometer. Miss Caldwell did not expect each child to read the thermometer independently, but several made progress and helped others.

Figure 11.4   Testing temperature with a thermometer.

The children also conducted a temperature scavenger hunt, suggesting places in the school to take the temperatures, then actually measuring it. They found the highest temperature in a closed storage room and the lowest in the school kitchen freezer. The children also engaged in the "Weather Reporters" activity.

 ## WEATHER REPORTERS

As primary children begin to use the thermometer, they can simulate weather reports and share their reports with other classes.

Focus: Measurement—standard units, communication, connecting to science and to the real world.

What To Do: Work with small groups of children to prepare weather reports. Children might watch videotaped segments of local weather reports to get ideas. Help the children gather weather data such as outdoor temperature, rehearse their weather reports, then make the reports to the class from a large box, decorated like a television screen.

Adjustments: Encourage the children to add props and pictures to their reports. After several groups have had turns making reports, videotape the reports to share with another class or report the weather on the school intercom.

Ongoing Assessment: As the children work with the thermometer, observe those who read the device independently and those who still need help. Encourage children to self-evaluate and improve their reports. Could they be heard? Did they speak in interesting ways? Do they think the audience understood them?

Angles

Picture a pair of scissors as you manipulate them to cut paper. The blades of the scissors rotate about a fulcrum or vertex, making various angles as they move. A more formal definition of angle, for adults, is a figure formed by two rays with a common vertex or meeting point. The standard measurement unit for angles is the degree. The common measurement tool for angles is the protractor calibrated in degrees. Young children can compare angles; they may use nonstandard units to measure them, but not until middle elementary school years are children expected to use degrees and protractors.

Amy Nyen worked in a preschool classroom for four-year-olds which was part of a primary school. As she attended in-service sessions addressing the NCTM standards, Amy became fascinated with the K–4 measurement standard's mention of angles as an attribute for young children. She decided to introduce the angle concept to her four-year-olds in informal ways.

As the children exercised and danced to music, Miss Nyen moved her arms at various angles—close to her body, straight out, and rotated to above the head. The children willingly "copycatted" her movements; several led the group in different poses. Miss Nyen commented, "We can make angles with our arms." After Miss Nyen observed two children playing "exercise" with dolls and saying, "Move your arms this way, 'round and 'round," she built on the idea of using a doll to model various funny poses. The children followed along; they seemed to understand and often used Miss Nyen's phrase, "Make a body angle like this."

To explore angle concepts further, a teacher of a primary class might gather the children near the classroom door and predict the appearance of the angle made by the door as it opens. When Miss Brock did this, she had the children draw predictions, then she laid a piece of tape just outside the door to define one side of the angle. As she opened the door "just a crack," the children could see a narrow angle outlined by the tape and the door. Miss Brock helped one child place a piece of yarn on the floor to make the angle clearer, then sketch the angle. Then as she opened the door wider and wider, the children laid more pieces of yarn to outline the angles. Miss Brock allowed time for the children to manipulate the door and talk about its angles.

Miss Brock extended attention to angles using notecards. The children traced around the corners of the notecards with their fingers and discussed their shapes. Miss Brock introduced the term "right angle" and encouraged the children to use this term as well as the phrase "square corners" that many of them used. As the children tested angles of classroom objects by holding their cards on top, they found many right angles.

Miss Brock continued to work with angles by letting the children find the angles or corners on pattern blocks and paper shapes. The children used paper strips fastened together with brads; they moved the strips to look like some of the angles they found (Figure 11.5). They also cut small, equal wedges of paper plate and used this nonstandard measure of angle to predict and find out how many wedges would fit within each angle. Miss Brock also planned an "Angle Search" described in the next activity.

Figure 11.5 *About two wedges cover each angle in the rectangle.*

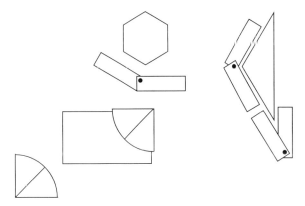

ANGLE SEARCH

Angles abound in most settings; they just need to be noticed!

Focus: Measurement—comparing, ordering, communicating, connecting to everyday life.

What To Do: With primary children, take a classroom walk, encouraging children to point out angles and describe them. Are some angles like square corners? Are some skinnier or narrower? Can the children find any angles that are wider or more spread out than square corners? Let the children sketch angles as you walk.

Adjustments: Extend the search to the school halls, playground, or to the neighborhood. Let the children sketch interesting examples of angles.

Ongoing Assessment: Let the children add words to their sketches, or copy the sketches and narratives in their math journals. Judge the children's insightfulness and interest in locating angles.

WHAT DO *YOU* THINK?

"Children are curious by nature. They are born problem solvers. From the earliest age, they delight in their interactions with the world around them, handling, manipulating, experimenting. . . . With each new encounter, they . . . begin to construct their own knowledge of the elements within the environment" (Rowan & Bourne, 1994, p. 18). How does this quote serve to summarize ideas about involving children in measurement activities? What are some examples of constructing knowledge as children measure?

SUMMARY

Measurement is a vital mathematics topic for young children because of its pertinence to everyday life, as well as its potential for involving children in interesting activities. Most physical objects have a variety of measurement attributes—length, area, volume, and angle, for example. Educators can help children focus on these attributes and learn more about how to describe, compare, and quantify the attributes with nonstandard and standard measurement units.

Children's understanding of measurement attributes grows slowly and must be based on experience and conversation about those experiences. Development of concepts such as telling time or the effects of temperature on people's activities should develop throughout the school year. School experiences are complemented by extensions at home and by activities where the teacher helps children set up and work with materials designed to focus attention to specific measurement attributes. Related literature, artwork, and graphs can complement other mathematics experiences as children explore measurement.

◆ *APPLICATIONS: THINKING AND COLLABORATING*

To help you further assimilate the ideas presented in this chapter, here are suggestions for professional development activities. Choose and carry out one or more of them that fit your interests and needs. Share results with your colleagues.

1. Many authors assert that measurement is often used in everyday life. Is this true for you? Find out by making notes for a weekday and weekend day. Jot down all your uses of measurement concepts and tools. Organize your list into categories. Plan ways to share your results with the children.

2. It's easy to connect measurement activities to other math topics, other curricular areas, and everyday life. Think of a topic you are teaching or have recently taught. Devise several ways you might have worked in measurement concepts with children. Choose two or three favorite ideas to share.

3. Choose a measurement attribute you feel less comfortable with—perhaps volume or angles. Read about enhancing children's knowl-edge of that attribute. Plan and implement activities with children. Seek the children's reactions to the experience. What did they learn? What did they like about the activities? What more could they explore? Add your own reactions as you write up results or share them with colleagues.

4. Examples of right angles abound in things that people have made. Find examples of some right angles and other angles in your sur-roundings. Draw and label sketches. You might want to compile your sketches in a booklet to show to others.

5. Many measurement experiences for children can be related to everyday life. Choose several learning experiences from this chapter that relate to everyday life, but have potential for relating to other areas of the curriculum as well. Describe how you might focus or extend each experience to relate it to areas such as science, art, music, social studies, or language arts.

6. This chapter suggests several children's books about measurement. Choose one or more books and share them with children. Extend the ideas from the book in learning activities focusing on measure-ment. Could children make their own book as one of your learning activities? Write up the results.

7. If you have started a mathematics autobiography in other chapters, finish it now, adding comments about teaching measurement, and discussions about areas of mathematics you feel confident about, and areas in which you would like to grow.

◆ REFERENCES

Carle, E. (1987). *Hermit crab finds a home.* New York: Harper Collins.

National Council of Teachers of Mathematics. (1989). *Curriculum and evaluation standards for school mathematics, K–12.* Reston, VA: Author.

Partridge, E., Austin, S., Wadington, E., and Bitner, J. (1996). Cooking up mathematics in the kindergarten. *Teaching Children Mathematics, 2,* 492–495.

Paul, A. W. (1991). *Eight hands round: a patchwork alphabet.* New York: Harper Collins.

Rowan, T. & Bourne, B. (1994). *Thinking like mathematicians: putting the K–4 NCTM standards into practice.* Portsmouth, NH: Heinemann.

Souviney, R. J. *Learning to teach mathematics.* New York: Macmillan.

Young, E. (1992). *Seven blind mice.* New York: Philomel.

◆ SELECTED CHILDREN'S BOOKS

Carle, E. (1987). *Hermit Crab Finds a Home.* New York: Harper Collins. Carle's famous cut paper and paint artwork creates a beautiful book which outlines the adventures of a hermit crab throughout the months of the year.

Jenkins, S. (1996). *Big and Little.* Boston: Houghton Mifflin. Animals vary greatly in size, and this book provides some impressive examples. With stunning, colorful collages, the book helps children develop a sense of scale and relative size in the animal world.

Paul, A. W. (1991). *Eight Hands Round: A Patchwork Alphabet.* New York: Harper Collins. This book shows 26 quilt patterns with historical stories, pictures of quilt blocks, and drawings of entire quilts.

Von Noorden, Djinn. (1994). *The Lifesize Animal Counting Book.* New York: Dorling Kindersley. This large attractive book features photos of a variety of animals. With a series of questions about the animal pictures, the author invites children to count and use various measurement concepts to compare the animals' sizes.

Wood, Douglas. (1996). *Northwoods Cradle Song.* New York: Simon and Schuster. This book features a Menominee Indian lullaby. It might be used at nap time or quiet time. Its vivid pictures, from different angles and perspectives, show many night events and creatures.

Young, E. (1992). *Seven Blind Mice.* New York: Philomel. Vivid colors and stylized mice give this book a dramatic appearance. Young also highlights days of the week and order in this amusing version of the old tale of identifying an elephant by its various parts.

Suppliers of Mathematics Education Materials Suitable for Young Children

Many companies supply mathematics education materials such as manipulatives, posters, activity and trade books for children, idea books for teachers, calculators, measuring tools, and other related supplies. Listed here are the names of several of these suppliers, their addresses, and telephone numbers.

Creative Publications
5040 West 11th Street
Oak Lawn, IL 60653
(800)624-0822

Cuisenaire Company of America
P. O. Box 5026
White Plains, NY 10602-5026
(800)237-0338

Dale Seymour
P. O. Box 10888
Palo Alto, CA 94303-0879
(800)827-1100

Delta Education
P.O. Box 3000
Nashua, NH 03061-3000
(800)442-5444

Didax
395 Main Street
Rowley, MA 01969-3785
(800)458-0024

ETA
620 Lakeview Parkway
Vernon Hills, IL 60061
(800)445-5985

Nasco
901 Janesville Avenue
Fort Atkinson, WI 53538-2446
(414)563-2446
or
4825 Stoddard Road
Modesto, CA 95356-9318
(209)545-1600

Mathematics Autobiography

Make marks on the lines to create a picture of your knowledge and skills for teaching mathematics to young children. (If you add to the lines at different times, use various colors and make a code for each date.)

	Very poor/Shaky	Excellent
Knowledge of Content		
Numeration and number sense		
Working with data		
Problem solving and reasoning		
Geometry		
Measurement		
Knowledge of Techniques for Teaching Young Children		
Selecting appropriate tasks		
Planning lessons and activities		
Organizing groups		
Using manipulatives and materials		
Assessing children's work		

Narrative. Write a paragraph or more each time you add to the autobiography. Tell about your past study of math and your feelings about it. Describe any mentors you may have had and the ways they—or other learning experiences—have helped you. Describe yourself as a future (or current) teacher of mathematics. Date your work.

Index

Page numbers in *italics* indicate topics that are covered in activities.